Moeller
Liedloff
Adolph
Hoecherl-Alden
Kirmse
Lalande

Deutsch heute
Grundstufe/Sixth Edition

Arbeitsheft

Workbook

Lab Manual

Self Tests

Silke Van Ness, State University of New York at Albany

Jack Moeller, Oakland University

Helmut Liedloff, Southern Illinois University

Barbara Beckman Sharon, Pacific Lutheran University

Video Workbook

Thomas F. Thibeault, Southern Illinois University

Proficiency Cards

Cynthia Hall Kouré

HOUGHTON MIFFLIN COMPANY   **BOSTON**   **TORONTO**

Geneva, Illinois   **Palo Alto**   **Princeton, New Jersey**

Credits

The authors and editors of the *Deutsch heute, Sixth Edition, Arbeitsheft* would like to thank the following companies and organizations for granting permission to reproduce or adapt copyrighted material:

p. 5	BOSE, Nordhorn.
p. 14	Zeleste Tanzbar, Berlin.
p. 21	GLOBUS-Kartendienst GmbH, Hamburg.
p. 28	Courtesy of Preisring-Markt.
p. 57	Egon Schiele Museum, Tulln.
p. 83	Deutsche Welle, Köln.
p. 90	Horn.
p. 113	Lexica Verlag, München.

Drawings by George Ulrich, Anne Burgess, and Tim Jones.

Sponsoring Editor: E. Kristina Baer
Project Development Editor: Amy Hatch Davidson
Development Editor: Barbara B. Lasoff
Art Editor: Linda Hadley
Editorial Assistant: Lisa Cutler
Senior Manufacturing Coordinator: Marie Barnes
Marketing Manager: Elaine Leary

Printed in the U.S.A.

ISBN: 0-395-76687-7

123456789-B-00 99 98 97 96

Contents

Video Workbook

Introduction

The *Arbeitsheft* to accompany *Deutsch heute: Grundstufe, Sixth Edition,* is designed to help you improve your reading and writing skills, reinforce your listening comprehension skills, and enhance your cognition of grammatical features of German. The *Arbeitsheft* consists of five components: (1) the Workbook, (2) the Lab Manual, (3) Self-Tests with an Answer Key, (4) the Video Workbook, and (5) a set of 56 Proficiency Cards. They have been bound together for your convenience. The pages have been perforated so they can be handed in for correction.

Workbook

The Workbook provides guided practice in writing German. Exercises include dialogue or sentence completion, rewriting sentences, answering questions, building sentences or paragraphs from guidelines, and creating short compositions. Some exercises encourage you to express your own moods, opinions, and ideas and to speculate on what you would do in a particular situation. Other exercises are based on line art and realia, including maps; some activities offer extra reading practice and new cultural information. Vocabulary sophistication is developed by exercises that require you to supply synonyms, antonyms or definitions, or to form new words with suffixes and prefixes. For the instructor's convenience, an Answer Key to the exercises in the Workbook is provided in the *Deutsch heute Instructor's Resource Manual.*

Lab Manual

The Lab Manual contains material that is coordinated with the **Übungen zum Hörverständnis** in the tape program. The exercises consist of new aural material based on the dialogues and readings in each chapter of the text. Exercises include true/false statements about the **Lesestück** and about conversations and stories heard on the tape, logical/illogical response, and dictations. In general, responses to the recorded material consist of checking off correct answers or writing short answers in the Lab Manual. For the instructor's convenience, the script for the listening comprehension exercises and an Answer Key are printed in the *Instructor's Resource Manual.*

Self-Tests

The Self-Tests are provided to help you determine whether you are ready for the chapter test by giving you an opportunity to review structures and vocabulary. Doing the Self-Tests, either individually or in class, will enable you to see whether you have understood the grammatical features introduced in the chapter and whether you can apply your understanding of the grammatical principles. You will need to use a separate answer sheet for the Self-Tests. An Answer Key to the Self-Tests follows the Self-Tests.

Video Workbook

The Video Workbook contains activities designed to be used in conjunction with the video *Einfach toll!* The Video Workbook is divided into eight sections to correspond to the modules of the video. There are also exercises to accompany each **Parkplatz** section, which presents additional images of daily life in Germany. The **Einführung** (introductory lesson) introduces you to the main characters in the video.

Each section of the Video Workbook begins with an **Einleitung** (introduction) section containing questions and vocabulary to help you bring focus to your viewing of the module and to introduce unfamiliar vocabulary. The video itself is broken into shorter segments for viewing. These segments are indicated on the video by a green and yellow **Haltestelle** (bus stop) symbol in the lower left-hand corner of the screen. In the Video Workbook you will often be asked to view the video segment first with the sound off, so that you can concentrate on visual cues. When you watch a TV program in English without the sound on, you can often still tell what is happening. You will find that the same is true when you are watching the video in German. Body language, people's facial expressions, and the scenery in the background all combine to let you know what is going on and anticipate what people are saying.

Video Workbook activities for guiding your viewing of the video with the sound on progress from requiring you to identify actual statements in the video to checking your understanding of the language and action. Cultural information is provided throughout the Video Workbook to further enhance your understanding of the video and of Germany itself.

Post-viewing activities encourage you to expand on what you have seen in the video and to call on your own experience and imagination, e.g., you may be asked to create a dialogue between two people having a disagreement or to arrange the furniture in your room. An Answer Key to the Video Workbook is included in the *Instructor's Resource Manual*.

Proficiency Cards

This set of 56 activity cards has been designed to help you develop oral proficiency in German. By providing a meaningful context and task for each interaction, the cards furnish suggestions to be used to stimulate spontaneous communication involving oral skills learned in the text.

There are four cards for chapters 1–13 and three for chapter 14 plus a summary. Within each chapter the tasks described on the cards are sequenced to move from controlled situations to free conversations. The first card for every chapter is a short warm-up activity, the second and third cards involve role-playing, directed dialogues, and pair work activities, and the fourth card, the **Kaffeestunde,** is intended for general conversation.

Workbook

Kapitel 1

A. Wie bitte? Stephan Meyer approaches the secretary in an office and is asked to provide information about himself. Use the following ideas to create the conversation.

Stephan responds to her greeting and states his name. The secretary asks him to spell it and then asks for his address and phone number. Stephan gives her the information. The secretary thanks him.

Sekretärin: Bitte?

Stephan: *Ich heisse Stephan Meyer.*

Sekretärin: *Wie schreibt man das? Und Ihre Adresse und Telefonnummer?*

Stephan: *STEPHAN MEYER. 18 Reiher Weg. 50259 Pulheim. 02238 - 7483*

Sekretärin: *Danke Herr Meyer.*

B. Wochentage. Answer each question by writing the appropriate *day* or *days of the week* in German.

1. Which two days constitute the weekend? *Samstag* und *Sonntag*

2. Which day is the middle of the week? *Mittwoch*

3. The German word for *moon* is **Mond.** Which day is named after the moon? *Montag*

4. **Freia** was the Germanic goddess of love. Which day is named after her? *Freitag*

5. The Germanic god of thunder was **Donar.** Which day is named after him? *Donnerstag*

C. Welcher Artikel? Give the *definite article* for each of the following nouns.

▶ *die* Frau

1. *das* Papier

2. *der* Bleistift

3. *die* Woche

4. *das* Wort

5. *die* Sekretärin

6. *das* Buch

7. *der* Computer

8. *das* Telefon

D. Wie ist ... ? For each conversational exchange first complete the question by supplying the pictured *noun and its definite article.* Then give an answer, using a complete sentence with the cue in parentheses.

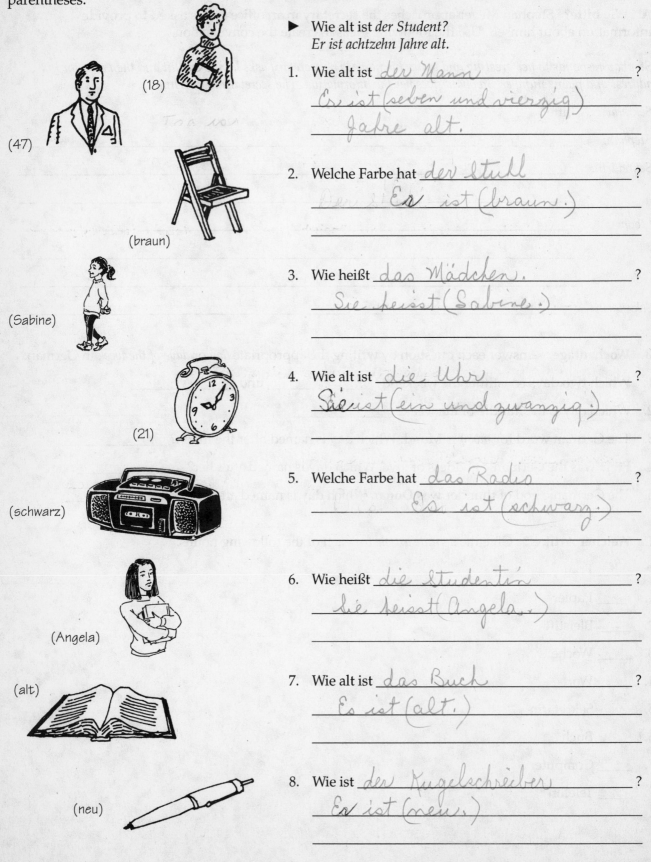

▶ Wie alt ist *der Student?*
Er ist achtzehn Jahre alt.

1. Wie alt ist *der Mann* ?
Er ist (seben und vierzig) Jahre alt.

2. Welche Farbe hat *der Stuhl* ?
Der Es ist (braun.)

3. Wie heißt *das Mädchen.* ?
Sie heisst (Sabine.)

4. Wie alt ist *die Uhr* ?
Sie ist (ein und zwanzig.)

5. Welche Farbe hat *das Radio* ?
Es ist (schwarz.)

6. Wie heißt *die Studentin* ?
Sie heisst (Angela.)

7. Wie alt ist *das Buch* ?
Es ist (alt.)

8. Wie ist *der Kugelschreiber* ?
Er ist (neu.)

E. Welche Farben? Complete the bilingual *color* guide for these road signs.

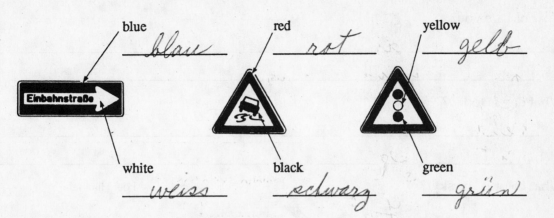

blue — *blau*

red — *rot*

yellow — *gelb*

white — *weiss*

black — *schwarz*

green — *grün*

F. Landeskunde°. Provide brief responses in English.

° the study of a country, its people, and its culture

1. Compare the academic year at a German university with the academic year at your school.

_____

_____

2. Write the German address for the Hamburg office of ADAC*, Germany's automobile association. It is located at number 39 Amsinckstraße. The postal code is 20097.

ADAC

neun und dreissig Ansinckstrasse

zwei, null, null, neun, sieben

3. Compare what you say when you answer the phone at home with how it is typically done in Germany.

_____

_____

*ADAC = Allgemeiner Deutscher Automobil-Club e.V.

G. Wie? Was? Express the following questions in German. Then answer each question with a complete sentence.

1. How old are you?

   Wie alt bist du?

   Ich bin neun und sechzig.

2. What day is today?

   Welcher Tag ist heute?

   Heute ist Donnerstag.

3. What color is the sky°?   I der Himmel

   Was ist die Farbe des Himmel?

   Es ist blau.

4. Your name is Kim, isn't it?

   Sie heissen Kim, nicht?

   Ja, das ist mein name.

5. Frau Köhler, what is your address?

   Frau Köhler, Wie ist Ihre Adresse?

6. Alex, what is your address? And your telephone number?

   Alex, wie ist deine Adresse?, und deine Telefonnummer?

H. Das Zimmer. An Austrian friend has asked you about typical dorm rooms on your campus. Using various *modifiers* (colors, size, age), write five sentences describing a room and objects in it.

▶ *Der Tisch ist zwanzig Jahre alt.*

4 _Der Stuhl ist grün._

2 _Das Bücherregal ist weiss_

5 _Ich habe keine Fernseher oder Computer._

3 _Die Wand sind also weiss._

1 _Die Zahl das zimmer ist 589_

I. Deutsch ist leicht°! You may be surprised to discover how much German you can understand without knowing every word. Since German and English are closely related linguistically, you will find many cognates that will help you get the gist of a reading. Look at the ad *Ja, Bose ist Musik in meinen Ohren* and answer the questions below.

° easy

1. List six German words you already know.

   _Ja_____   _in_____

   _ist_____   _meinen_____

   _Musik_____   _Ohren_____

2. List five German words that look *similar* to English words.

   _Musik_____   _Informationen_____

   _meinen_____   _Radio_____

   _senden_____

3. What is this ad about? _sound_____

4. In the ad, fill in the requested personal details so that you can receive more information from *Bose.*

5. Wie heißt die Firma? _Bose_____

6. Wie heißt die Stadt? _Nordhorn_____

7. Wie ist die Faxnummer? _05921 - 833 250_____

Kapitel 2

A. Wie geht es Ihnen? While shopping in the morning Ms. Gärtner and Ms. Ziegler meet. Reconstruct their conversation using the following ideas:
Ms. Ziegler greets Ms. Gärtner. Ms. Gärtner responds and asks how Ms. Ziegler is doing. Ms. Ziegler replies.

Frau Ziegler: _____

Frau Gärtner: _____

_____

Frau Ziegler: _____

_____

B. Gehen wir tanzen? Philipp wants to go dancing in the evening. In the afternoon he happens to run into Linda and he asks her about her plans. Use the following questions to help you reconstruct their conversation.
How are you? What are you doing tonight? Do you like to . . . ? At what time? See you later.

Philipp. Tag, Linda!

Linda: _____

_____

Philipp: _____

_____

Linda: _____

Philipp: _____

C. Wie sind Sie? Complete the personality chart for yourself and others. For each person select three *adjectives* from the following list and enter them under the appropriate headings.

fleißig, faul, freundlich, unfreundlich, froh, kritisch, intelligent, praktisch, lustig, ernst, ruhig, tolerant, nett

	sehr	**manchmal°**	**nicht**	I sometimes
► ich bin	[*intelligent*]	[*faul*]	[*kritisch*]	
1. meine Mutter° ist	_____	_____	_____	I mother
2. mein Vater° ist	_____	_____	_____	I father
3. meine Freundin° ist	_____	_____	_____	I friend (f.)
4. mein Freund° ist	_____	_____	_____	I friend (m.)
5. meine Professorin/ mein Professor ist	_____	_____	_____	

D. Wann? While staying in Luzern, you plan an excursion on the lake. Use the steamer schedule to answer the questions, spelling out the times. Use Method 1 for a., and official time and Method 2 for b. (*ab* = departure; *an* = arrival)

Luzern	(ab)	9.30
WEGGIS X	(an)	10.09
	(ab)	10.32
KEHRSITEN X	(an)	10.50
	(ab)	11.00
ALPNACHSTAD	(an)	12.00
	(ab)	15.10
Luzern	(an)	16.45
	ab	

▶ Wann fahren wir von° Luzern ab°? | from / **fahren ab:** depart

a. Um *halb zehn*

b. Um *neun Uhr dreißig*

1. Wann kommen wir in Weggis an°? | **kommen an:** arrive

a. Um _____

b. Um _____

2. Wann fahren wir von Kehrsiten ab?

a. Um _____

b. Um _____

3. Wann kommen wir in Luzern an?

a. Um _____

b. Um _____

E. Gespräche. Complete the mini-conversations by filling in the cued verb.

▶ *Bernd:* Was _____ du heute? (machen)   *Was machst du heute?*

1. *Frau Lange:* Was ___machen___ Sie heute, Herr Professor? (machen)

2. *Professor Klug:* Ich ___wandere___ heute nachmittag. (wandern)

3. *Kevin:* ___tanzt___ du gern, Natalie? (tanzen)

4. *Natalie:* Ja, ich ___tanze___ sehr gern. (tanzen)

5. *Tanja und Thomas:* Was ___macht___ ihr heute abend? (machen)

6. *Alex und Melanie:* Wir ___hören___ Jazz. (hören)

7. *Boris:* ___Bist___ du heute krank? (sein)

8. *Sarah:* Nein, aber ich ___bin___ sehr müde. (sein)

F. Nein, nein. Answer each question in the *negative.*

▶ Ist das Radio alt?   *Nein, das Radio ist nicht alt.*

1. Sind Gabi und Michael fleißig?

_____

2. Glaubt sie das?

_____

3. Arbeitet Herr Wagner in Bonn?

_____

4. Gehst du heute nachmittag ins Kino?

_____

5. Spielt ihr gern Basketball?

___Nein, wir spielen nicht gern___

6. Ist das Frau Kraft?

_____

7. Wandern Gabi und Erika oft?

_____

Wer? Was? Wann? Write specific questions, using the cues provided. Remember that a verb must agree with its subject.

▶ wann / gehen / Thomas / ?   *Wann geht Thomas?*

1. wer / glauben / das / ?

   _____

2. warum / schwimmen / ihr / nicht auch / ?

   _____

3. wann / gehen / Sie / ins Kino / ?

   _____

4. wie / machen / ich / das / ?

   _____

5. was für Musik / hören / du / gern / ?

   _____

6. wie alt / sein / Ute und Monika / ?

   _____

7. wann / machen / wir / das / ?

   _____

H. Sie, du oder ihr? Use the cues provided to write a question addressed to the person in parentheses, using **du, ihr,** or **Sie** as appropriate.

▶ (Frau Braun)   glauben / das / ?   *Glauben Sie das?*

1. (Erika)   spielen / oft / Tennis / ?

   _____ spielst du _____

2. (Mark und Lutz)   gehen / ins Kino / ?

   _____ ihr _____

3. (Herr Wagner)   wandern / gern / ?

   _____ Sie _____

4. (Jürgen)   treiben / viel / Sport / ?

   _____ st du _____

5. (Frau Ruland)   hören / das / nicht / ?

   _____ Sie _____

I. Was? Wann? Your Austrian neighbor, Andrea, asks you about various activities. Check your calendar and respond in German using complete sentences with **Ja, ...** or with **Nein, ...** and the correct activity.

Montag	Volleyball
Dienstag	mit Max Schach spielen
Mittwoch	mit Tanja Musik hören
Donnerstag	mit Inge arbeiten
Freitag	mit Andrea tanzen
Samstag	mit Frank schwimmen
Sonntag	Kino

► *Freitag:* Wir gehen schwimmen, nicht?   *Nein, wir gehen tanzen.*

1. *Montag:* Wir spielen Fußball, nicht?

   _____

2. *Dienstag:* Du spielst Schach, nicht?

   _____

3. *Mittwoch:* Gehst du heute abend schwimmen?

   _____

4. *Donnerstag:* Gehen wir ins Kino?

   _____

5. *Samstag:* Spielen wir heute morgen Tennis?

   _____

6. *Sonntag:* Du arbeitest heute viel, nicht?

   _____

sagt man das? Give the *German equivalent* of each of the following sentences.

Petra is working this afternoon.

Arbeitet heute

2. Do you believe that, Karin?

_____

3. Does Mr. Klein like to play chess?

Spielt H.K. gern Schach

4. When are they going to the movies?

Wann gehen sie ins Kino

5. Do you like to hike, Erik and Ute?

Wandert ihr gern

6. Are you working today, Ms. Becker?

Arbeiten sie heute

7. Fritz likes to swim, doesn't he (isn't that so)?

_____

K. Landeskunde. Provide brief responses in English.

1. Give one example of a standard German expression for *good-bye,* and two examples of farewells reserved for friends. Compare with English—do you hear or use informal good-byes with friends? If yes, give an example.

_____

_____

_____

2. What are the general guidelines for using **du** and **Sie?**

_____

_____

_____

3. Compare how people in Germany and people in your country may participate in competitive sports.

_____

_____

_____

L. Wer sind Sie? You are going to study abroad for a year. The chart and questionnaire were sent to you by the exchange agency. Use the chart to complete the questionnaire so that your German host family will know who you are and what you like to do.

EIGENSCHAFTEN°		HOBBIES / AKTIVITÄTEN			characteristics
(Was für ein Mensch bist du?)		*(Was machst du gern?)*		
✓klein	freundlich	✓wandern	✓schwimmen
groß	✓ruhig	tanzen	Sport treiben
✓ernst	kritisch	Volleyball	schreiben
fleißig	✓praktisch	✓Tennis ⎫	Musik hören
✓tolerant	✓nett	Basketball ⎬ spielen	Gitarre spielen
intelligent	natürlich	Schach ⎭	Videospiele spielen
lustig	faul	joggen	Gewichte heben

1. Name: _____

2. Adresse: _____

3. Telefon: _____

4. *Eigenschaften:*

   Was für ein Mensch sind Sie? _____

   _____

5. *Aktivitäten:*

   Was machen Sie gern? _____

   _____

   Was machen Sie nicht gern? _____

   _____

...e Beate! Kerstin has moved and is writing a brief note to her girlfriend. Read the letter and ...ver the questions below:

Liebe Beate,
wie geht's? Heute ist Montag und ich bin jetzt° in Hamburg. Meine Adresse ist Eggers | now
Allee 38, 22763 Hamburg. Heute abend gehen Dieter und ich ins Kino und später hören wir
Musik. Dieter tanzt gern und oft, aber, Du weißt°, ich tanze nicht gern. Es ist jetzt sieben | know
Uhr, und Dieter kommt gleich°. | soon
     Viele Grüße
        Deine° Kerstin | your

1. Wo ist Kerstin? _____

2. Welcher Tag ist heute? _____

3. Was machen Dieter und Kerstin heute abend? _____

4. Tanzt Kerstin gern? _____

5. Wer kommt gleich? _____

6. Wie heißt Kerstins Freundin? _____

Kapitel 3

A. Das Wetter. Use the following ideas to write a short conversation in German.

You comment on today's weather.
Sabine gives an appropriate response.
You make a prediction about tomorrow's weather.
Sabine agrees (or disagrees) with you.

Sie: _____

Sabine: _____

Sie: _____

Sabine: _____

B. Wo waren Sie? Complete each sentence with the correct form of the simple past tense of **sein.**

1. Wir _____ in Frankreich.

2. _____ das Mädchen in Belgien?

3. Ich _____ in Dänemark.

4. _____ Frau Kohl wieder in der Schweiz?

5. Ihr _____ in Polen, nicht?

6. _____ Sie in Österreich?

7. Wer _____ in Kanada?

8. Du _____ in Spanien, nicht?

C. Wetterprobleme. Tell about problems with the weather. Rewrite each sentence, beginning with the cued word. Be sure not to delete any of the original words in rewriting the sentences.

▶ Das Wetter ist furchtbar. (heute)   *Heute ist das Wetter furchtbar.*

1. Der Wind ist sehr kalt. (im Winter)

_____

2. Es schneit in München. (vielleicht)

_____

3. Es regnet wieder. (morgen)

_____

4. Es ist aber schön warm. (im Süden)

_____

5. Ich bleibe in Italien. (jetzt)

_____

D. Was machst du (nicht) gern?   Write down two things you like to do and two things you do not like to do. Then tell about your friends. The following expressions will give you some ideas.

Gitarre spielen, Gewichte heben, joggen, Schach spielen, Tennis spielen, tanzen, wandern, arbeiten, Musik (Rock 'n Roll, Jazz, Rap) hören, schwimmen, Sport treiben, Basketball/Volleyball/Fußball spielen

▶ *Ich jogge gern.*

1. _____

2. _____

▶ *Ich höre nicht gern Jazz.*

3. _____

4. _____

▶ *Meine Freunde heben gern Gewichte.*

5. _____

6. _____

E. Etwas über Deutschland.   Below are several statements about Germany. In each sentence underline the *subject* once. Some of the sentences contain a predicate noun. Underline each *predicate noun* twice.

▶ Berlin ist die Hauptstadt von Deutschland.

1. Für Amerikaner ist Deutschland sehr klein.

2. In Deutschland ist das Wetter anders.

3. Heute ist es aber heiß in Deutschland.

4. Die Deutschen sagen das.

5. Die Frau da ist Deutsche, nicht?

6. Nein, sie ist Amerikanerin.

7. Sie heißt Carol Jones.

F. Wie ist das Wetter? Construct a question about the weather from each set of guidelines below. Add articles where necessary. Be sure the subject and verb agree.

▶ wann / scheinen / Sonne / wieder / ?   *Wann scheint die Sonne wieder?*

1. wo / regnen / es / sehr viel / ?

   _____

2. wer / finden / Wetter / schön / ?

   _____

3. wie / sein / Sommer / in Deutschland / ?

   _____

4. was / denken / ihr / ?

   _____

5. wo / sein / Winter / warm / ?

   _____

6. wann / sein / es / heiß / ?

   _____

G. Wer hat was? Elke, Karin, Krista, Udo, and Torsten are comparing items in their apartments. Using the following chart, write statements about who owns how many of what.

	Elke	Karin und Krista	Udo	Torsten
das Bild	4	7	2	6
der Fernseher	—	2	1	2
das Telefon	1	2	1	—
das Buch	30	80	20	60
das Bett	1	2	1	1
der Computer	—	2	2	1
der Stuhl	2	4	3	4
das Videospiel	—	5	10	2

▶ das Bild: Elke; Torsten   *Elke hat vier Bilder. Torsten hat sechs Bilder.*

▶ das Telefon: Karin und Krista   *Karin und Krista haben zwei Telefone.*

1. das Buch: Karin und Krista _____

_____

2. der Fernseher: Torsten; Karin und Krista _____

_____

3. das Videospiel: Udo; Torsten _____

_____

4. der Stuhl: Elke; Torsten _____

_____

5. der Computer: Karin und Krista _____

_____

6. das Bett: Karin und Krista; Elke _____

_____

7. das Telefon: Udo; Karin und Krista _____

_____

H. Ist das dein Heft?   At the end of a club project you try to sort out what belongs to whom. Complete each sentence with the German equivalent of the cued word.

▶ Da liegt ___*mein*___ Heft. (*my*)

1. Wo sind _____ Bücher, Kai und Markus? (*your*)

2. Ist das _____ Poster? (*Rita's*)

3. Hier ist _____ Lampe. (*her*)

4. Ist das _____ Bleistift, Herr Winter? (*your*)

5. Ist das auch _____ Kuli? (*his*)

6. Hier ist _____ Uhr, Anni. (*your*)

7. Wo ist _____ Radio? (*our*)

I. Ja, so ist es.   Patrick is checking to see if his information about places and people is correct. Answer each question in the affirmative, replacing the noun phrase with its corresponding *demonstrative pronoun*.

▶ Das Land ist klein, nicht?   *Ja, das ist klein.*

1. Die Schweiz ist sehr schön, nicht?

   Ja, _____

2. Die Städte sind sehr alt, nicht?

   Ja, _____

3. Herr Schneider arbeitet in Bern, nicht?

   Ja, _____

4. Kirstin arbeitet jetzt in Luzern, nicht?

   Ja, _____

5. Die Nachbarn bleiben eine Woche in St. Moritz, nicht?

   Ja, _____

J. Kein oder ein? Look at the pictures and then answer the questions.

▶ Ist das eine Tür? *Nein, das ist keine Tür. Das ist ein Fenster.*

1. Ist das ein Stuhl? _____

_____

2. Ist das ein Kugelschreiber? _____

_____

3. Ist das ein Buch? _____

_____

4. Ist das ein Heft? _____

_____

5. Ist das eine Lampe? _____

_____

6. Ist das ein Videospiel? _____

_____

7. Ist das ein Tisch? _____

_____

8. Ist das eine Tür? _____

_____

Name _____ Date _____

K. Landeskunde. Provide brief responses in English.

1. Between 1945 and 1990 Berlin enjoyed an unusual status. Explain.

_____

_____

_____

_____

2. Identify two typical birthday customs in German-speaking countries that are the same as those in your country and one custom that is different.

_____

_____

_____

3. What are **Namenstage?** In which German-speaking areas are **Namenstage** often celebrated? Are such days celebrated in your community?

_____

_____

_____

4. When is **Hochdeutsch** used in German-speaking countries?

_____

_____

_____

A B C J M Z

Von Alma mater bis Zeitung

Unser Minilexikon für das erste Studienjahr

L. Wie ist das Wetter? Wieviel Grad ist es? Have a look at the weather map below and familiarize yourself with the symbols. Then answer the questions in complete sentences.

| heiter | *pleasant* | bewölkt | *partially cloudy* | bedeckt | *cloudy* |
| Nebel | *fog* | Schauer | *showers* | Gewitter | *thunderstorms* |

Heute noch warm und trocken, allmähliche Bewölkungszunahme

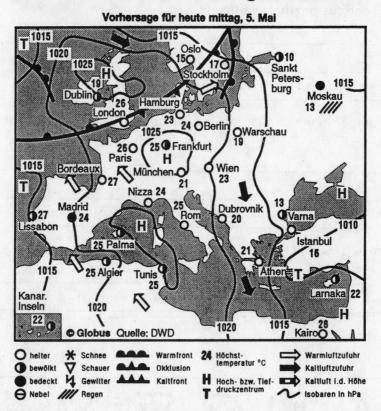

Vorhersage für heute mittag, 5. Mai

○ heiter	✳ Schnee	▲▲▲ Warmfront	**24** Höchst-temperatur °C	⟹ Warmluftzufuhr
◑ bewölkt	▽ Schauer	▲▲▲ Okklusion		➡ Kaltluftzufuhr
● bedeckt	⩔ Gewitter	▲▲▲ Kaltfront	**H** Hoch- bzw. Tief-	⟹ Kaltluft i.d. Höhe
⊖ Nebel	///// Regen		**T** druckzentrum	∿ Isobaren in hPa

▶ Wie ist das Wetter in Moskau?   *Es ist in Moskau bedeckt. / In Moskau ist es bedeckt.*

▶ Wieviel Grad ist es in Paris?   *Es sind (ist) in Paris 26 Grad. / In Paris sind (ist) es 26 Grad.*

1. Wie ist das Wetter in München? _____

2. Wieviel Grad ist es in Hamburg? _____

3. Wie ist das Wetter in Frankfurt? _____

4. Wieviel Grad ist es in Oslo? _____

5. Wo regnet es? _____

6. Wo ist es sehr warm? _____

7. In Berlin sind es 24 Grad. Wieviel Grad Fahrenheit sind das? (*Use the quick estimate.*) _____

_____

M. Deutsche Städte. Identify the five rivers (*Flüsse*) and fifteen cities marked on the map of Germany. Refer to the map on the inside cover of your textbook as necessary.

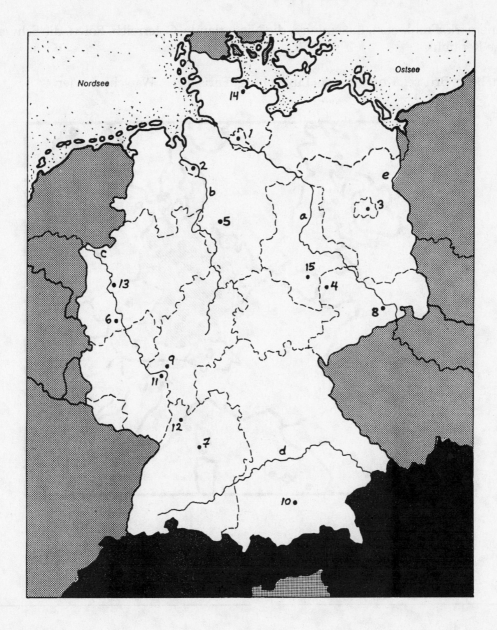

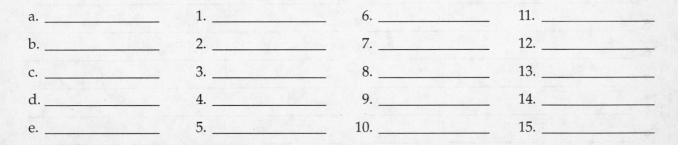

Flüsse	**Städte**		
a. _____	1. _____	6. _____	11. _____
b. _____	2. _____	7. _____	12. _____
c. _____	3. _____	8. _____	13. _____
d. _____	4. _____	9. _____	14. _____
e. _____	5. _____	10. _____	15. _____

N. Deutschlands Nachbarn. The following lists provide the names and the capital cities of the countries numbered on the map. On the lines below, write the name of each country beside its map number, and match the country with its capital.

Belgien, Dänemark, Frankreich, Luxemburg, die Niederlande, Österreich, Polen, die Schweiz, die Tschechische Republik

Amsterdam, Bern, Brüssel, Kopenhagen, Luxemburg, Paris, Prag, Warschau, Wien

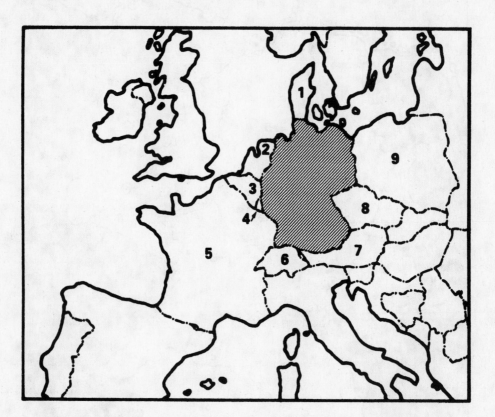

Land	**Hauptstadt**
1. _____	_____
2. _____	_____
3. _____	_____
4. _____	_____
5. _____	_____
6. _____	_____
7. _____	_____
8. _____	_____
9. _____	_____

Kapitel 4

A. Wo kauft man was? Make up your shopping list, organizing it by store and item. For each store, list at least 3 items that you intend to purchase.

Aspirin	Bier	Butter	Spaghetti	Kaffee	Hefte
Kämme	Apfelsaft	Shampoo	Milch	Wein	Bleistifte
Gemüse	Gurken	Karotten	Kartoffeln	Salat	Tomaten
Obst	Bananen	Fernseher	Trauben	Orangensaft	Hähnchen
Rinderbraten	Brötchen	Nudeln	Schinken	Wurst	Eier
Make-up	Kuchen	Margarine	Brot	Käse	Videospiele

Beim Bäcker

Brötchen

_____

_____

Beim Metzger

_____

_____

_____

In der Drogerie

_____

_____

_____

Im Supermarkt

_____

_____

_____

Auf dem Markt

_____

_____

_____

Im Kaufhaus

_____

_____

_____

B. Was essen Sie zum (Frühstück)? Write what you eat at the following meals.

▶ *Zum Frühstück esse ich ein Ei und trinke etwas Milch.*

1. Zum Frühstück: _____

_____

2. Zum Mittagessen: _____

_____

3. Zum Abendessen: _____

_____

C. Neue Wörter. Form a compound from each pair of nouns. Write the compound with its definite article and give the English equivalent.

		Compound	English Equivalent
▶ der Kaffee und das Haus	*das*	*Kaffeehaus*	*coffee shop, café*
1. die Wand und die Uhr			
2. die Butter und das Brot			
3. der Sommer und der Abend			
4. der Frühling (+ s) und der Tag			
5. das Haus und die Tür			
6. der Herbst und der Wind			
7. der Geburtstag (+ s) und das Kind			

D. Was ißt man gern? Rewrite each sentence, using the cue as the new subject.

▶ Nehmt ihr Tee? (du)   *Nimmst du Tee?*

1. Gibst du mir° das Brot, bitte? (Sie)

   ° I me

   _____

2. Frau und Herr Schneider geben Erika den Wein. (Klaus)

   _____

3. Essen Sie keinen Fisch? (du)

   _____

4. Sie nimmt einen Liter Milch. (ich)

   _____

5. Gebt ihr Frau Ahrend nichts? (Renate)

   _____

6. Ißt er gern Spaghetti? (ihr)

   _____

Name _____ Date _____

E. Mach das! Give advice or instructions to the persons indicated in parentheses by inserting the appropriate form of each cued verb.

▶ _____ doch die Professorin.   (Anni und Kai / fragen)

  Fragt _____ doch die Professorin.

1. _____ nicht so kritisch!   (Gabi und Frank / sein)

2. _____ mir bitte zwei Pfund Kaffee.   (Herr Winter / geben)

3. _____ bitte Tee.   (Michael und Sonja / nehmen)

4. _____ den Kuchen nicht.   (Paul / essen)

5. _____ mir bitte die Adresse.   (Frau Klein / geben)

6. _____ doch nett!   (Lutz / sein)

7. _____ den Stuhl.   (Helga / nehmen)

8. _____ bitte am Montag.   (Frau und Herr Weiß / kommen)

F. Einkaufen im Preisring-Markt. You and your housemate are preparing a shopping list by looking at the offers at the Preisring-Markt. Tell your housemate what you need and how much it will cost.

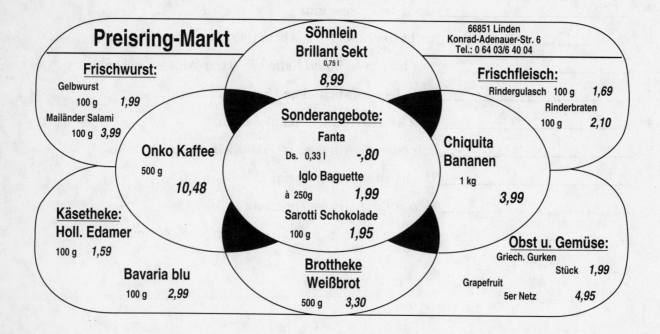

Preisring-Markt

Frischwurst:
Gelbwurst
100 g   *1,99*
Mailänder Salami
100 g   *3,99*

Onko Kaffee
500 g
    10,48

Käsetheke:
Holl. Edamer
100 g   *1,59*

Bavaria blu
100 g   *2,99*

Söhnlein Brillant Sekt
0,75 l
8,99

Sonderangebote:
Fanta
Ds. 0,33 l   *-,80*
Iglo Baguette
à 250g   *1,99*
Sarotti Schokolade
100 g   *1,95*

Brottheke Weißbrot
500 g   *3,30*

66851 Linden
Konrad-Adenauer-Str. 6
Tel.: 0 64 03/6 40 04

Frischfleisch:
Rindergulasch 100 g   *1,69*
Rinderbraten
100 g   *2,10*

Chiquita Bananen
1 kg
    3,99

Obst u. Gemüse:
Griech. Gurken
Stück   *1,99*
Grapefruit
5er Netz   *4,95*

▶ (250 Gramm Kaffee, 200 Gramm Schokolade): *Wir brauchen 250 Gramm Kaffee und 200 Gramm Schokolade. Das macht neun Mark vierzehn.*

1. (300 Gramm Käse, Holl. Edamer): _____

_____

Das macht _____

2. (500 Gramm Rindergulasch, 200 Gramm Gelbwurst): _____

_____

Das macht _____

3. (1 Kilo Bananen, 2 Gurken, 4 Dosen° Fanta): _____ | cans

_____

Das macht _____

Name _____ Date _____

G. Einkaufen gehen. Underline each *subject* once and each *direct object* twice.

▶ Im Tante-Emma-Laden kennt <u>man</u> <u><u>Monika und Andrea</u></u>.

1. Monika findet Herrn Meier freundlich.

2. Wieviel Gramm Käse braucht sie heute?

3. Frag doch Andrea!

4. Die Mädchen haben heute viele Fragen.

5. Auf dem Markt kaufen wir Blumen, nicht?

6. Monika nimmt Obst für ihre Freunde mit.

H. Akkusativ. Complete each sentence with the correct form of the word or phrase in parentheses.

▶ Ich arbeite für _____ . (Herr Reiger)

Ich arbeite für _*Herrn Reiger*_____ .

1. Er geht jetzt durch _____ . (die Buchhandlung)

2. Kennst du _____ ? (Herr Reiger)

3. _____ fragst du? (wer)

4. Herr Reiger ist _____ . (unser Nachbar)

5. Er geht um _____ . (sein Haus)

6. Wir haben _____ besonders gern. (unser Nachbar)

7. Ohne _____ kommen wir nicht! (unsere Nachbarn)

8. Ihr habt also nichts gegen _____ ? (die Leute)

I. Gehen wir einkaufen? Make each sentence negative. Use **kein** if the noun has an indefinite article or no article, and **nicht** if the noun has a definite article or possessive adjective.

▶ Hast du Kaffee? *Hast du keinen Kaffee?*

▶ Katja braucht ihr Buch. *Katja braucht ihr Buch nicht.*

1. Jürgen findet seine Einkaufstasche. _____

2. Nimmst du den Tee? _____

3. Ich habe Geld. _____

4. Gibt es hier Bäckereien? _____

5. Julia kauft einen Kuchen. _____

6. Diane findet die Apotheke. _____

7. Sie kauft Aspirin. _____

J. Bitte nicht. You are telling Rudi that no one wants to lend him a car. Complete each sentence with the *accusative pronoun* that corresponds to the noun or pronoun in parentheses.

▶ Frag _____ bitte nicht. (Max)

   Frag *ihn* _____ bitte nicht.

1. Frag _____ bitte nicht. (ich)

2. Frag _____ bitte nicht. (wir)

3. Frag _____ nicht. (Thomas)

4. Frag _____ nicht. (Jan und Inge)

5. Frag _____ nicht. (Frau Lange)

K. Warum machen Sie das (nicht)? State in German two things you will do and two things you will not do and why. Suggested verbs: **essen, trinken, brauchen, kaufen, nehmen.**

▶ *Ich kaufe (Bananen). Ich esse gern (Bananen).*

▶ *Ich kaufe keine (Bananen). Ich esse nicht gern (Bananen).*

1. _____

2. _____

3. _____

4. _____

L. Das Picknick. Erika and Anja want to pack a picnic but encounter setbacks. Express their conversation in German.

Anja: We need fruit and cheese.

_____

Erika: Buy the cheese at Neumann's.

_____

Anja: It's better and cheaper there, isn't it?

_____

Erika: We also don't have any rolls.

_____

Anja: Those I'll buy at the bakery.

_____

Erika: Do we have enough money for the wine?

_____

Anja: No. As always!

_____

M. Landeskunde. Provide brief responses in English.

1. State two ways in which **Supermärkte** in Germany differ from supermarkets in your country.

    _____

    _____

2. Name two things you would find particularly enjoyable about shopping at an outdoor market in a German-speaking country.

    _____

    _____

3. State two differences between weekend shopping hours in Germany and in your community.

    _____

    _____

N. Haben Sie das? While vacationing in Germany, you decide to check out a Tante Emma Laden. Frau Schlemmer, the owner, answers your many questions about what the store does and does not sell. Write down Frau Schlemmer's replies in complete sentences, following the model below.

▶ Haben Sie Obst? (Ja)   *Ja, das haben wir.*

   Haben Sie Apfelsaft? (Nein)   *Nein, den haben wir nicht.*

1. Haben Sie Tee? (Ja) _____

2. Haben Sie Hefte? (Nein) _____

3. Haben Sie einen Kamm? (Nein) _____

4. Haben Sie Mineralwasser? (Ja) _____

5. Haben Sie Butter? (Ja) _____

6. Haben Sie Schinken? (Nein) _____

7. Haben Sie Kaffee? (Ja) _____

8. Haben Sie Brot? (Ja) _____

O. Der bekannteste° Hamburger hat Geburtstag. Read the following
passage and then answer the questions below. Some of the information
is from an article that appeared in the widely-read German daily
newspaper, the Frankfurter Allgemeine (197/93).

| best known

Der Big Mäc ist über 25 Jahre alt. Von 1968 bis zu seinem fünfundzwanzigsten
Geburtstag (1993) verkaufte° McDonald's weltweit° über 14 Milliarden°
Big Mäcs. Auch in Deutschland ißt man den Protagonisten amerikanischer°
Eßkultur° sehr gern und nicht nur, weil sein Name deutsch ist. Sein Name
kommt von Hamburger Steak, denn er kommt aus der norddeutschen Stadt
Hamburg. McDonald's Deutschland hat 442 Restaurants und hier kaufen
jeden° Tag eine Million Gäste° Hamburger. Aber auch in anderen Ländern
ist das Geburtstagskind populär. Es gibt nicht nur den Big Mäc und Fischmäc,
sondern° auch Hamburger Royal mit° Käse und Pommes frites°, McSundae
Eisbecher°, Milchshake mit Vanille-, Schokoladen- oder
Erdbeer°-Geschmack° und Heiße Apfel- und
Kirschtaschen°. Man trinkt dazu° Coca-Cola, Fanta, Sprite, Milch,
Mineralwasser, Orangensaft oder auch Bier. Guten Appetit!

| sold / worldwide / billion
| American
| culinary habits

| every / guests or
customers

| but / with / french fries
| ice cream sundae
| strawberry / flavor
| cherry pockets / with it

1. Wer hat Geburtstag? _____

2. Wie alt war das Geburtstagskind im Jahr 1993? _____

3. Wie alt ist McDonald's heute? _____

4. Wie viele Deutsche kaufen jeden Tag Hamburger bei McDonald's? _____

5. Wie viele McDonald's gibt es in Deutschland? _____

6. Was trinkt man nicht bei McDonald's in Amerika? _____

_____

Kapitel 5

A. Mußt du arbeiten? Sabine and Andreas are talking about the work they have to do. Express their conversation in German.

Sabine: Hi, Andreas. What are you doing this afternoon?

_____

Andreas: I have to read an article for my report. And you?

_____

Sabine: I have to study for the test.

_____

Andreas: Would you like to work together?

_____

Sabine: Glad to. Afterwards we can go for coffee.

_____

B. Was sagen Sie? Respond appropriately to the following statements or questions. You may wish to consult the Supplementary Expressions on page R-22 of your textbook.

Expressing Agreement

1. *Freundin / Freund:* Kannst du mir dein Deutschbuch leihen?

   Du: _____

2. *Freundin / Freund:* Kann ich deine Notizen für das Drama-Seminar haben?

   Du: _____

Expressing Regret

3. *Freundin / Freund:* Willst du um vier Kaffee trinken gehen?

   Du: _____

4. *Freundin / Freund:* Kannst du mir morgen deine Diskette leihen?

   Du: _____

C. Wer ist denn das? You are showing family photos to a roommate who is far-sighted. First correct the mistaken identifications as you wish. Then supply your own answers concerning *professions* and *nationality*. (You may refer to the Supplementary Word Sets on page R-32 in your textbook.)

▶ Ist das deine Kusine? *Nein, das ist meine Tante.*

Ist sie Sozialarbeiterin? *Nein, sie ist Professorin.*

1. Ist das dein Bruder? _____

Ist er Apotheker? _____

2. Das ist deine Mutter, nicht? _____

Ist sie Spanierin? _____

3. Sind das deine zwei Vettern? _____

Sind sie Elektriker? _____

4. Ist das dein Großvater? _____

Ist er Frankfurter? _____

5. Das ist deine Kusine, nicht? _____

Was will sie werden? _____

D. Das Studentenleben. People react differently to upcoming major exams. Complete each sentence with the correct form of the verb in parentheses.

▶ — _____ du gern Krimis? (lesen)   Ja, ich _____ sie auch gern im Fernsehen. (sehen)

Liest du gern Krimis?   Ja, ich sehe sie auch gern im Fernsehen.

1. — _____ du nervös? (werden)

— Klar. Und ich _____ auch sehr müde. (werden)

2. — _____ du den Studenten da? (sehen)

— Ja. Der _____ jeden Tag in der Bibliothek. (lesen)

3. — _____ er für die Literaturprüfung? (lesen)

— Das _____ ich nicht. (wissen)

E. Wißt ihr, wo die Mozartstraße ist? Meike meets two students and asks them for information. Complete each sentence with the correct form of **wissen** or **kennen**.

1. _____ du diese Stadt wirklich gut?

2. _____ ihr denn nicht, wo die Universität ist?

3. _____ du den Professor da?

4. Ja, ich _____ aber nicht, wie er heißt.

5. Er denkt, er _____ alles, aber wir _____ nichts.

6. Ich _____ sein Buch über moderne Kunstgeschichte. Es ist wirklich gut.

7. Du _____ doch, ich mache jetzt Geschichte als Hauptfach.

F. An der Uni. Complete the following sentences by supplying the correct forms of the cued der-words.

▶ Findest du _____ Vorlesung gut? (dies-)   *Findest du diese Vorlesung gut?*

1. _____ Studenten machen Germanistik als Hauptfach. (manch-)

2. Wir lesen jetzt _____ Artikel über den neuen deutschen Film. (dies-)

3. _____ Filme kennst du schon? (welch-)

4. _____ Buch über den Film ist besonders interessant. (dies-)

5. _____ Student muß ein Referat vorbereiten. (jed-)

6. Findet ihr _____ Kurs schwer? (dies-)

7. _____ Fächer sind nicht leicht. (solch-)

G. Fragen. David, an American student studying in Hamburg, has questions for his new German acquaintances, Sabine and Ursel. Form sentences, using the cues below.

▶ ihr / möchten / arbeiten / im Sommer / ?   *Möchtet ihr im Sommer arbeiten?*

1. du / mögen / Hamburg / ?

   _____

2. ihr / dürfen / studieren / zehn Semester / ?

   _____

3. Studenten / müssen / schreiben / viele Klausuren / ?

   _____

4. man / müssen / zurückzahlen / BAföG / ?

   _____

5. du / möchten / studieren / in Amerika / ?

   _____

6. wir / können / gehen / jetzt / in die Bibliothek / ?

   _____

H. Schönes Wochenende. Complete each sentence with the proper form of the cued verb.

▶ David _____ Sabine an der Uni _____ . (kennenlernen)

   David lernt Sabine an der Uni kennen.

1. David _____ heute nachmittag mit Sabine _____ . (spazierengehen)

2. Dann _____ sie ihre Vorlesungsnotizen _____ . (wollen / durcharbeiten)

3. Sabine _____ nachher _____ . (müssen / einkaufen)

4. Dann _____ sie mit Ursel und Andreas das Abendessen _____ . (vorbereiten)

5. David _____ Wein _____ . (mitbringen)

6. Später _____ sie zusammen _____ . (fernsehen)

I. Deutsch oder amerikanisch? Decide which system of higher education and which culture each of the following statements describes. Write **a** for **amerikanisch** or **d** for **deutsch** in each blank.

1. _____ An den Unis gibt es viele Studentenjobs.

2. _____ Es gibt zuwenig Studienplätze.

3. _____ Es gibt viele Privatuniversitäten.

4. _____ Nach acht oder zehn Semestern macht man Examen.

5. _____ Fast° alle Studenten müssen Kurse wie Englisch und Geschichte nehmen. | almost

6. _____ Es gibt keine Studiengebühren.

7. _____ Nur wenige Kurse haben jedes Semester Prüfungen.

8. _____ Man studiert nur ein oder zwei Fächer.

J. Ich brauche Deine Notizen. Write a note to Ilse asking if she can lend you her lecture notes. Tell her you have to prepare your report, and that you were sick yesterday and still have a lot to do. Ask if she can bring the notes along tomorrow.

Liebe Ilse,

_____

_____

_____

_____

Dein/Deine

_____

K. Landeskunde.   Provide brief responses in English.

1. Define the following types of classes briefly: **Vorlesung, Übung, Seminar.**

   _____

   _____

   _____

2. What factors determine whether a university applicant in Germany may study a subject such as law or medicine?

   _____

   _____

3. What is **BAföG**? Does your country have a similar law?

   _____

   _____

4. Describe briefly the three main types of schools German young people attend after the **Grundschule.**

   _____

   _____

   _____

L. Wo wohnen Studenten in Hamburg? Read the passage and then answer the questions in German.

Früher°, bis 1960 oder 1965, war das typische° Studentenzimmer eine „Studentenbude". Eine Studentenbude war ein Zimmer bei Privatleuten. Heute wohnen nur noch sehr wenige Studenten so. Warum ist das heute anders? Es gibt heute nicht mehr so viele alte Häuser mit extra Zimmern. Auch möchten die Studenten machen können, was sie wollen und nicht, was der Wirt° oder die Wirtin° will. Sie wollen nicht mehr hören: „Ihr Freund (oder Ihre Freundin) darf aber nur bis zehn Uhr in Ihrem Zimmer bleiben." Die Studenten wollen aber nicht nur von Wirt und Wirtin unabhängig° sein. Sie wollen auch von ihren Eltern unabhängig sein. Deshalb wohnen heute auch weniger° Hamburger Studenten als früher bei ihren Eltern.	formerly / typical landlord / landlady independent fewer
Heute haben die meisten Studenten ihre eigene° Wohnung°. Eine eigene Wohnung kostet° natürlich viel Geld. Daher mieten° oft mehrere° Studenten zusammen eine große Wohnung. Sie bilden° eine Wohngemeinschaft°. Die Wohnungen in alten Häusern sind oft billiger° als in neuen. Deshalb findet man solche Wohngemeinschaften mehr in alten und weniger° in neuen Häusern.	own / apartment costs / rent several / form group of people sharing an apartment / cheaper less
Für einige° Studenten hat die Universität Hamburg Studentenheime. Studentenheime haben in Deutschland aber noch keine lange Tradition. Daher gibt es auch in Hamburg nicht genug Plätze in Universitäts-studentenheimen. So kommt es, daß viele Studenten oft mehrere Monate auf° einen Platz warten° müssen.	some for / wait

1. Bis wann war das typische Studentenzimmer bei Privatleuten?

_____

2. Warum gibt es heute nicht mehr so viele Studentenbuden?

_____

3. Warum wohnen heute nicht mehr so viele Studenten bei ihren Eltern?

_____

4. Was ist eine Wohngemeinschaft?

_____

5. Warum mieten Studenten Wohnungen in alten Häusern?

_____

6. Warum müssen Studenten oft mehrere Monate auf einen Platz im Studentenheim warten?

_____

Kapitel 6

A. Pläne. Complete the discussion between Dieter and Petra about vacation plans. Add *articles* and *prepositions* as necessary.

▶ *Dieter:* du / haben / Pläne / für / Ferien / ?　　*Hast du Pläne für die Ferien?*

Petra: ja, / ich / fahren / nach / Österreich

_____

Dieter: du / fahren / mit / Zug / ?

_____

Petra: nein, / ich / fliegen

_____

Dieter: wann / du / kommen / wieder / Hause / ?

_____

Petra: ich / wissen / noch nicht

_____

B. Identifizieren Sie. For the following English and German sentences, underline each *independent clause* once and each *dependent clause* twice.

1. a. I hope that you'll be going home today.

    b. I'm sure that it won't be before three o'clock.

    c. My car isn't running again, and it's too far to walk.

    d. I'll be glad to take you, but I have to stop at the bookstore.

2. a. Weißt du, daß Rita in die Ferien fährt?

    b. Fährt sie nach Österreich, oder fährt sie nach Italien?

    c. Glaubst du, daß sie mit dem Zug fährt?

    d. Ich kann nicht mitfahren, weil ich nicht genug Geld habe.

C. Dänemark. Complete the sentences with **aber** or **sondern,** as appropriate.

1. Ullas Großeltern kommen nicht aus Norwegen, _____ aus Dänemark.

2. Ulla kann Dänisch verstehen, _____ sie kann es nicht gut sprechen.

3. Ihre Tante wohnt noch in Dänemark, _____ ihr Vetter wohnt jetzt in Österreich.

4. In den Ferien arbeitet Ulla nicht in Innsbruck, _____ sie fährt nach Kopenhagen.

D. Christel studiert in England. Tell about Christel's plans for studying next year. Combine the sentences using the conjunctions **daß, wenn,** or **weil,** as appropriate.

▶ Christel jobbt im Sommer. Sie braucht Geld.   *Christel jobbt im Sommer, weil sie Geld braucht.*

1. Sie geht jeden Tag spazieren. Das Wetter ist gut.

    _____

2. Im Herbst studiert sie in London. Sie möchte besser Englisch lernen.

    _____

3. Es ist gut. Sie kann in England studieren.

    _____

4. Sie bleibt ein ganzes Jahr. Sie hat genug Geld.

    _____

5. Nach dem Jahr in London kommt sie nach Linz zurück. Sie will in Linz ihr Examen machen.

    _____

    _____

6. Sie findet vielleicht einen guten Job bei einer Exportfirma. Sie kann gut Englisch.

    _____

    _____

E. Akkusativ und Dativ. For each of the following English and German sentences first circle the *subject.* Then underline the *direct object* once and the *indirect object,* when present, twice.

1. a.   The rental agency promised us the car for next week.

    b.   The travel agent gave George and me several brochures.

    c.   Don't forget the tickets! (*subject understood*)

2. a.   Der Deutsche fragt eine Österreicherin.

    b.   Diesen Dialekt kann er aber nicht verstehen.

    c.   Ein Freund erklärt ihm alles.

    d.   Kauft Alex seiner Freundin dieses Buch über Wien?

    e.   Nein, er schenkt ihr ein Buch über Salzburg.

F. Demonstrativpronomen. Complete the answers to the following questions, using a *demonstrative pronoun*.

▶ Kann man mit diesem Bus nach Oberndorf fahren?

Ja, mit *dem* kann man nach Oberndorf fahren.

1. Kann man bei deinen Freunden in Graz übernachten?

Ja, bei _____ kann man übernachten.

2. Kann man mit deinen Freunden sprechen?

Ja, mit _____ kann man sprechen.

3. Können wir Erik Geld leihen?

Ja, _____ können wir Geld leihen.

4. Wem gehört dieses Fahrrad hier? Birgit?

Nein, _____ gehört das Fahrrad nicht.

5. Gehört es Sebastian?

Ja, _____ gehört es.

G. Was macht Anja in den Ferien? Answer each question with the *possessive adjective* in the *dative case*. Use the cues provided.

▶ Mit wem zeltet Anja in Österreich? (ihre Familie)   *Anja zeltet mit ihrer Familie in Österreich.*

1. Wem gibt sie das Buch über Tirol? (ihr Bruder)

_____

2. Mit wem wandert sie in Kärnten? (ihre Eltern)

_____

3. Wem gehören die Videos über Salzburg? (ihre Schwestern)

_____

4. Wem kauft sie Blumen? (ihre Tante)

_____

5. Von wem hat sie das Geld für die Ferien? (ihr Onkel und ihre Großmutter)

_____

H. Stimmt das? You are trying to locate the owners of certain items. Complete each sentence with a *dative personal pronoun*.

▶ Die Poster gehören _____ (wir).   *Die Poster gehören uns.*

▶ Die Poster gehören _____ (Tanja).   *Die Poster gehören ihr.*

1. Der Computer gehört _____ (du), nicht wahr?

2. Ja, der gehört _____ (ich).

3. Aber der CD Spieler gehört _____ (Tanja und Max)?

4. Nein, der CD Spieler gehört _____ (wir).

5. Glaubst du _____ (Tanja)?

6. Nein, aber ich glaube _____ (Max).

I. Wem schenkst du das? Your friend Thomas asks you about several gifts. Answer affirmatively, using *pronouns* for the *direct objects*.

▶ Schenkst du deiner Schwester diese CD?   *Ja, ich schenke sie meiner Schwester.*

1. Kaufst du deinen Eltern dieses Radio? _____

2. Schenkst du deiner Mutter diesen Roman? _____

3. Kaufst du deinem Bruder dieses Poster? _____

4. Schenkst du deinem Freund diese CDs? _____

5. Kaufst du Alex diesen Krimi? _____

6. Schenkst du deinen Freunden diese Karten? _____

J. Landeskunde. Provide brief responses in English.

1. Briefly discuss **Jugendherbergen:** where are they located, and who uses them?

_____

_____

2. Compare public transportation in German-speaking countries with that in your own country (or city): Is it efficient? well-utilized?

_____

_____

3. Name two ways in which Austria is actively involved in world affairs.

_____

_____

4. List four names that are associated with Vienna as an important cultural center.

_____

_____

Name _____ Date _____

K. Identifizieren Sie. Identify the two rivers° and eight cities marked on the map of Austria. Refer to the map on the inside cover of your textbook as necessary.

° Flüsse

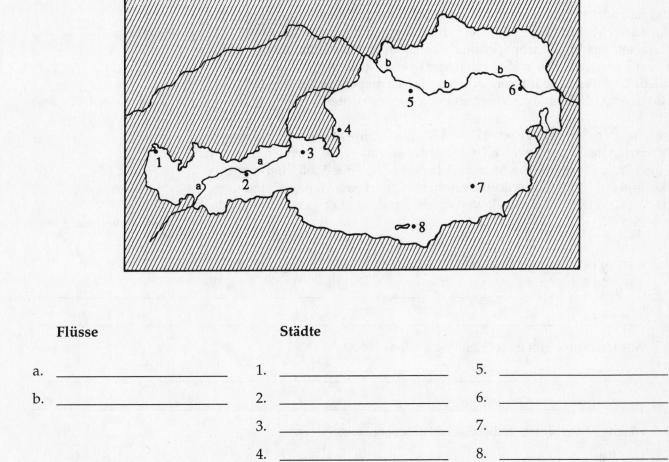

Flüsse	**Städte**	
a. _____	1. _____	5. _____
b. _____	2. _____	6. _____
	3. _____	7. _____
	4. _____	8. _____

L. Schubert und Mozart. Read the passage and then answer the questions.

Für viele Leute gehören Österreich und Musik zusammen. Im Sommer kann man in Österreich „Musikferien" machen, denn es gibt jeden Sommer über 50 Festspiele°, bekannte° und nicht so bekannte, vom Bodensee im Westen bis zum Neusiedler See im Osten. Es gibt Oper, Operette und Musical, Ballett und Konzerte mit klassischer und moderner Musik.

° festivals / well-known

In Hohenems bei Bregenz gibt es jeden Sommer die „Schubertiade", ein Musikfest° für die Musik von Franz Schubert (1797–1828). Schubert ist durch seine Lieder°, Symphonien, Kammermusik° und Klavierstücke° bekannt. Aber besonders wichtig sind seine Lieder. Es gibt über 600 von ihm.

° music festival
° songs / chamber music / piano pieces

Schubert war in seinem Leben° nicht sehr erfolgreich° und hatte° immer wenig Geld. Er wohnte° oft bei Freunden. Hier und da arbeitete° er als Klavierlehrer°. In seinem ganzen Leben hatte er aber kein eigenes° Klavier.

° life / successful / had
° lived / worked
° piano teacher / own

Man erzählt von ihm diese Anekdote: Einmal will ein Freund mit ihm ins Kaffeehaus gehen, aber Schubert kann keine Strümpfe° ohne Löcher° finden. Er sucht und sucht und sagt endlich°: „Es scheint°, daß man in Wien die Strümpfe nur mit Löchern fabriziert."

| stockings / holes
| finally / seems

Die Salzburger Festspiele sind vor allem Mozartfestspiele. Wolfgang Amadeus Mozart (1756–1791) ist in Salzburg geboren°. Er ist für fast° alle Gebiete° der° Musik sehr wichtig. Seine Opern gehören zum internationalen Repertoire. Die großen Orchester spielen seine Symphonien. Immer wieder° gibt es neue Interpretationen von seinen Serenaden, von seinen Klavier-° und Violinkonzerten° und von seinen Sonaten.

| born / almost
| areas / of
| **Immer wieder:** again and again
| piano / **Konzert:** concerto

Von dem großen Beethoven (1770–1827) gibt es eine kleine Geschichte zu° Mozarts Musik: Beethoven geht mit dem bekannten Pianisten Cramer durch einen Park. Da spielt man Mozarts Klavierkonzert in c-Moll°. Bei einem bestimmten Motiv bleibt Beethoven stehen°, hört eine Weile zu° und sagt dann: „Cramer, solche Musik werde° ich in meinem Leben nicht zustande bringen°."

| about

| C minor
| **bleibt stehen:** stops / **hört zu:** listens / will

| **zustande bringen:** accomplish

1. Warum kann man in Österreich besonders gut Musikferien machen?

   _____

   _____

2. Was für Musik gibt es bei den Festspielen?

   _____

   _____

3. Welche Musik von Schubert ist besonders bekannt?

   _____

4. Warum kann Schubert keine Strümpfe ohne Löcher finden?

   _____

5. Wo ist Mozart geboren?

   _____

6. Für welche Gebiete der Musik ist Mozart wichtig? Nennen° Sie drei.

   | name

   _____

   _____

7. Wie findet Beethoven Mozarts Musik?

   _____

Kapitel 7

A. Wie war es? Christine asks Klaus about his dinner with Gerd. Give their conversation, based on the guidelines. Use the *present perfect tense* where appropriate.

▶ *Christine:* wo / ihr / essen / gestern / zu Abend / ?   *Wo habt ihr gestern zu Abend gegessen?*

Klaus: wir / gehen / ins Café an der Uni

_____

Christine: Essen / schmecken / ?

_____

Klaus: ja / die Pizza / sein / ganz toll

_____

Christine: ihr / Wein / trinken / ?

_____

Klaus: Ja / Gerd / mich / einladen

_____

B. Was haben Sie als Kind (nicht) gern gemacht? Check off those things that you liked or didn't like to do as a child.

	gern	nicht gern	
▶ Fisch essen		X	
1. Sport treiben			
2. früh aufstehen			
3. Comics lesen			
4. Hausaufgaben° machen				homework
5. mit dem Lehrer° / der Lehrerin° sprechen				teacher

Now form complete sentences in the *present perfect tense.*

▶ *Ich habe nicht gern Fisch gegessen.*

1. _____

2. _____

3. _____

4. _____

5. _____

C. Kurze Gespräche. Use the verbs **gefallen, mögen,** and **gern haben** to complete the mini-dialogues below.

1. — Warum _____ du dieses Café nicht?

   __ Ich _____ die Musik nicht.

2. — _____ euch ihre Wohnung?

   — Mir _____ die sehr, aber Markus

   _____ die Nachbarn nicht _____ .

D. Das hat Daniela heute gemacht. Tell what Daniela did at specific times during the day by using the *present perfect tense.* Use the pictures as cues.

▶ *Sie ist um 7.50 Uhr aufgestanden.*
Or: Um 7.50 Uhr ist sie aufgestanden.

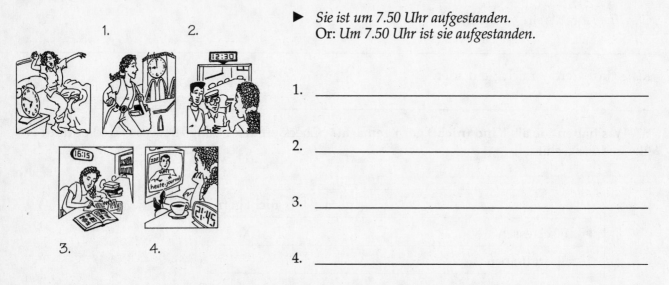

1. _____

2. _____

3. _____

4. _____

E. Auf englisch, bitte. Write the English equivalents of the following sentences.

1. Anton sagt, daß er zum Studieren zu alt ist.

   _____

2. Zuviel Essen macht krank.

   _____

3. Das Wandern am Morgen und am Abend macht Brigitte müde.

   _____

4. Warten ist oft schwer.

   _____

F. Das Spiel. Jan substitutes in a soccer game. Restate each sentence in the *present perfect tense*.

▶ Thomas ruft mich um elf an.   *Thomas hat mich um elf angerufen.*

1. Ich mache gerade Pläne für den Nachmittag.

   _____

2. Das Spiel interessiert mich sehr.

   _____

3. Aber ich spiele ziemlich schlecht.

   _____

4. Das gefällt mir nicht.

   _____

5. Leider fotografieren meine Freunde mein Spielen.

   _____

6. Sie finden das lustig.

   _____

7. Nach dem Spiel feiern wir.

   _____

G. Geburtstagskaffee. Describe Gabi and Daniel's party for their father. Form six sentences in the *present perfect tense* by combining subjects from list **A** with predicates from list **B.** Put your sentences into a logical sequence.

A. Daniel und Gabi; die Großeltern; der Käsekuchen; Kim; die Mutter, Onkel Max und Tante Hanni; die Pizza; Sebastian

B. Pizza machen; bis acht Uhr bleiben; einige Freunde zum Essen einladen; Käsekuchen bringen; lustige Geschichten erzählen; erst um zehn nach Hause gehen; bei der Arbeit helfen; allen schmecken; zuviel Kuchen essen

▶ *Daniel und Gabi haben einige Freunde zum Essen eingeladen.*

1. _____

2. _____

3. _____

4. _____

5. _____

6. _____

H. Ein Abend bei uns. Gerritt tells what his family did on a Saturday evening. Give his account in the past, using the *present perfect tense*.

▶ Ich mache keine Hausaufgaben, weil ich keine Lust habe.

Ich habe keine Hausaufgaben gemacht, weil ich keine Lust gehabt habe.

1. Laura ißt zwei Wurstbrote, weil sie Hunger hat.

   _____

2. Tobias sieht fern, obwohl ihn der Krimi nicht interessiert.

   _____

3. Weil Julian Freitagabend spät nach Hause kommt, ißt er Samstagmorgen kein Frühstück.

   _____

4. Meine Eltern gehen ins Konzert, weil Placido Domingo singt.° | **singen: gesungen**

   _____

5. Das Konzert gefällt ihnen.

   _____

I. Wie waren die Ferien? David is talking with Valerie about his trip to Austria. Give the *German equivalents*.

1. We traveled by train to Austria.

   _____

2. Did you hike a lot?

   _____

3. Yes, although it often rained.

   _____

4. Did your friend (*m.*) like the trip?

   _____

5. Yes. He found the mountains beautiful.

   _____

J. Landeskunde. Provide brief responses in English.

1. Describe the work week and vacation time of German industrial workers and compare the system with the one in your country.

_____

_____

_____

2. Name three customs pertaining to eating at home or in a restaurant in German-speaking countries, which are not generally observed in your country.

_____

_____

_____

3. Contrast getting a driver's license in German-speaking countries with the situation in your state or province.

_____

_____

_____

4. Name three things that you've learned about the German movie industry.

_____

_____

_____

K. Freizeit ein Problem? Read the passage and then answer the questions.

„Alle gehen in ihr Zimmer, machen die Tür zu und tun eine oder
eineinhalb Stunden, was sie wollen. Unsere eine Tochter will Musik
hören. Unsere andere Tochter will fernsehen. Meine Frau will lesen.
Ich will etwas schlafen. So verbringen° wir alle einen sehr schönen | spend
Sonntagnachmittag", erzählt Dr. Feldgen vom Institut für
Freizeitforschung° in Hamburg. | research on leisure

Man möchte fragen: „Ja und? Ist das etwas Besonderes?°" Nach° Dr. Feldgen, | special / according to
ja. Viele Leute finden nämlich, daß Freizeit ein Problem ist.
In den meisten Familien wollen die Menschen vor allem zwei Dinge°. Sie | things
wollen Kontakt mit anderen, wollen etwas zusammen machen. Sie wollen
aber auch allein sein, weg° von den anderen. In diesem Dilemma ist | away
Fernsehen oft der einzige° Ausweg°. Man weiß nicht, was man machen soll. | only / way out
So sieht man eben fern. Wenn der Fernseher kaputt ist, gibt's eine
Familienkrise.

Für viele ist Freizeit keine freie Zeit. Am Wochenende machen sie
Hausarbeit, waschen das Auto oder arbeiten im Garten. Für diese

Aktivitäten gibt man seine freie Zeit auf°. Oder man macht einen großen Plan für die ganze Familie. Dieser Plan soll dann alle in der Familie zufriedenstellen°. Statt° Zufriedenheit° gibt's aber oft Unzufriedenheit, Frustration, Aggression, Streß.

| **gibt auf:** give up

| satisfy / instead of / satisfaction

Für viele ist Freitag der schönste° Tag der Woche. Man denkt daran, was man am Wochenende machen kann. Die Wirklichkeit ist dann aber oft gar nicht so schön. Warum? Dr. Feldgen sagt: „Weil wir nicht gelernt haben, was wir brauchen. Wir brauchen freie Zeit für persönliche Wünsche. Wir brauchen freie Zeit für Kontakt mit anderen. Und wir brauchen freie Zeit, nichts zu tun, ohne Langeweile° und ohne Schuldgefühle°."

| the best

| boredom
| feelings of guilt

1. Warum ist der Sonntagnachmittag für alle in Dr. Feldgens Familie sehr schön?

   _____

2. Warum ist ein schöner Sonntagnachmittag für alle in Dr. Feldgens Familie etwas Besonderes?

   _____

3. Was wollen die Menschen in den meisten Familien?

   _____

4. Warum sehen viele Menschen am Wochenende oft fern?

   _____

5. Was machen viele Leute am Wochenende?

   _____

6. Warum ist für viele Freitag der schönste Tag der Woche?

   _____

L. Was machen Sie in Ihrer Freizeit? Write a paragraph of five complete sentences of activities you enjoy doing in your free time. Below are some ideas you may want to use. (You may also want to consult the Supplementary Word Sets in the Reference Section of your textbook for additional terminology.)

samstags, sonntags, morgens, nachmittags, abends, Karten (Golf, Tennis, Basketball) spielen, schwimmen, wandern, Freunde besuchen / einladen; ins Restaurant (Kino, Theater, Konzert, Museum) gehen; in die Kneipe / Disko gehen; zum Einkaufszentrum° gehen; spät aufstehen, faulenzen, ... gefällt mir, ... mag ich gern.

| shopping center

In meiner Freizeit _____

_____

_____

_____

Kapitel 8

A. Das Fest. Read the following conversation and then make up five questions about it. Answer your own questions.

Susanne: Du, hier sieht es aber furchtbar aus!

Ingrid: Und in einer Stunde kommen schon die Gäste.

Susanne: Wie viele Leute kommen eigentlich?

Ingrid: Ich habe fünfzehn Leute eingeladen.

Susanne: Ich räume schnell auf.

Ingrid: Hoffentlich bringt Jan seine neuen CDs mit.

Susanne: Hast du jetzt einen neuen CD-Spieler?

Ingrid: Ja, sieh mal, das Geburtstagsgeschenk° meiner Eltern. | birthday present

Susanne: Na, dann muß das Fest ja toll werden.

1. _____

_____

2. _____

_____

3. _____

_____

4. _____

_____

5. _____

_____

B. Was sagen Sie? Respond appropriately. See Reference Section #6 and #3 on page R-23 of your textbook.

Expressing Good Wishes

1. *Freund/in:* Ich habe gestern Geburtstag gehabt.

   Du: _____

2. *Freund/in:* Morgen fahre ich mit Anne und Erik in die Berge.

   Du: _____

Expressing Annoyance

3. *Freund/in:* Ich habe zwölf Leute für heute abend eingeladen.

   Du: _____

4. *Freund/in:* Max hat Jan deinen CD-Spieler geliehen.

   Du: _____

C. Was meinen Sie? Decide whether each sentence is a subjective
judgment or generalization, or an objective observation. Write **U** for **Urteil°** | judgment
or **B** for **Beobachtung°**. | observation

1. _____ Die Amerikaner sehen den ganzen Tag fern.

2. _____ In Deutschland findet man fast überall Blumen.

3. _____ Die Amerikaner benutzen den Vornamen mehr als die Deutschen.

4. _____ Die Deutschen fahren wie die Wilden.

5. _____ In Amerika kann man das ganze Wochenende einkaufen gehen.

6. _____ Die deutschen Züge sind fast immer pünktlich.

7. _____ Die Deutschen essen zuviel Wurst.

8. _____ Die Amerikaner sind sehr freundlich.

D. Bei Rita. Friends are gathering at Rita's. Describe their activities and locations by supplying
appropriate *prepositions*. Contract the two definite articles in parentheses.

Claudia steht _____ dem Sofa. Paul steht _____ ihr. Sie sprechen

_____ einen Roman.

Drei Freunde sitzen _____ (dem) Tisch. Uwe schreibt eine Karte _____

seine Freundin. Hans redet _____ seine Ferien. Anni sitzt _____ ihnen.

Gisela kommt gerade _____ (das) Zimmer.

E. Peters Plan. Complete the following passage about Peter's plan, using the cued *prepositions and articles.*

Peter arbeitet _____ _____ (*in a*) Café, aber er möchte gern _____ _____

(*at the*) Universität studieren. Er spricht oft mit Studenten _____ _____ (*about the*)

Universität.

Er will Physik studieren. _____ _____ (*on his*) Schreibtisch zu Hause liegt ein Buch

von Einstein. Darin liest er gern _____ (*in the*) Abend. Und _____ _____ (*in front*

of the) Fenster hat er eine kleine Statue von dem Physiker Werner Heisenberg gestellt. _____

_____ (*next to the*) Bücherregal steht sein Computer.

Letzte Woche hat Peter _____ _____ (*to his*) Eltern geschrieben. Er möchte wissen,

was sie _____ _____ (*of his*) Plan halten.

F. Fragen, Fragen! Oldenburg's information center receives many inquiries about events in the city. Complete the answers below with the appropriate *accusative and dative time expressions.*

1. Wie lange spielt „Figaros Hochzeit°"? | Marriage of Figaro

    Es spielt _____ . (*one month*)

2. Wann ist der erste Winterflohmarkt°? | winter flea market

    Er ist _____ . (*on Saturday*)

3. Wann ist das Winterkonzert im Schloß°? | castle

    Es tut mir leid, das war schon _____ . (*a week ago*)

4. Kommt das Hazen-Quartett wieder?

    Ja, es kommt bestimmt _____ wieder. (*next year*)

5. Wann kann man Karten fürs Staatstheater kaufen?

    Man kann sie _____ ab 14 Uhr kaufen. (*every day*)

G. Viele Fragen über Judith. Daniel wants to meet Judith and gets information about her from her friend Katja. Fill in their dialog with **ob, wenn, wann.**

1. *Daniel:* Weißt du, _____ Geographie Judiths Hauptfach ist?

2. *Katja:* Das weiß ich nicht, aber ich kann sie fragen, _____ ich sie sehe.

3. *Daniel:* Kannst du mir sagen, _____ ihre nächste Vorlesung ist und _____ sie im Herbst weiter studiert?

4. *Katja:* Ich glaube, sie studiert nur weiter, _____ sie im Sommer jobben kann.

5. *Daniel:* Weißt du, _____ wir drei ein Glas Wein zusammen trinken können?

6. *Katja:* Ich glaube, _____ das Wetter schön wird, können wir in den Biergarten am Main gehen.

H. Was Markus macht, macht Daniel auch. Show that Markus and Daniel have the same interests by rewriting each prepositional phrase in the following sentences, replacing the preposition and the noun with a **da**-compound or a *preposition and personal pronoun* as appropriate.

▶ Markus spricht gern *über Computer.*   *Daniel spricht auch gern darüber.*

▶ Markus redet wieder von Isabella, *seiner Computerfreundin.*
   Daniel redet auch wieder von ihr.

1. Markus hat keine Angst *vor der Technik.*

   _____

2. Markus spricht viel *über seinen Informatik-Professor.*

   _____

3. Am Wochenende arbeitet Markus *an seinem Computer.*

   _____

4. Er wartet immer *auf neue Software-Programme.*

   _____

5. Markus hält sehr viel *von seinen Computerfreunden.*

   _____

I. Worüber hat Katja gesprochen? A friend of Katja's retells her conversation with her. The surroundings are noisy and Birgit inquires what Katja has been saying. Rewrite the prepositional phrase in italics in the following sentences. Form a question by replacing the preposition and the noun with a **wo**-compound or *preposition and personal pronoun* as appropriate.

▶ Katja hat *über ihr neues Auto* gesprochen.   *Birgit: Worüber hat sie gesprochen?*

▶ Katja hat *von ihrem Freund* Peter geredet.   *Birgit: Von wem hat sie geredet?*

1. Katja hat keine Angst *vor der nächsten Klausur.*

   Birgit: _____

2. Katja denkt meistens *an das Wochenende.*

   Birgit: _____

3. Sie kann dann *mit ihrem Freund Peter* Tennis spielen.

   Birgit: _____

4. Später haben Katja und Peter *über das Spiel* gesprochen.

   Birgit: _____

5. Abends sind sie *mit Katjas Eltern* zum Restaurant Rosenau gefahren.

   _____

Name _____ Date _____

J. Gerrit muß sein Zimmer aufräumen. Gerrit is very messy. His father leaves him a detailed note of what he wants done by the time he comes home. Use **legen/liegen, setzen/sitzen, stellen/stehen, stecken,** and **hängen** where appropriate. (Imperative forms of the verb are indicated by "Imp.")

▶ Bitte _____ (Imp.) die Lampe in die Ecke!   *Bitte stell die Lampe in die Ecke!*

1. Gerrit, bitte _____ (Imp.) den Fernseher neben den Schrank, dann

_____ er nicht mehr vor dem Bücherregal. 2. Deine Hefte _____

auf dem Boden. _____ (Imp.) sie bitte in deine Büchertasche! 3. Das Claudia

Schiffer Poster _____ an der Wand, und ich möchte, daß du es jetzt in den großen

Schrank _____ . 4. Deine Schuhe _____ unter dem Bett. Du

sollst sie putzen, und sie dann in den Schrank _____ . 5. Heute abend

_____ wir nach dem Essen zusammen,

und ich helfe dir bei deinen Hausaufgaben°, wenn du willst. | homework

K. Landeskunde. Provide brief responses in English.

1. When did immigration of Germans to America begin? Why did they come? Where did they settle? What has been their numerical impact? Name four states with large German populations.

   _____

   _____

   _____

2. With whom do German-speaking people use the word **Freund**? Name two or three adjectives that English speakers often use with the noun *friend*.

   _____

   _____

   _____

3. Name three things you learned about apartments and private homes in Germany.

   _____

   _____

   _____

4. Name three features of home design or layout in German-speaking countries that promote a sense of privacy.

   _____

   _____

   _____

L. Deutschland ist nicht Amerika. Read the passage and then answer the questions.

Robert Jones erzählt von seiner Reise nach Deutschland. Er sagt: „Also, wissen Sie, ich bin ja ganz gern in Deutschland gewesen. Aber ich möchte in diesem Land nicht leben. Ich fahre zum Beispiel gern mit dem Auto. Aber das Land ist zu klein. In *einem* Tag bin ich von Hamburg im Norden nach München im Süden gefahren. Nicht ganz 800 Kilometer!

„Ich weiß, die Deutschen wandern gern, oder sie gehen spazieren, in den Parks, an den Seen° und auch in den Stadtzentren°. Wirklich! Aber ich arbeite die ganze Woche. Also will ich am Wochenende doch nicht auch noch wandern.

| lakes / city centers

„Und dann die Restaurants! Das Essen war ja nicht schlecht. Darüber will ich ja nichts sagen. Aber nie° steht kaltes Wasser auf dem Tisch. Und wenn die Kellner° kaltes Wasser bringen, ist es ein Miniglas, und darin schwimmt dann ein klitzekleines° Eisstück°. Ich will aber trinken und keine Tabletten nehmen. Das deutsche Bier habe ich aber zu schwer und zu bitter und zu warm gefunden. Und der deutsche Wein war mir zu sauer°.

| never
| waiters
| tiny / ice cube

| sour

„Und dann habe ich immer ‚Herr Schmidt' gesagt und ‚Frau Meyer'. Wie kalt das ist. Und zu mir haben alle Leute ‚Herr Jones' gesagt. Ich habe das furchtbar unpersönlich gefunden. Daher habe ich auch keine Freunde in diesem Land, obwohl ich doch drei Wochen da war. Wenn Sie mich fragen, ob ich eines Tages wieder dahin will, so muß ich sagen, ich weiß nicht."

1. Wo möchte Robert Jones nicht leben?

_____

2. Warum kann er in diesem Land nicht so gut mit dem Auto fahren?

_____

3. Warum will er am Wochenende nicht wandern?

_____

4. Was hat ihm beim Essen im Restaurant nicht gefallen?

_____

5. Warum hat ihm das Bier nicht geschmeckt?

_____

6. Wie findet er es, wenn er „Herr" und „Frau" benutzen muß und wenn die Leute zu ihm „Herr Jones" sagen?

_____

7. Warum hat er keine Freunde in Deutschland?

_____

M. Schreiben Sie.   Answer the following questions and give a brief explanation.

1. An wen denken Sie oft? Warum?

   _____

   _____

2. Wovor haben Sie (keine) Angst? Warum (nicht)?

   _____

   _____

3. Auf wen müssen Sie manchmal warten? Warum?

   _____

   _____

4. Wohin gehen Sie gern mit Freunden? Warum?

   _____

   _____

Geöffnet: **TÄGLICH** - außer
Montag: 9-12 und 14-18 Uhr

AN DER DONAULÄNDE

**Von Wien aus in
30 Minuten zu erreichen!**

90 Originalwerke
und die Dokumentation:
"SCHIELE UND SEINE ZEIT."

IM ALTEN STADTGEFÄNGNIS

Kapitel 9

A. Eine neue Stelle. Imagine you are interviewing for a summer job as a typist. Answer the following questions.

Personalchef/in: Haben Sie schon einmal bei einer Firma gearbeitet?

Sie: _____

_____

Personalchef/in: Warum möchten Sie bei uns arbeiten?

Sie: _____

_____

Personalchef/in: Können Sie mit dem Wortprozessor oder Computer arbeiten?

Sie: _____

_____

Personalchef/in: Was möchten Sie gern verdienen?

Sie: _____

_____

B. Was sagen Sie? Respond appropriately. See Reference Section #2 and #9 on pages R-23 and R-24 of your textbook.

Expressing Doubt

1. *Freund/in:* Bei einer größeren Firma bekomme ich mehr Verantwortung.

   Du: _____

2. *Freund/in:* Ich habe gehört, daß deine Chefin fünf Jahre in Kanada gearbeitet hat.

   Du: _____

Expressing Surprise

3. *Freund/in:* Ich wollte eigentlich Pilotin/Pilot werden.

   Du: _____

4. *Freund/in:* Sebastian hat seine Stelle schon wieder gewechselt.

   Du: _____

C. -heit und -keit. Write the adjective from which each noun is derived, and then guess the meaning of the noun.

	Adjective	Meaning
1. Mehrheit	_____	_____
2. Genauigkeit	_____	_____
3. Trockenheit	_____	_____
4. Gleichheit	_____	_____
5. Freiheit	_____	_____
6. Lustigkeit	_____	_____
7. Richtigkeit	_____	_____

D. Ferienreise. Complete the information about the Kohls' trip to Austria by providing the proper *genitive forms* of the *noun phrases* in parentheses.

▶ Sie hatten die Adresse _____ in Salzburg. (ein Freund)

Sie hatten die Adresse eines Freundes in Salzburg.

1. Auf einem Fest haben Kohls den Nachbarn _____ kennengelernt. (ihre Freunde)

2. Sie haben den Sohn _____ auch kennengelernt. (der Nachbar)

3. Während _____ mußte Frau Kohl manchmal arbeiten. (die Abendstunden)

4. Wegen _____ war sie oft müde. (ihre Arbeit)

5. Wegen _____ sind Kohls nicht viel gewandert. (das Wetter)

6. Kohls konnten nur fünf Tage statt _____ in Österreich bleiben. (eine Woche)

7. Trotz _____ haben die Ferien der Familie gefallen. (die Probleme)

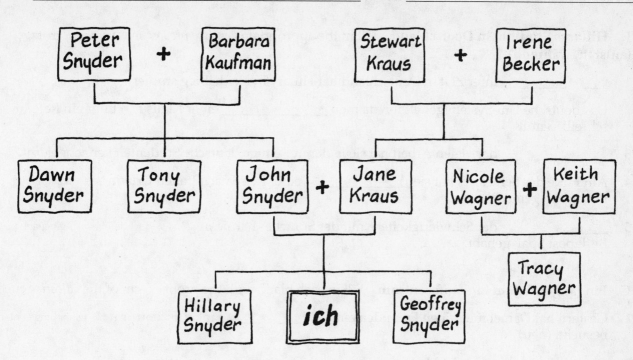

E. Wessen Kusine ist das? Locate yourself („ich") in the above **Stammbaum** and then answer the questions about your family using *genitive constructions* as appropriate.

▶ Wessen Kusine ist Tracy Wagner?

Tracy ist meine Kusine und die Kusine meiner Schwester Hillary und meines Bruders Geoffrey.

1. Wessen Mutter ist Irene Becker?

_____

2. Wessen Großvater ist Peter Snyder?

_____

3. Wessen Tochter ist Nicole Wagner?

_____

4. Wessen Onkel ist Tony Snyder?

_____

5. Wessen Mutter ist Barbara Kaufman?

_____

F. Hillarys Studium in Deutschland. Fill in the appropriate *genitive prepositions* (**wegen, trotz, (an)statt, während**).

1. _____ ihrer Zeit in Deutschland hat Hillary in Heidelberg studiert.

2. Das deutsche Uni-System gefällt ihr, da man _____ einer Klausur oft nur ein Referat schreiben muß.

3. _____ der vielen Arbeit hat sie leider nur einige deutsche Studenten kennengelernt.

4. Am Ende des Semesters hat sie _____ einer Reise nach Italien Urlaub° | vacation
   in Ungarn gemacht.

5. _____ der Schwierigkeiten° mit der Sprache° hat sie in | difficulties / language
   Budapest Spaß gehabt.

G. Ein langer Tag im Einkaufszentrum. Fill in each blank with the proper form of the *adjective* cued.

1. Gestern hat Daniel mit seinen Freunden ein _____ Einkaufszentrum° | shopping center
   besucht. (neu)

2. Obwohl sie nur wenig Geld haben, wollen sie doch _____ aber _____
   Sachen kaufen. (toll, billig)

3. Weil Peter gern am Abend joggt, kauft er einen _____ , _____
   Jogginganzug. (weiß, japanisch)

4. Annika sieht eine _____ , _____ Handtasche. (klein, praktisch) Die muß sie
   haben.

5. Sascha findet eine _____ CD von der _____ Opernsängerin Maria Callas.
   (interessant, berühmt)

6. Da Daniel ein _____ , _____ Mann ist, (schwierig, jung) mit

   _____ , _____ Wünschen, kauft er nichts. (kompliziert, teuer)

7. Am Ende des _____ Tages (lang) gehen alle ins Kino und sehen einen

   _____ , _____ Film. (modern, amerikanisch)

H. Was meinen Sie? State your opinion by choosing one or more of the *adjectives* in parentheses, or provide your own.

1. Ich möchte ein _____ Auto haben. (klein, groß, billig, teuer)

2. Ich gehe gern zu _____ Festen. (lustig, klein, laut, interessant)

3. Ich möchte einen _____ Pulli kaufen. (warm, blau, leicht, toll)

4. Ich sehe gern _____ Filme. (modern, alt, gut, lustig)

5. Herr X ist ein _____ Professor. (gut, ernst, ausgezeichnet, nett)

I. Was haben Sie? Wie sieht es aus? Describe the rooms and items below using *attributive adjectives.*

▶ Wohnung: groß / freundlich   *Ich habe eine große, freundliche Wohnung.*

1. Küche: modern / schön

_____

2. Schlafzimmer: klein / unordentlich° | messy

_____

3. Bücherregal: groß / lang

_____

4. Kommode: modern / neu

_____

5. Wohnzimmer: groß / gemütlich

_____

6. Teppich: alt / grau

_____

7. Computer: teuer / toll

_____

J. Landeskunde. Provide brief responses in English.

1. Name the four women whose portraits appear on Germany's bank notes, and indicate for each woman the field in which she achieved prominence. Compare Germany's bank notes with those in your country—are women represented?

    _____

    _____

    _____

    _____

2. Describe two benefits established by federal legislation in Germany to aid parents. Do similar benefits exist in your country?

    _____

    _____

    _____

3. Describe where some progress has been made in the professional lives of German women toward equality and where inequalities still exist.

    _____

    _____

    _____

4. Name two well-known female German film directors.

    _____

    _____

K. Frauen in Spitzenpositionen°. Read the passage and then answer the questions.

| leading positions

Vor kurzer Zeit hat eine deutsche Zeitung eine Studie° über Frauen in Spitzenpositionen in Deutschland geschrieben. Die Studie zeigt, was diese Frauen erfolgreich° gemacht hat, und wie ihr Familienleben ist. Man hat nur Frauen in traditionellen Männerberufen wie Professor, Rechtsanwalt, Direktor eines Krankenhauses° und Geschäfts-eigentümer° interviewt. Diese Frauen haben studiert und verdienen mehr als einhunderttausend Mark im Jahr. Zu dieser Zeit haben weniger° als zehn Prozent der Frauen einen dieser Berufe.

| study

| successful

| hospital
| owner of a business

| less

Die Studie hat gefunden, daß mehr als fünfzig Prozent dieser Frauen nicht verheiratet sind. Frauen mit eigenem Geschäft sind öfter verheiratet. Diese Frauen nehmen dann ihr Kind mit zur Arbeit — mit ins Geschäft. Die Mutter eines jungen Mädchens sagt: „Meine kleine Sonja hat oft im Büro auf dem Schreibtisch geschlafen." Für die meisten berufstätigen Frauen ist das natürlich unmöglich.

Wenn Frauen verheiratet sind, dann brauchen sie auch viel Energie für die Familie. Eine der Frauen hat gemeint: „Wir haben es im Beruf sehr schwer. Wir haben nicht das, was für den Erfolg im Beruf sehr wichtig ist: eine Frau."

Fast alle Frauen meinen, daß man eine gute Ausbildung° haben muß und auch den Willen° zum Erfolg. Dafür müssen sie oft ihre privaten Interessen aufgeben und auch Pläne für eine eigene Familie. Was ist für diese erfolgreichen Frauen wichtig? Sie suchen weniger das Geld und die Sicherheit°, sondern mehr ihre Unabhängigkeit° und eine interessante Arbeit.

| training
| determination

| security / independence

1. Auf welche Fragen will die Studie Antworten finden?

   _____

   _____

2. Was für Frauen hat man interviewt?

   _____

3. Wieviel Prozent Männer gibt es in diesen Berufen?

   _____

4. Warum ist es für Frauen mit Kindern leichter, wenn sie ihr eigenes Geschäft haben?

   _____

5. Was müssen Frauen in Spitzenpositionen oft aufgeben?

   _____

6. Was finden sie im Beruf wichtig und was weniger wichtig?

   _____

L. Liebes Tagebuch°. Keep a diary for three days. Follow the model
below for the dates, and use the *present perfect tense* in your entries.

I diary

▶ *Freitag, den zwölften Februar: Heute habe ich Valerie im Café getroffen. Am Abend bin ich mit ihr ins Kino gegangen.*

_____ , den _____ _____ : _____

_____

_____ , den _____ _____ : _____

_____

_____ , den _____ _____ : _____

_____

_____

Kapitel 10

A. Morgens oder abends machen Jasmin und Florian das. Describe what Jasmin and Florian are doing in the illustrations and when.

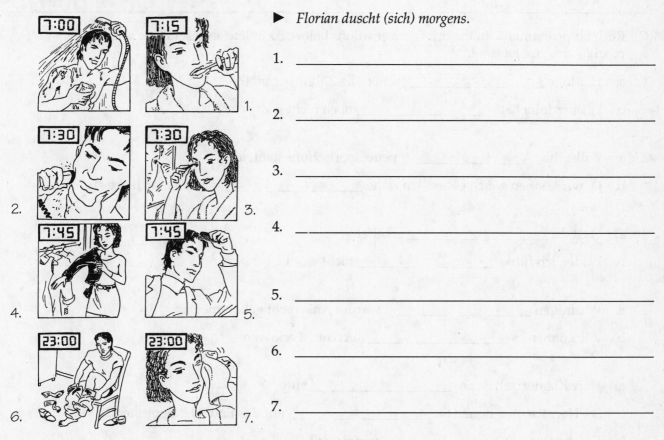

▶ *Florian duscht (sich) morgens.*

1. _____

2. _____

3. _____

4. _____

5. _____

6. _____

7. _____

B. Schreiben Sie über Ihr Morgenprogramm. Describe your morning routine. Use *reflexives* where appropriate. Suggested vocabulary:

zuerst	baden	Radio / Kassetten hören
dann	(sich) duschen	Zeitung kaufen / lesen
jetzt	sich waschen	Bett machen
später	sich die Zähne putzen	joggen gehen
	sich anziehen	frühstücken° l to eat breakfast
	sich rasieren	Freund / Freundin anrufen
	sich schminken	
	sich kämmen	

Ich stehe um _____ Uhr auf. Zuerst _____

_____

_____

_____

_____

_____

_____

C. Reflexivpronomen. In the brief conversations below, complete each sentence with the appropriate *reflexive pronoun*.

1. a. Hat Inge _____ schon die Zähne geputzt?

   b. Ja, aber Julia hat _____ noch nicht geduscht.

2. a. Willst du _____ neue Sportschuhe kaufen?

   b. Ja, wir können gleich gehen. Ich ziehe _____ schnell eine Jacke an.

3. a. Hast du _____ erkältet?

   b. Leider, ich fühle _____ nicht wohl.

4. a. Wir fragen _____ , warum Anja nicht gekommen ist.

   b. Wir können es _____ auch nicht erklären.

5. a. Herr Kleiner, setzen Sie _____ bitte.

   b. So, Herr Kleiner, freuen Sie _____ auf das Ende des Semesters?

   c. Ja, ich freue _____ sehr darauf.

D. Was sagen Sie? Respond appropriately. See Reference Section #12 and #14 on page R-24 of your textbook.

Expressing Regret

1. *Freund/in:* Jan tut das Bein sehr weh.

   Du: _____

2. *Freund/in:* Ich bin furchtbar erkältet. Ich kann nicht mit zum Skifahren.

   Du: _____

Expressing Indifference

3. *Freund/in:* Dein Bekannter will morgen kommen.

   Du: _____

4. *Freund/in:* Uwe hat immer noch deinen CD-Spieler.

   Du: _____

E. Auf der Uni. Tell about Tanja's first semester. Write new sentences using the *modal + infinitive*, **zu** *+ infinitive*, or **um ... zu** *+ infinitive* constructions, as appropriate. Begin each sentence with the phrase in parentheses.

▶ Tanja lernt Japanisch. (Es ist schwer, ...)

Es ist schwer, Japanisch zu lernen.

1. Sie arbeitet mehr in der Bibliothek. (Sie beginnt, ...)

_____

2. Tanjas Freunde reden oft über ihre Kurse. (Tanjas Freunde wollen ...)

_____

3. Tanja schreibt ein Referat. (Tanja muß ...)

_____

4. Sie sieht nicht fern. (Sie hat keine Zeit ...)

_____

5. Sie kommt schneller zur Uni. (Sie hat sich ein Rad gekauft, ...)

_____

F. Identifizieren Sie. Identify the two rivers (**Flüsse**) and eight cities marked on the map of Switzerland. Refer to the map on the inside cover of your textbook as necessary.

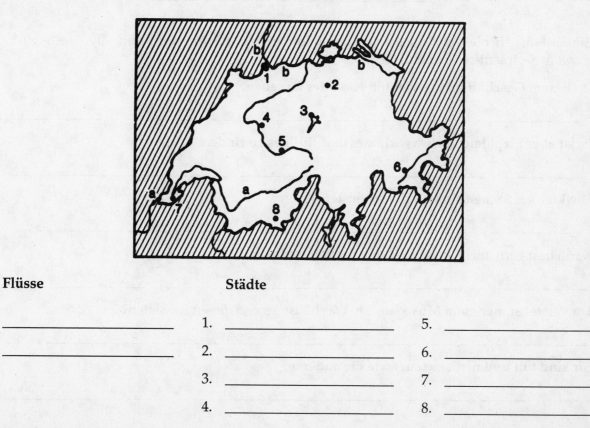

Flüsse   **Städte**

a. _____   1. _____   5. _____

b. _____   2. _____   6. _____

                       3. _____   7. _____

                       4. _____   8. _____

G. Eine tolle Mannschaft°. Complete each sentence with the *comparative* and then the *superlative* of the adjective or adverb.

| team

▶ Die ganze Mannschaft läuft schnell.

Aber Michael läuft schneller.

Und Markus läuft am schnellsten.

1. Alle springen° sehr hoch.

| jump

   Aber Heidi _____

   Und Sabrina _____

2. Alle joggen lange.

   Aber Johannes _____

   Und Karl _____

3. Alle trainieren° viel.

| train

   Aber Sebastian _____

   Und Cordula _____

4. Alle reden gern über Sport.

   Aber Jörn _____ über Autos.

   Und Sabrina und Kerstin _____ über Musik.

H. Einkaufen. Nicole and Daniel are shopping for birthday presents for Karin. Give the *English equivalent* of each sentence in boldface.

1. **In diesem Geschäft gibt es viel Interessantes zu sehen.**

   _____

2. **Es ist aber nicht leicht, etwas Schönes und Billiges zu finden.**

   _____

3. **Die kleinen Sachen sind oft die schönsten.**

   _____

4. Karin liest gern, nicht?—**Ja, aber sie hört lieber Musik.**

   _____

5. **Du verstehst mehr von Musik als ich.** Was hältst du von diesen Kassetten?

   _____

6. **Sie sind toll und nicht so teuer wie die anderen.**

   _____

Name _____ Date _____

I. Landeskunde. Provide brief responses in English.

1. Give the four *national* languages of Switzerland, and indicate which are the three *official* languages. What is the official language / are the official languages of your country?

_____

_____

2. Describe military service in Switzerland. Which aspects are different from those in your country?

_____

_____

3. Name one major political similarity and one major political difference between Switzerland and your country.

_____

_____

J. Die Sage° von Wilhelm Tell. Read the passage and then answer the questions. | legend

Was Robin Hood für die Engländer ist, das ist Wilhelm Tell für die Schweizer —
ein tapferer° Kämpfer° für die Freiheit und gegen die Ungerechtigkeit°. | brave / fighter / injustice
Lesen Sie bitte die Sage von Wilhelm Tell.

Im dreizehnten Jahrhundert haben sich die Schweizer Kantone Schwyz, Uri
und Unterwalden zusammengetan, um gegen Österreich zu kämpfen°. | fight
Die Schweizer wollten° frei sein und nicht zu Österreich gehören. In drei | wanted
Kriegen° haben sie dann ihre Freiheit gewonnen. Aus dieser Zeit kommt | wars
auch die Sage von Wilhelm Tell.

Zu Tells Zeiten ist Geßler der österreichische Gouverneur in der Schweiz.
Um die Treue° der Schweizer zu prüfen°, hängt Geßler einen Hut auf eine | loyalty / test
Stange° in Altdorf, Kanton Uri. Wer an diesem Hut vorbeigeht, muß ihn | pole
grüßen° und so Respekt für Geßler und Österreich zeigen. Eines Tages | greet
geht Tell mit seinem Sohn an dem Hut vorbei, ohne ihn zu grüßen.
Ein Soldat sieht das und bringt Tell zum Gouverneur. Dieser ist sehr böse
und sagt: „Tell, als Strafe° mußt du einen Apfel vom Kopf deines Sohnes | punishment
schießen°.“ Tell antwortet: „Das mach' ich nicht. Ich schieße nicht.“ | shoot
Geßler ist jetzt noch böser: „Tell, ich sage dir, du schießt oder du stirbst° | die
zusammen mit deinem Sohn.“

Etwas später legt der Gouverneur selbst dem Jungen den Apfel auf
den Kopf. Jetzt kann Tell wirklich nichts mehr machen als schießen.
Tell schießt und trifft° den Apfel. Geßler sagt ihm, daß er das gut gemacht | hits
hat und daß er gut schießen kann. Geßler will aber auch wissen, warum
Tell nicht einen Pfeil°, sondern zwei genommen hat. Tell fürchtet sich, | arrow
die Wahrheit zu sagen und meint: „Man braucht immer zwei Pfeile,
wenn man schießt.“ Geßler glaubt ihm aber nicht, und sagt: „Du brauchst
keine Angst zu haben. Dein Leben ist sicher. Sag' mir aber die Wahrheit.“
Tell antwortet: „Der zweite Pfeil war für dich, wenn ich meinen Sohn
getroffen hätte°.“ | would have

Als Geßler das hört, wird er zornig° und schreit°: „Dein Leben sollst du behalten aber nicht die Freiheit." Dann fesseln° die Soldaten Tell, und bringen ihn auf das Schiff des Gouverneurs. Kaum sind sie auf dem See°, da kommt ein starker Sturm°. Alle haben große Angst, weil sie das Schiff nicht mehr steuern° können. Nur Tell kann sie retten°. Die Soldaten binden ihn los, und Tell steuert das Schiff sicher ans Land. Als sie ankommen, springt Tell aus dem Schiff, stößt es wieder auf den See und läuft weg°.

| enraged / shouts
| chain
| lake
| storm
| steer / save

| **wegstoßen:** to shove

Später hört der Sturm auf, und Geßler und seine Leute kommen auch an Land. Tell steht hinter einem Busch und wartet auf den Gouverneur. Als dieser vorbeireitet°, hört Tell, wie Geßler einige Pläne gegen ihn macht, und er schießt. Mit dem Tod° des Gouverneurs beginnt jetzt der Kampf°, um den Schweizern Freiheit zu bringen. Obwohl diese Geschichte nur eine Sage ist, steht eine Statue von Tell in Altdorf. Für die Schweizer bedeutet der Name „Tell" auch heute noch Freiheit und Unabhängigkeit°.

| rides by
| death
| struggle

| independence

1. Wer ist Wilhelm Tell?

   _____

2. Zu welcher Zeit hat er gelebt?

   _____

3. Wer ist Geßler?

   _____

4. Warum haben die Soldaten Tell zum Gouverneur gebracht?

   _____

5. Was sagt Geßler, soll Tell machen?

   _____

6. Was will Tell mit dem zweiten Pfeil machen?

   _____

7. Warum fürchten sich die Soldaten auf dem See?

   _____

8. Wann beginnt der Kampf um die Freiheit?

   _____

9. Was bedeutet der Name „Tell" für die Schweizer?

   _____

Kapitel 11

A. Gespräch mit Rebecca.   You went to see the musical "Das Phantom der Oper." Write a short dialogue in German in which you discuss your evening with Rebecca. Use the following guidelines.

▶   Ask what Rebecca did over the weekend.

Sie: Was hast du am Wochenende gemacht?

▶   Rebecca said she had lots of fun.

Rebecca: Ich hatte viel Spaß.

1.   Rebecca said she saw the musical "Das Phantom der Oper."

Rebecca: _____

2.   Ask if she would recommend it.

Sie: _____

3.   She says, "Without reservation. I found it absolutely great."

Rebecca: _____

_____

4.   Tell her you would like to see it but you're broke.

Sie: _____

_____

5.   Rebecca asks if you feel like going along to a beer garden with her friends.

Rebecca: _____

_____

6.   Say you're glad to go along. You can talk more about the musical.

Sie: _____

_____

B. Was sagen Sie?   Respond appropriately. For additional responses see Reference Section #16 and #22 on page R-25 of your textbook.

Expressing Rejection

1.   *Freund/in: Ich habe zwei Karten für Das Leben des Galilei. Willst du mit?*

Du: _____

2.   *Freund/in: Die Filmschauspielerin° Katharina Koch ist toll, nicht?* | actress

Du: _____

Expressing Expectation

3. *Freund/in:* Du kommst mit ins Theater, nicht?

   Du: _____

4. *Freund/in:* Ich bin froh, daß wir Karten für das Open-Air-Konzert bekommen haben. Es soll sehr gut sein.

   Du: _____

C. Ein neues Leben. Describe what occurs when Mrs. Gerber returns to the work force once her children are all in school. Rewrite each sentence in the *present tense*.

1. Der Vater mußte lernen, wie man kocht.

   _____

2. Klaus wusch jeden Tag ab.

   _____

3. Seine Schwester trocknete immer ab.

   _____

4. Alle lernten zu helfen.

   _____

5. So fing für die Gerbers ein neues Leben an.

   _____

6. Die Nachbarn redeten über Frau Gerber.

   _____

7. Sie kannten nur die alten Rollen.

   _____

D. An der Uni. Describe Robert's experiences as a student in Germany. Use the simple past tense forms of the verbs in parentheses.

1. Während Robert an einer deutschen Universität _____ ,

   _____ er in einem Studentenheim. (studieren, wohnen)

2. Als er wieder nach Hause _____ , _____

   er seiner Familie, wie es in Deutschland auf der Uni _____ .

   (kommen, erzählen, sein)

3. Die Universität _____ nichts. (kosten)

4. Viele Studenten _____ Geld vom Staat. (bekommen)

5. Die Studenten _____ nur ein oder zwei Fächer studieren. (müssen)

6. Sie _____ nicht jedes Semester ein Examen. (machen)

7. Das _____ Robert sehr. (gefallen)

E. Eine Reise nach Berlin.   Kevin tells about his trip to Berlin. In telling you about his trip to Berlin, Kevin uses the present tense to make it more direct. But in writing to a friend about Kevin's trip you use the *simple past*. Rewrite each sentence in the *simple past*.

▶   Kevin macht im Herbst eine Reise nach Berlin.   *Kevin machte im Herbst eine Reise nach Berlin.*

1.   Er kommt am Wochenende in Berlin an.

_____

_____

2.   Am Sonntagmorgen geht er auf der berühmten Straße „Unter den Linden" spazieren.

_____

_____

3.   Nachmittags besucht er das Deutsche Historische Museum.

_____

_____

4.   Hier sieht er eine neue Ausstellung° über die Nachkriegszeit in Deutschland. | exhibit

_____

_____

5.   Er lernt auch etwas über die Zeit der Berliner Blockade.

_____

_____

6.   Zu seinen Freunden sagt er: „Berlin ist wirklich eine Reise wert." | worth

_____

_____

F. Samstagabend.   Michael couldn't join you at the movies, but he did make it later to the pub. Give the English equivalents of the following sentences.

1.   Michael war nicht gekommen, weil er arbeiten mußte.

_____

2.   Er hatte sein Referat noch nicht geschrieben.

_____

3.   Wir hatten das schon gehört, bevor° er uns davon erzählte. | before

_____

4.   Nachdem wir Michael geholfen hatten, konnte er mit in eine Kneipe.

_____

G. Eine Reise nach Italien. While Susi's and Nadja's first trip to Italy was fun, it wasn't a total success. Tell about their vacation by rewriting each sentence in the *past perfect*.

▶ Im August fuhren wir nach Italien.   *Im August waren wir nach Italien gefahren.*

1. Susi und Nadja waren noch nie in Italien.

_____

2. Sie lernten kein Italienisch in der Schule.

_____

3. Sie übernachteten in einer Jugendherberge.

_____

4. Beide aßen jeden Tag Spaghetti oder Pizza.

_____

5. Susi trank nur Cola.

_____

6. Nadja hatte Heimweh°, und sie schrieb jeden Tag eine Karte nach Hause. | homesick

_____

_____

H. Das Rad. Petra has written about the use of bicycles in Germany. Combine the sentences using **als, wann,** or **wenn,** as appropriate.

1. Ich war in Deutschland. Es gab einen Fahrradboom.

_____

2. Ich weiß nicht. Der Boom hat angefangen.

_____

3. Man fuhr mit dem Rad. Man mußte in die Stadt.

_____

4. Niemand fand das komisch°. Ich fuhr einmal mit dem Rad zum Einkaufen. | odd

_____

5. Ich fuhr immer mit. Meine Freunde machten eine Radtour.

_____

6. Am Freitag fragte ich sie immer. Wir sollten uns am Sonntag treffen.

_____

I. Landeskunde. Provide brief responses in English.

1. Why is Bertolt Brecht regarded as a prominent figure in 20th-century literature?

_____

_____

2. Why and when was the Berlin Wall erected and subsequently demolished?

_____

_____

3. Describe some of the problems Germany faced **Nach der Einigung**—after unification.

_____

_____

_____

4. Describe the selection process and function of the **Bundespräsident** and the **Bundeskanzler.**

_____

_____

_____

J. So war es. Ms. Bunge recalls the problems her son encountered in East Berlin before German unification—all for love. Read the passage and then answer the questions.

Als mein Sohn Erik Ingenieurstudent in Berlin war, lernte er eine Frau aus dem Westen kennen. Es war die große Liebe°. Die beiden wollten heiraten°. Das Problem war nur: Wie konnte mein Sohn legal aus der DDR in den Westen?

| love / to marry

Erik war in der FDJ, der Freien Deutschen Jugend, der staatlichen Jugendorganisation, aktiv. Er machte gerade bei einer Firma in Berlin sein Praktikum°, als er beantragte°, in den Westen gehen zu dürfen. Zwei Tage danach wurde er exmatrikuliert° und verlor° Arbeit und Zimmer. Der Direktor der Ingenieurschule fuhr zu uns. Wir sollten unsren Sohn beeinflussen. Wir konnten es aber nicht. Er wollte zu seiner Inge.

| internship / applied

| expelled / lost

Lange Zeit hörte Erik nun nichts. Er mußte also ein neues Zimmer finden. Das war schwer. Eine neue Stelle war gar nicht zu finden. Er fand einige freie Stellen. Aber wenn man hörte, daß er beantragt hatte, in den Westen zu gehen, kamen Antworten wie: „Es tut uns leid, aber die Stelle ist doch nicht frei." Oder: „Wir brauchen doch etwas andere Qualifikationen." In *einer* Firma sagte man ihm ganz offen: „Leute, die in den Westen wollen, können hier nicht einmal° als Hilfsarbeiter° arbeiten."

| **nicht einmal:** not even / unskilled worker

Kein Mensch wußte, wann er eine Antwort erwarten konnte. Einige Leute hatten nach kurzer Zeit eine Antwort bekommen. Bei anderen wieder war

es sehr langsam° gegangen. Waren diese Unterschiede nun Teil des | slowly
politischen Systems, oder war es einfach die Schlamperei° der Bürokratie? | bungling
Es war schwer zu sagen.

Eines Nachmittags mußte es dann plötzlich° sehr schnell gehen. Er mußte | suddenly
in drei Stunden reisefertig sein. Er hatte nicht einmal Zeit, zu uns zu fahren.

Erst am 9. November 1989° konnten wir unseren Sohn endlich wiedersehen, | Berlin wall was opened.
und seine westdeutsche Frau, unsere Schwiegertochter°, endlich | daughter-in-law
kennenlernen.

1. Wo war Erik Bunge zu Hause?

    _____

2. Warum konnte er Inge nicht einfach heiraten?

    _____

3. Warum sprach der Direktor der Ingenieurschule mit Eriks Eltern?

    _____

4. Warum konnte Erik keine Arbeit finden?

    _____

5. Wann konnte Erik eine Antwort auf seinen Antrag° erwarten? | application

    _____

6. Warum war der 9. November 1989 ein wichtiges Datum° für die Familie Bunge? | date

    _____

Kapitel 12

A. Eine Frage der Qualität.   Ms. Meister is trying to sell a previous customer her company's new computer. In a short German paragraph, write a summary of what happened at a recent meeting.

Frau Meister: So, Herr Kohl, was halten Sie von unseren Preisen?

Herr Kohl: Sie wissen, es ist keine Frage des Preises. Ihre Computer sind nicht gerade billig, aber darüber können wir später reden. Am wichtigsten ist die Frage der Qualität.

Frau Meister: Bei unserem Namen, Herr Kohl? Alle kennen den „Solo".

Herr Kohl: Trotzdem. Die Computer, die wir vor fünf Jahren bei Ihnen gekauft haben, haben wir ziemlich oft reparieren müssen.

Frau Meister: Leider. Aber jetzt haben wir keine Bildprobleme mehr. Der neue Solo Personal Computer 97 arbeitet auch schneller. Sie werden also viel Zeit sparen. Außerdem kann man mit unserem Software-Packet ohne Programmierer programmieren. Sie brauchen kein kompliziertes Programm zu schreiben, Sie brauchen nur ein paar Worte zu tippen. Ich bin sicher, Sie werden zufrieden° sein. | satisfied

Herr Kohl: Hm, ja … . Ich rufe Sie am Montag in einer Woche an und sage Ihnen, ob wir uns für den „Solo" interessieren. Dann können wir noch einmal über die Preise reden, nicht?

B. Was sagen Sie?   Respond appropriately. See Reference Section #21 and #25 on pages R-25 and R-26 of your textbook.

Making Surmises

1. *Kollegin:* Bringt Frau Richter eine Preisliste mit?

   Du: _____

2. *Kollege:* Ich habe gehört, wir kaufen dreißig neue Solo Computer.

   Du: _____

Correcting Misunderstandings

3. *Freund/in:* Glaubst du wirklich, ich verdiene zuviel?

   Du: _____

4. *Freund/in:* Willst du damit sagen, ich arbeite zuwenig?

   Du: _____

C. Verben, Verben. Give the *subjunctive forms* of the following verb phrases in both present and past time.

	Present time	Past time
▶ ich tue	*ich täte* _____	*hätte getan* _____
1. er denkt	_____	_____
2. ich komme	_____	_____
3. du weißt	_____	_____
4. es gibt	_____	_____
5. er geht	_____	_____
6. sie bleibt	_____	_____
7. Sie bringen	_____	_____
8. ihr habt	_____	_____
9. sie schläft	_____	_____
10. sie tun	_____	_____
11. es wird	_____	_____
12. du bist	_____	_____

D. Schwierigkeiten. Michael and Sabine are trying to schedule a rehearsal. Complete each sentence below to express politeness, using the *present-time subjunctive* of the cued modal.

▶ Michael: *Könntest* du um sieben zur Probe kommen? (können)

Sabine: _____ es um sieben sein? (müssen)

Michael: Die Probe _____ vier Stunden dauern. (sollen)

Sabine: _____ ich vielleicht um acht kommen? (dürfen)

Michael: Sicher _____ du das, aber... . (können)

Sabine: Morgen _____ ich um sieben kommen. (können)

E. Am Bodensee. Stephanie is on vacation at Lake Constance. She wishes conditions were different. Express her sentences as *wishes in the subjunctive.* Begin with **Ich wollte ...** .

▶ Das Wetter ist nicht schön.   *Ich wollte, das Wetter wäre schön.*

1. Ich kann nicht windsurfen gehen.

_____

2. Es gibt kein Fest hier.

_____

3. Ich habe zuwenig Geld. (use *mehr*)

_____

4. Kurt ist nicht mitgekommen.

_____

5. Er hat nicht geschrieben.

_____

F. Wenn wir das anders gemacht hätten ... Klaus and his friends discuss how things might have been if they shared an apartment. Give the *English equivalents.*

▶ Ich hätte nicht immer kochen müssen.   *I wouldn't have always had to cook.*

1. Wir hätten nicht immer Spaghetti essen müssen.

_____

2. Bernd hätte bei der Hausarbeit helfen können.

_____

3. Thomas hätte nicht immer so lange schlafen dürfen.

_____

4. Du hättest die Küche nicht so oft saubermachen müssen.

_____

5. Wir hätten zusammen ins Theater gehen können.

_____

G. Wenn ... dann. Provide conclusions for the conditional sentences below, telling what you might do or might have done during a holiday or leisure time.

▶ Wenn es nicht geregnet hätte, _____ .

Wenn es nicht geregnet hätte, dann wären wir spazierengegangen.

1. Wenn diese Woche Ferien wären, _____

   _____

2. Wenn ich abends nicht arbeiten müßte, _____

   _____

3. Wenn wir im Juli an einem See° gewesen wären, _____   l lake

   _____

4. Wenn ich letzten Sommer mehr Zeit [Geld] gehabt hätte, _____

   _____

H. Landeskunde. Provide brief responses in English.

1. Give one example of social legislation in Germany for which your country has similar legislation. Give two examples of German social legislation for which your country has no legislative equivalents. (You may also refer to your textbook, p. 386.)

   _____

   _____

   _____

2. Explain the term **Mitbestimmung** (codetermination). Does your country have such a policy?

   _____

   _____

   _____

3. State the goals and achievements of the European Union.

   _____

   _____

   _____

4. Describe the apprenticeship system in Germany.

   _____

   _____

   _____

   _____

I. Die Welt der Kinder — ein großes Geschäft. Read the passage and then answer the questions.

Gisela Weinbauer, eine Reporterin aus Düsseldorf, interessiert sich für die Werbung° und ihren Einfluß° auf die deutschen Familien. Sie interviewte einige Personen für ihren Bericht. Lesen Sie, was diese Leute zu dem Thema „Werbung" zu sagen haben.

| advertising / influence

Zuerst sprach Gisela Weinbauer mit Frau Greif, die die Werbung kritisierte. Frau Greif sagte, daß sie, als Mutter von drei Kindern, sich wirklich wünschte, es gäbe gar keine Werbung mehr. Zum Geburtstag und zu Weihnachten° kauft sie natürlich Geschenke° für ihre Kinder, aber wegen der ewigen Werbung im Fernsehen, ist es schwer „nein" zu sagen, wenn die Kinder zu anderen Zeiten Wünsche haben. Sobald die Werbung neue Spielsachen° empfiehlt, haben ihre Kinder kein Interesse mehr für die alten Dinge; sofort wollen sie das Neue haben. Frau Greif meinte auch, daß sie keine Freude mehr daran hat, ins Kaufhaus zu gehen, denn es heißt immer nur: „Mami, das möcht' ich gern haben, und dieses möcht' ich haben." Da sie aber arbeitslos ist und ihr Mann nicht viel verdient, haben sie wenig Geld. Wenn sie könnte, würde sie lieber das Geld sparen, anstatt soviel für teure Spielsachen zu bezahlen.

| Christmas / presents

| toys

Als Gisela Weinbauer sich mit Herrn Voss, dem Chef eines Spielzeughauses, unterhielt, hörte sie, was ein typischer Geschäftsmann zu sagen hat. Für ihn ist die Werbung eben etwas Gutes, ein Boom. Zum Beispiel, wenn die Werbung am Wochenende etwas Neues im Fernsehen zeigt, dann müssen die Kinder das am Montag gleich haben. Das ist ganz selbstverständlich. Herr Voss war der Meinung, daß der Lebensstandard der Deutschen sehr hoch ist, sogar einer der höchsten der Welt. Das Resultat ist also, daß die Deutschen Geld haben, um ihren Kindern kaufen zu können, was sie haben möchten. Nicht nur die Eltern kaufen den Kindern sehr viel, sondern auch die Verwandten — Tanten, Onkel und Großeltern — kaufen Spielsachen und geben den Kindern Geld. Vielleicht wäre es besser, wenn sie einen Teil des Geldes sparen würden, aber es gefällt Herrn Voss, daß sie es für Spielsachen ausgeben°. Für die Geschäftsleute ist die Werbung etwas ganz Tolles.

| spend

Kara, ein neunjähriges Mädchen, hat keine Idee, warum man soviel von der Werbung redet. Sie weiß nur, daß sie ihre Barbi-Puppen° liebt. Obwohl sie nur zwölf Barbis hat, hat ihre Freundin Ulrike fünfundzwanzig. Außerdem hat Ulrike jetzt für ihre Barbis ein super Haus, ein tolles Auto und neue, französische Sportkleidung bekommen. Das muß Kara auch unbedingt haben, denn schließlich kann sie keinen Spaß haben, wenn ihre Barbis nicht auch neue Sachen bekommen, genauso wie Ulrikes.

| dolls

Was für Mädchen die Barbi-Puppen sind, das sind für Jungen die Dinosaurier. Überall gibt es Dinosaurier, im Kino, im Fernsehen, als Puzzle, als Plastikfigur und natürlich auch als Videospiel. Alle Kinder, jung und alt, lieben Werbespots — sie sind bunt° und voller Action. Was das Kind haben will und was das Kind glücklich° macht, sagen heute die großen Firmen mit ihrer Werbung. Obwohl Lehrer und Eltern sich Sorgen machen über den negativen Einfluß der Werbung, freut sich die Wirtschaft über die jungen Kunden mit dem vielen Geld.

| colorful
| happy

1. Wofür interessiert sich Gisela Weinbauer?

_____

_____

2. Was ist Frau Greifs Meinung über die Werbung?

_____

_____

3. Warum hat Frau Greif keine Lust mit ihren Kindern einkaufen zu gehen?

_____

_____

4. Was sagt Herr Voss über die Deutschen und ihre Kinder?

_____

_____

5. Warum muß Kara neue Sachen für ihre Barbis haben?

_____

_____

6. Was machen die großen Firmen mit ihrer Werbung?

_____

_____

J. Write a ten sentence essay about what you would do if your life were different. Some suggestions: **Wenn Sie mehr Zeit (Geld, Talent) hätten; wenn Sie weniger Arbeit (Streß, Probleme) hätten; wenn Sie reich°** | rich
(toll aussehend, berühmt) wären.

Wenn ich (berühmt) wäre, würde ich _____

_____

_____

_____

_____

_____

Kapitel 13

A. Etwas Persönliches.   Here is the opportunity to talk about some plans, likes, and dislikes.

1. Was haben Sie nächste Woche vor?

   a. _____

   b. _____

   c. _____

2. Nennen Sie

   a. zwei Bands oder Musiker, die Sie gern hören möchten.

      1. _____   2. _____

   b. zwei Filme, die Sie sehen möchten.

      1. _____   2. _____

   c. zwei Bücher, die Sie dieses Jahr gelesen haben.

      1. _____   2. _____

3. Nennen Sie die Vorlesung,

   a. die Sie am interessantesten gefunden haben. _____

   b. die Ihnen am wenigsten gefallen hat. _____

   c. die Sie ihren Freunden empfehlen würden. _____

B. Was sagen Sie?   Respond appropriately. See Reference Section #11 and #24 on pages R-24 and R-26 of your textbook.

Responding to a Request

1. *Freund/in:* Mein Auto ist kaputt. Könntest du mich morgen abholen?

   Du: _____

2. *Freund/in:* Könnte ich deine Notizen von der Psychologie-Vorlesung borgen?

   Du: _____

Giving Advice

3. *Freund/in:* Heute schneit es sehr. Soll ich trotz des Wetters Jogging gehen?

   Du: _____

4. *Freund/in:* Du wolltest doch mit ins Open-Air-Konzert. Wann sollen wir uns treffen?

   Du: _____

C. Was wird Anja nach ihrem Examen machen? Describe Anja's future plans by using the *future tense.*

▶ Ich suche mir meine eigene Wohnung.   *Ich werde mir meine eigene Wohnung suchen.*

1. Ich spare Geld, um mir ein neues Auto zu kaufen. (*Do not change* **zu kaufen.**)

_____

2. Dann mache ich Ferien in Italien und Griechenland.

_____

3. Meine beiden Freundinnen kommen auch mit.

_____

4. Wenn wir zurückkommen, suche ich mir einen interessanten Job beim Fernsehen. (*Do not change* **zurückkommen.**)

_____

_____

5. Vielleicht studiere ich aber erst noch zwei Jahre im Ausland.

_____

6. Es ist möglich, daß ich in zehn Jahren heirate. (*Do not change* **ist.**)

_____

D. So war es möglich. Mr. and Mrs. Wieland both worked full time while raising their children. Give the English equivalents of Mrs. Wieland's statements with the different meanings of **lassen.** (You may wish to refer to textbook p. 425.)

1. Als die Kinder klein waren, haben wir sie nicht allein gelassen.

_____

2. Wir haben immer einen Babysitter kommen lassen.

_____

3. Als die Kinder älter waren, sagten sie oft: „Laß uns dies oder das machen."

_____

4. Wir haben die Kinder immer abwaschen lassen.

_____

5. Wir haben auch viel Hausarbeit einfach liegenlassen.

_____

6. Wir haben den Kindern immer genug Zeit gelassen, ihre Hausaufgaben zu machen.

_____

E. Relativpronomen. Complete the following definitions by supplying the relative pronouns.

▶ Ein Mann, _____*der*_____ Brot und Kuchen backt, ist ein Bäcker.

1. Eine Frau, _____ aus Deutschland kommt, ist eine Deutsche.

2. Ein junger Mann, _____ an einer Universität studiert, ist ein Student.

3. Das Essen, _____ man zu Abend ißt, ist das Abendessen.

4. Leute, für _____ man arbeitet, sind Chefs oder Chefinnen.

5. Ein Geschäft, in _____ man Brot kauft, ist eine Bäckerei.

6. Ein Instrument, mit _____ man Musik machen kann, ist ein Musikinstrument.

F. Unterschiede. Claudia and Robert are discussing differences they noted between German and American culture. Complete the sentences with a *relative clause*, using the guidelines provided.

▶ Claudia spricht mit einem Freund, (sie hat ihn in Deutschland kennengelernt).

Claudia spricht mit einem Freund, den sie in Deutschland kennengelernt hat.

1. Sie sprechen über kulturelle Unterschiede, (sie haben die Unterschiede bemerkt°).   I noticed

_____

2. Die Fahrer, (die Fahrer hat Robert in Deutschland gesehen), sind wie die Wilden gefahren.

_____

3. Die Züge, (er ist mit den Zügen gefahren), waren meistens pünktlich.

_____

4. Claudia hat Hunger auf Brot, (das Brot ist schwerer als amerikanisches Brot).

_____

5. Sie hat auch Hunger auf den Kuchen, (sie hat von dem Kuchen in Bonn immer drei Stücke gegessen).

_____

G. Landeskunde. Provide brief responses in English about **Ausländer** in Germany.

1. Who are the **ausländische Arbeitnehmer** and where do they come from?

_____

_____

_____

2. Briefly describe **Aussiedler.**

_____

_____

3. Tell briefly about the **Asylanten.**

   _____

   _____

4. With which groups of foreigners does integration into German life work best?

   _____

   _____

   _____

H. Brief aus Deutschland. Sue is an American living in Germany and working in a factory in Berlin. Read her letter to her former German instructor and then answer the questions.

Berlin, den 5. Mai

Liebe Frau Hill!

Ich danke Ihnen für Ihren freundlichen Brief. Es geht mir gut. Mein Deutsch wird langsam° besser, aber leider eben nur langsam. Wenn ich abends aus der Fabrik° nach Hause komme, bin ich müde. Und in der Fabrik habe ich viel Kontakt zu Türkinnen, die kein oder wenig Deutsch können. | slowly
| factory

Da ich mehr Deutsch kann als die Türkinnen, aber natürlich weniger als die Deutschen, stehe ich ein bißchen zwischen beiden Gruppen. Ich kann gut verstehen, warum die Türkinnen Schwierigkeiten mit Deutsch haben. Ich sehe, wie schwer es ist, Deutsch zu lernen, wenn man den ganzen Tag mit Türkinnen zusammen ist. Die deutschen Kolleginnen sehen aber nur, daß so viele Türkinnen kein oder wenig Deutsch können. Ich habe von den Deutschen daher oft gehört, daß die Ausländer eben nicht wirklich versuchen, Deutsch zu lernen. Wirkliche Gespräche mit den Ausländern finden sie unmöglich. Also sprechen die Deutschen vor allem miteinander. Ich glaube aber, daß die Türkinnen sicher mehr Deutsch lernen könnten, wenn die Deutschen sich mehr Zeit nehmen würden.

Dies sollte ja eigentlich ein Brief über Deutschland und Berlin werden. Aber ich sehe schon, daß es ein Brief über mich zwischen Deutschen und Türken wird. Na ja, das ist vielleicht auch nicht uninteressant.

Besonders interessant finde ich das türkische Familienkonzept. Meine türkischen Kolleginnen haben z.B. oft vier, fünf oder mehr Kinder, während die Deutschen meistens nur eins oder zwei haben. Während die deutschen Frauen ihre kleinen Kinder während des Tages in Kindergärten bringen, sagen die Türkinnen, daß sie ihre Kinder lieber bei Verwandten in der Türkei lassen. Sie sagen, daß das ihre Liebe° zu ihren Kindern zeigt. Sie lassen ihre Kinder lieber bei Tanten, Onkeln, Großeltern, d.h. in der Familie zu Hause. Das ist besser für die Kinder als nach Deutschland zu kommen. Hier wären sie den ganzen Tag allein, oder sie müßten bei fremden Leuten sein. Natürlich wären sie, die Mütter, auch lieber mit ihren Kindern zusammen. Aber das geht nun leider eben nicht. | love

Ich habe durch meine türkische Freundin Emine sehr viel gelernt: z.B. über türkische Traditionen, die Sprache, das Essen, die Musik. Und dann ist da die Gastfreundlichkeit° der Türken. Immer wieder laden sie mich zum Kaffee oder zum Abendessen ein. Ich habe mich bei ihnen schnell | hospitality

wie zu Hause gefühlt. Die Wärme° meiner türkischen Freunde war für
mich ein besonders schönes Erlebnis°.

| warmth
| experience

   Ich könnte noch viel von meiner deutschen (und türkischen) Welt hier
erzählen. Aber es ist spät, ich bin müde, und morgen früh um sieben muß
ich wieder in der Fabrik sein. Wenn Sie im Sommer wirklich nach
Deutschland kommen, bitte besuchen Sie mich!

Herzliche Grüße
Sue

1. Warum wird Sues Deutsch nur langsam besser? Geben Sie zwei Gründe°!

| reasons

_____

_____

2. Warum hat Sue Kontakt zu deutschen und ausländischen Arbeiterinnen?

_____

_____

3. Warum ist es für manche Türkinnen schwer, Deutsch zu lernen?

_____

_____

4. Wie könnten die Deutschen ihnen helfen, mehr Deutsch zu lernen?

_____

_____

5. Welche Unterschiede gibt es zwischen dem deutschen und türkischen Familienkonzept?

_____

_____

6. Was hat Sue durch ihre Freundin Emine gelernt?

_____

7. Warum hat Sue die Türkinnen besonders gern?

_____

I. Write a ten-sentence essay about your own *future plans*. What will you be doing in about 20 years from now? Do include adverbs like **schon, sicher, wohl.** Suggestions of areas to write about: **Beruf, Wohnung, Reisen, Kinder, Geld, Hobbys, Partnerin / Partner, berühmt sein.**

In zwanzig Jahren werde ich wohl _____

_____

_____

_____

_____

_____

Viel Spaß und Freude
am Geburtstag...

Kapitel 14

A. Umweltbewußtsein. List four things you do for the environment and three things you should do but don't.

▶ *Ich recycle Zeitungen.*

▶ *Ich sollte eigentlich langsamer fahren.*

Das mache ich:

1. _____

2. _____

3. _____

4. _____

Ich sollte eigentlich ...

1. _____

2. _____

3. _____

B. Von wem wird was in Annikas Familie gemacht? Everyone in Annika's family has chores. You decide what they are. Use *present passive.*

▶ Tante - Gartenarbeit machen.   *Die Gartenarbeit wird von der Tante gemacht.*

Wer?	**Was?**		
Vater	Blumen pflanzen	Hund füttern°	I feed
Mutter	Badezimmer putzen	Garage aufräumen	
Uwe	Essen kochen		
Oma	Hausaufgaben machen		
Opa	Pfandflaschen zurücktragen		
Annika	Auto waschen		

1. _____

2. _____

3. _____

4. _____

5. _____

6. _____

C. Von wem wurde das erfunden° oder geschrieben? Use the cues below | invented
and provide the appropriate verb. Use the *simple past passive.*

▶ das Telefon — Alexander Graham Bell.   *Das Telefon wurde von Alexander Graham Bell erfunden.*

1. *Huckleberry Finn*—Mark Twain. _____

   _____

2. das Dynamit—Alfred Nobel. _____

   _____

3. die amerikanische Verfassung—Thomas Jefferson. _____

   _____

4. das Musical *West Side Story*—Leonard Bernstein. _____

   _____

5. die Buchdruckerkunst (*printing*)—Johann Gutenberg. _____

   _____

D. Die Umwelt wird verschmutzt. Complete each sentence with the appropriate *form of werden* and
indicate the *use of werden.* Then give the English equivalent of the sentence.

▶ Die Flaschen _____ gesammelt.

   Die Flaschen werden gesammelt. (passive); *The bottles are (being) collected.*

1. Es _____ (past) sehr spät, und Familie Meister mußte noch den Müll sortieren.

   _____

2. Dienstags _____ Altpapier und leere Glas- und Plastikflaschen abgeholt.

   _____

3. In dieser Familie _____ alles recycelt.

   _____

4. Nicht nur Recycling, sondern auch die Umwelt und ihre Probleme sind ein wichtiges Thema

   _____ .

   _____

5. Durch die Abgase der vielen Autos ist die Luft schlechter _____ , aber es

   _____ immer mehr Autos gekauft.

   _____

6. Wie _____ die Zukunft aussehen?

   _____

7. Vielleicht _____ Julia Meister Recyclingingenieurin, und dann _____ sie

   der Umwelt helfen können.

   _____

E. Lebensstandard in Ostdeutschland. Bärbel has made notes for a report on the standard of living in the eastern part of Germany. Rewrite her sentences in the active voice, using **man.**

▶ Neue Straßen werden gebaut.   *Man baut neue Straßen.*

1. Ein hoher Lebensstandard wird erwartet.

   _____

2. In den letzten Jahren sind viele Autos gekauft worden.

   _____

3. Neue Jobs müssen gefunden werden.

   _____

4. Die Wirtschaftsprobleme können nicht leicht gelöst werden.

   _____

F. Lebensstandard in Westdeutschland. Martin also has notes on the economic situation in the western part of Germany. Rewrite his sentences, using **sein** + **zu** + *infinitive*, with the original object as the new subject.

▶ Man kann den hohen Lebensstandard leicht erklären.

   Der hohe Lebensstandard ist leicht zu erklären.

1. Man kann Qualitätsprodukte leichter verkaufen.

   _____

2. Die Inflationsrate muß man so niedrig wie möglich halten.

   _____

3. Man kann die geographischen Fakten nicht ändern°. | change

   _____

4. Probleme der Arbeitslosigkeit° kann man nicht leicht lösen. | unemployment

   _____

G. Lassen sich die Probleme lösen? Answer these questions, using a form of **sich lassen** + *infinitive*.

▶ Kann man die Umweltprobleme lösen?

   Ja (Nein), die Umweltprobleme lassen sich (nicht) wirklich lösen.

1. Kann man das in zehn Jahren machen?

   _____

2. Kann man Bücher über die Luftverschmutzung finden?

   _____

3. Kann man die Bücher leicht lesen?

_____

4. Kann man aber das Problem mit den vielen Autos lösen?

_____

H. Landeskunde. Provide brief responses in English.

1. List three ways in which Germany's recycling system differs from the one in your country.

_____

_____

_____

_____

2. During which decade and with which issues did the Green party first gain prominence?

_____

_____

_____

3. Why and how has the political agenda of the Greens shifted?

_____

_____

_____

I. Alternative Energie. Read the passage and then answer the questions.

Michael Mahler ist Mechaniker°. Seine Frau Marianne ist Studentin. Sie ° mechanic
wohnen in Zürich und leben mit alternativer Energie. Und das ist so
gekommen: Das Elektrizitätswerk° hat, so glauben sie, mit dem Geld der ° power company
Kunden ein Atomkraftwerk° finanziert. Um zu zeigen, daß sie dagegen ° nuclear power plant
waren, haben sie jeden Monat nur 90 Prozent ihrer Rechnung° bezahlt. ° bill
Sie waren dagegen, als Kunden des Elektrizitätswerks ein Atomkraftwerk
zu finanzieren. Nach einiger Zeit hat ihnen das Elektrizitätswerk die
Elektrizität abgestellt°. ° turned off

Nun machen sie ihre eigene mit einem Fahrrad auf einem Stand im
Wohnzimmer. Ein Dynamo° produziert 100 bis 150 Watt. Die gehen in ° generator
fünf Autobatterien auf einem Bücherregal. Am Fenster haben sie noch
einen Generator. Der arbeitet mit Solarenergie. Jeden Tag müssen sie eine
halbe Stunde „radfahren", um ihre tägliche Elektrizität zu produzieren.

Natürlich sind sie jetzt viel vorsichtiger° mit der Elektrizität. Ihren ° more careful
Fernseher haben sie verkauft. Die meisten Sendungen waren sowieso° ° anyhow
nicht sehr gut. Einen Kühlschrank brauchen sie auch nicht, denn sie
essen vor allem frisches Obst und Gemüse. Sie benutzen noch elektrisches

Licht und einen Staubsauger. Ihren CD-Spieler spielen sie viel weniger
als früher. Sie haben sich ein besseres Radio mit Batterie gekauft. Sie
finden es nicht mehr so furchtbar, sich kalt zu duschen. Wenn sie heiß
baden wollen, stellen sie die Badewanne° ins Wohnzimmer und machen | bath tub
Wasser auf dem Herd heiß. Am schwierigsten ist es mit der
Waschmaschine, weil das Wasser meistens nicht richtig warm wird.

Auf die Frage, ob das ein Modell für andere ist, antworten die Zwei:
„Es ist keine Frage, daß unsere Elektrizitätsproduktion umweltfreundlicher
ist. Die Frage ist eben, was man wichtiger findet, persönlichen Komfort
oder Umwelt. Auf diese Frage muß jeder für sich selbst eine Antwort geben."

1. Mit was für Energie leben Michael und Marianne?

   _____

2. Warum haben sie nur 90 Prozent ihrer Rechnungen bezahlt?

   _____

3. Warum machen sie ihre eigene Energie?

   _____

4. Wie produzieren sie Energie?

   _____

5. Warum haben sie ihren Fernseher verkauft?

   _____

6. Warum brauchen sie keinen Kühlschrank?

   _____

7. Was benutzen sie oft anstatt ihres CD-Spielers?

   _____

8. Wie duschen sie sich?

   _____

9. Was meinen Marianne und Michael—wer produziert umweltfreundlichere Energie, sie oder das
   Elektrizitätswerk?

   _____

J. Schreiben Sie, was man für die Umwelt tun kann. Write a short essay (ten sentences) about what you or all of us could do to improve the environment. For ideas you may want to refer to Kapitel 14 of your textbook, especially pages 441, 442, and 455 (Ex. 13).

Um die Umwelt zu schützen, sollte man _____

_____

_____

_____

_____

_____

_____

_____

Lab Manual

Kapitel 1

In the directions you will hear the following new words:

Übung   *exercise*
Beispiel   *example*
Fangen wir an.   *Let's begin.*

A. Frage und Antwort°. You will hear six questions, each followed by two | question and answer
responses. If both responses are the same, place a check mark in the column
marked same. If the responses are different, place a check mark in the column
marked *different*.

	same	different		same	different		same	different
▶	___	✓						
1.	✓	___	3.	___	✓	5.	✓	___
2.	___	✓	4.	✓	___	6.	___	✓

B. Welche Nummer? You will hear ten statements about the items pictured below. Put the number
of each statement under the picture to which it refers.

▶ ___1___   a. ___8___   b. ___5___   c. ___4___

d. ___10___   e. ___3___   f. ___7___   g. ___2___

  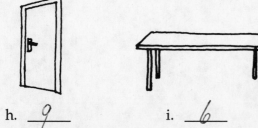

h. ___9___   i. ___6___

C. Farben. You will hear eight statements about colors. If a statement is correct, place a check mark in the column marked **richtig.** If the statement is false, place a check mark in the column marked **falsch.**

richtig (true)	falsch (false)		richtig	falsch	
✓		(der Ozean)			
1. ✓		(die Maus)	5.	✓	(die Banane)
2.	✓	(der Asphalt)	6. ✓		(das Gras)
3. ✓		(die Schokolade)	7.	✓	(die Tomate)
4.	✓	(das Gras)	8. ✓		(das Papier)

D. Frage und Antwort. You will hear five questions, each followed by two responses. Place a check mark by the letter of the answer that makes sense. You will hear each set of questions and answers twice.

▶ a. _____ b. ✓

1. a. _____ b. ✓   3. a. ✓ b. _____   5. a. _____ b. ✓
2. a. _____ b. ✓   4. a. ✓ b. _____

E. Diktat°. Write the words you hear spelled. | dictation

▶ *Lampe*

1. TSCHÜS   2. DANKE   3. HERSSEN
                                      ESS - ZETT

Copy down the numbers you hear.

1. 4 vier   3. 23   5. _____
2. 11 elf   4. 112

Kapitel 2

In the directions you will hear the following new words:

Übung	*exercise*
Beispiel	*example*
Fangen wir an.	*Let's begin.*

A. Eine Studentin in Berlin. Listen to the reading of the *Lesestück* "Eine Studentin in Berlin."

B. Richtig oder falsch? You will hear eight statements based on the *Lesestück* "Eine Studentin in Berlin." Check **richtig** if the statement is correct according to the information in the reading passage. Check **falsch** if the statement is incorrect.

richtig   **falsch**

▶ _____   ✓_____

1. _____   5. _____

2. _____   6. _____

3. _____   7. _____

4. _____   8. _____

C. Ist das logisch? You will hear seven pairs of questions and responses. Place a check mark in the column marked **logisch** if the response is logical. Place a check mark in the column marked **unlogisch** if the response to the question is not logical.

logisch   **unlogisch**   **logisch**   **unlogisch**   **logisch**   **unlogisch**

▶ ✓_____   _____

1. _____   _____   4. _____   _____   6. _____   _____

2. _____   _____   5. _____   _____   7. _____   _____

3. _____   _____

D. Das Gegenteil°. You will hear six questions containing an adjective or an adverb. Complete the answer printed in your lab manual by checking the antonym of the adjective or adverb you hear.

| the opposite

▶ Nein, er ist ...   ✓ a. faul   _____ b. ernst

1. Nein, es geht mir ...   _____ a. schlecht   _____ b. ruhig

2. Nein, sie ist ...   _____ a. krank   _____ b. freundlich

3. Nein, er ist ...   _____ a. lustig   _____ b. müde

4. Nein, es ist ...   _____ a. klein   _____ b. nett

5. Nein, er ist ...   _____ a. gut   _____ b. neu

6. Nein, sie ist ...   _____ a. freundlich   _____ b. kritisch

E. Jürgen. You will hear a brief description of Jürgen and learn what he likes to do. Afterwards, you will hear eight statements. Place a check mark in the column marked **richtig** if the statement is correct. Place a check mark in the column marked **falsch** if the statement is incorrect. You will hear the description twice.

	richtig	falsch
▶ Jürgen ist 22 Jahre alt.	_____	✓
1. Er ist faul.	_____	_____
2. Er spielt gern Schach.	_____	_____
3. Er treibt nicht gern Sport.	_____	_____
4. Er spielt Fußball.	_____	_____
5. Er spielt Tischtennis.	_____	_____
6. Er geht oft tanzen.	_____	_____
7. Er geht heute abend ins Kino.	_____	_____
8. Er ist heute müde.	_____	_____

F. Diktat. What are Susi and Oliver doing? Oliver runs into Susi on the street, and they talk about various things. Complete their conversation by supplying the missing words, which you will hear on the tape. You will hear the entire dialogue twice.

▶ Tag, Susi, wie _____ *geht's* _____ ?

— Tag, Susi, wie geht's?

— Tag, Oliver, danke, _____ _____ .

— Du, was _____ du _____ ?

— Ich _____ .

— Hm ... Und _____ _____ ?

— Nichts _____ .

— Spielst du gern _____ ?

— Ja, _____ gern.

— _____ du mit mir?

— Ja, gern.

G. Übungen zur Aussprache°. Listen and repeat the word pairs. You may wish | pronunciation
to review the pronunciation of long and short **u** and **o** in the Reference Section
of your textbook, page R-4.

long $\bar{u}$	short u	long $\bar{o}$	short o
Mus	muß	Moos	Most
buk	Buckel	bog	Bock
Schuster	Schuß	Schote	Schotte
Stuhle	Stulle	Ofen	offen
tun	Tunnel	Tone	Tonne

Now listen and repeat the sentences, paying special attention to the way you pronounce long and short **u** and **o** in the boldfaced words.

1. Spielt **Monika oft Rockmusik?**
2. Ist heute **Mittwoch oder Donnerstag?**
3. Es ist **Montag.**

4. Geht es Ihnen **gut?**
5. Ja, danke. **Und** Ihnen?

Kapitel 3

A. Groß oder klein? Alles ist relativ! Listen to the reading of the *Lesestück* "Groß oder klein? Alles ist relativ!"

B. Richtig oder falsch? In your lab manual you will see five questions based on the *Lesestück* "Groß oder klein? Alles ist relativ!" You will hear the questions and three possible answers to each question. Each answer is said twice. Check the letter of each correct answer. A question may have more than one correct answer.

		a	b	c
▶	Wo liegt Deutschland?	✓	✓	
1.	Wo liegt Berlin?			
2.	Wie ist das Wetter in Deutschland?			
3.	Wie groß ist Deutschland?			
4.	Wie viele Einwohner hat Deutschland?			

C. Das Wetter. You will hear six short conversational exchanges about the weather. In your lab manual you will see a statement based on each exchange. Check **richtig** if the statement is correct; check **falsch** if it is incorrect.

		richtig	falsch
▶	Es regnet heute.		✓
1.	Heute ist es kalt.		
2.	Heute ist es schön.		
3.	Es ist heute kalt.		
4.	Morgen ist es bestimmt warm.		
5.	Es schneit.		
6.	Hoffentlich regnet es morgen wieder.		

D. Welches Wort?   You will hear seven words. Check the word in each printed pair that you hear pronounced.

►   ✓   bleiben   _____ treiben

1. _____ nett   _____ Bett

2. _____ mehr   _____ sehr

3. _____ Schnee   _____ schön

4. _____ morgen   _____ Norden

5. _____ wieder   _____ weiter

6. _____ heiß   _____ weiß

7. _____ scheinen   _____ schneien

E. Entgegnungen°. You will hear four statements about the weather. In your lab   I responses
manual you will see two possible replies for each statement. Check the letter of
the reply that makes sense.

►   ✓   a. Ja, vielleicht regnet es morgen.

      _____ b. Ja, morgen regnet es bestimmt auch.

1. _____ a. Ja, leider, und gestern war es noch so schön.

      _____ b. Aber morgen regnet es vielleicht.

2. _____ a. Ja, der Wind ist so kalt.

      _____ b. Hoffentlich bleibt es so schön.

3. _____ a. Ja, es bleibt bestimmt so heiß.

      _____ b. Ja, bestimmt, der Wind ist so kalt heute.

4. _____ a. Jetzt bleibt es bestimmt warm.

      _____ b. Aber heute ist es leider wieder so heiß.

F. Ein Telefongespräch°. Dieter calls Ingrid on the telephone. Listen to | telephone conversation
their conversation, then check the correct answers to the questions printed
in your lab manual. You will hear the conversation twice. You will hear two
new words: **warum** (*why*) and **mit** (*with*).

1. Was macht Ingrid?

    _____ a. Sie spielt Schach.

    _____ b. Sie ist im Bett und hört Musik.

2. Wie war das Wetter gestern?

    _____ a. Naß und kalt.

    _____ b. Schön warm.

3. Warum spielt sie nicht mit Dieter Tennis?

    _____ a. Sie spielt nicht gern Tennis.

    _____ b. Sie ist krank.

4. Wie ist das Wetter heute?

    _____ a. Es ist schönes Wetter.

    _____ b. Es regnet.

5. Was macht Dieter?

    _____ a. Er geht ins Kino.

    _____ b. Er spielt vielleicht mit Barbara Tennis.

G. Übungen zur Aussprache. Listen and repeat the word pairs. You may wish to review the
pronunciation of long and short **o** and **ö** in the Reference Section of your textbook, pages R-4 and R-5.

long $\bar{e}$	long $\bar{ö}$	short e	short ö	long $\bar{o}$	long $\bar{ö}$	short o	short ö
Hefe	Höfe	Gent	gönnt	schon	schön	konnte	könnte
Lehne	Löhne	helle	Hölle	Ofen	Öfen	Frosch	Frösche
Sehne	Söhne	kennen	können	losen	lösen	Koch	Köche
beten	böten	Beller	Böller	hohe	Höhe	Bock	Böcke
hehle	Höhle	Bäcker	Böcke	tot	töten	Kopf	Köpfe

Now listen and repeat the sentences, paying special attention to the way you pronounce long and
short **o** and **ö** in the boldfaced words.

1. Wie ist der **Sommer** in **Österreich?**
2. Im **Sommer** ist es **oft schön.**
3. Deutschland liegt weiter **nördlich** als Amerika.
4. Er **hört** die **Wörter** nicht.

Kapitel 4

A. Einkaufen am Wochenende. Listen to the reading of the *Lesestück* "Einkaufen am Wochenende."

B. Richtig oder falsch? You will hear eight statements based on the *Lesestück* "Einkaufen am Wochenende." Check **richtig** if the statement is correct according to the information in the reading passage. Check **falsch** if the statement is incorrect.

richtig	falsch		richtig	falsch		richtig	falsch
1. _____	_____	4. _____	_____	7. _____	_____
2. _____	_____	5. _____	_____	8. _____	_____
3. _____	_____	6. _____	_____		

C. Der richtige Laden°. You will hear four short dialogues. For each one, in your lab manual you will see the names of two possible shops or stores where the dialogue might take place. Place a check mark beside the correct location. | the right store

1. _____ Bäckerei   _____ Buchhandlung

2. _____ Supermarkt   _____ Tante-Emma-Laden

3. _____ Metzger   _____ Markt

4. _____ Apotheke   _____ Drogerie

D. Entgegnungen°. You will hear six questions or statements. In your lab manual you will see two possible responses to each. Place a check mark beside the response that makes sense. | responses

1. _____ a. Ja, ich gehe in den Supermarkt.

   _____ b. Ja, ich gehe ins Kino.

2. _____ a. Nein, wir haben noch viel Brot.

   _____ b. Ja, wir brauchen Wurst.

3. _____ a. Gut, ich gehe in den Supermarkt.

   _____ b. Das Brot ist besser bei Müller.

4. _____ a. Ja, geh doch in die Apotheke!

   _____ b. Ich glaube ja.

5. _____ a. Wieviel brauchst du?

   _____ b. O.K., ich gehe in die Buchhandlung.

6. _____ a. Gut, ich kaufe drei Pfund.

_____ b. Sonst noch etwas?

E. Diktat: Gabis Geburtstag. Complete the following story about Gabi's birthday by supplying the missing words, which you will hear on the tape. You will hear the entire story twice.

Gabi hat heute _____ . Drei _____ kommen zum

Kaffee. Angelika geht in _____ _____ und kauft für Gabi

ein _____ über Frankreich. Das ist leider nicht ganz

_____ . Karin hat nicht so viel Geld. Sie geht auf _____

_____ und kauft schöne _____ . Sie sind ganz

_____ . Und Susanne kauft beim _____ viel

_____ . Jetzt hat auch sie _____

_____ _____ . Aber bei Gabi ist es sehr

_____ . Sie _____ Kuchen, hören Musik und finden

_____ wirklich schön.

F. Übungen zur Aussprache. Listen and repeat the word pairs. You may wish to review the pronunciation of long and short **ü** and **u** in the Reference Section of your textbook, page R-5.

long ī	long ǖ	short i	short ü
Biene	Bühne	Kiste	Küste
diene	Düne	Lifte	Lüfte
Kiel	kühl	Kissen	küssen
liegen	lügen	missen	müssen
fielen	fühlen	Binde	Bünde

long ǖ	short ü	long ū	long ǖ	short u	short ü
Füße	Flüsse	Huhn	Hühner	Fluß	Flüsse
Mühle	Müll	Hut	Hüte	Bund	Bünde
Sühne	Sünde	Fuß	Füße	Kuß	Küsse
Blüte	Bütte	Zug	Züge	Luft	Lüft
Düne	dünne	Blut	Blüte	Kunst	Künste

Now listen and repeat the sentences, paying special attention to the way you pronounce long and short **ü** and **u** in the boldfaced words.

1. **Für** ihren Mann kauft sie einen **Butterkuchen.**
2. Der **Student** kann seine **Bücher** nicht finden.
3. **Jürgen sucht** ein **Buch über Musik.**
4. Im **Frühling** sind die **Blumen** auf dem Markt besonders schön.

Name _____ Date _____

Kapitel 5

A. Studieren in Deutschland. Listen to the reading of the *Lesestück* "Studieren in Deutschland."

B. Richtig oder falsch? You will hear eight statements based on the *Lesestück* "Studieren in Deutschland." Check **richtig** if the statement is correct. Check **falsch** if it is incorrect.

	richtig	falsch		richtig	falsch		richtig	falsch
1.	_____	_____	4.	_____	_____	7.	_____	_____
2.	_____	_____	5.	_____	_____	8.	_____	_____
3.	_____	_____	6.	_____	_____			

C. Der richtige Ort°. You will hear six questions concerning the location ┃ the right place of certain activities. For each question you will hear two possible answers. Check the letter of the correct answer.

1. a. _____	b. _____		4. a. _____	b. _____		
2. a. _____	b. _____		5. a. _____	b. _____		
3. a. _____	b. _____		6. a. _____	b. _____		

D. Die richtige Entgegnung°. You will hear five questions which might ┃ response begin a conversation. In your lab manual are two possible responses to each question. Check the reply that makes sense.

1. _____ a. Ich kann leider nicht. Ich muß in die Bibliothek.

 _____ b. Ich mache Physik als Hauptfach.

2. _____ a. Mein Referat ist jetzt fertig.

 _____ b. Im Wintersemester mache ich Examen.

3. _____ a. Anglistik und Sport. Und du?

 _____ b. Ich muß in acht Semestern fertig werden.

4. _____ a. Ich muß noch zwei Semester studieren.

 _____ b. Diese Woche muß ich ein Referat schreiben.

5. _____ a. Ja, natürlich, gern.

 _____ b. Ich studiere Musik und Sport.

E. Das richtige Wort. You will hear ten words. Check the word in each printed pair that you hear pronounced.

1. _____ Arbeit   _____ Abitur   6. _____ werden   _____ wohnen

2. _____ sollen   _____ wollen   7. _____ Klausur   _____ Kurs

3. _____ müssen   _____ wissen   8. _____ können   _____ kennen

4. _____ leihen   _____ bleiben   9. _____ Fach   _____ Fisch

5. _____ seit   _____ Zeit   10. _____ zahlen   _____ erzählen

F. Eine deutsche Studentin. You will hear a short paragraph about a German student named Dagmar, her studies, and her activities. Listen, then check the correct answers to the questions printed in your lab manual. You will hear the story twice.

1. Was studiert Dagmar?

   _____ a. Sie studiert Physik.

   _____ b. Sie studiert in Marburg.

   _____ c. Sie studiert Germanistik und Geschichte.

2. Warum studiert sie nicht Medizin?

   _____ a. Sie findet es nicht interessant.

   _____ b. Ihre Noten vom Gymnasium waren nicht gut.

   _____ c. Es gibt keinen Numerus clausus in Medizin.

3. Was macht sie dieses Semester?

   _____ a. Sie schreibt viele Klausuren.

   _____ b. Sie leiht Michael ihre Notizen.

   _____ c. Sie schreibt ein Referat.

4. Wo arbeitet Dagmar für die Klausuren?

   _____ a. Im Seminar.

   _____ b. Im Café.

   _____ c. Sie geht in die Bibliothek.

5. Was kann Dagmar nicht oft machen?

   _____ a. In ein Café gehen und ihre Freunde sehen.

   _____ b. Ins Kino gehen.

   _____ c. Einkaufen gehen.

G. Übungen zur Aussprache.   Listen and repeat the word pairs. You may wish to review the pronunciation of long and short **a** in the Reference Section of your textbook, page R-4.

long a̅	short a	short a	short o
Bahn	Bann	Bann	Bonn
kam	Kamm	Kamm	komm
Staat	Stadt	Matte	Motte
Schlaf	schlaff	knalle	Knolle
lahm	Lamm	falle	volle

Now listen and repeat the sentences, paying special attention to the way you pronounce long and short **a** and short **o** in the boldfaced words.

1. **Komm doch** mit in die **Stadt!**
2. **Was soll** ich **noch machen?**
3. Der **Abend war aber interessant.**
4. Wer **sagt das?**
5. Mußt du heute **nachmittag noch** viel **arbeiten?**
6. Ich **habe noch** eine **Frage** für **Professor Bachmann.**

Kapitel 6

A. Eine Amerikanerin in Österreich. Listen to the reading of the *Lesestück* "Eine Amerikanerin in Österreich."

B. Richtig oder falsch? You will hear eight statements based on the *Lesestück* "Eine Amerikanerin in Österreich." Check **richtig** if the statement is correct. Check **falsch** if it is incorrect.

	richtig	**falsch**		**richtig**	**falsch**		**richtig**	**falsch**
1.	_____	_____	4.	_____	_____	7.	_____	_____
2.	_____	_____	5.	_____	_____	8.	_____	_____
3.	_____	_____	6.	_____	_____			

C. Ist das logisch? You will hear eight pairs of questions and responses. If the response is a logical reply to the question, check **logisch.** If the response is not logical, check **unlogisch.**

	logisch	**unlogisch**		**logisch**	**unlogisch**		**logisch**	**unlogisch**
1.	_____	_____	4.	_____	_____	7.	_____	_____
2.	_____	_____	5.	_____	_____	8.	_____	_____
3.	_____	_____	6.	_____	_____			

D. Die richtige Wortbedeutung°. You will hear six statements. For each statement, you will see two words printed in your lab manual. Indicate to which of the two words the recorded statement refers.

° the correct meaning

▶ _____ Flugzeug   ✓ Rad

1. _____ Bern   _____ Wien

2. _____ Ferien   _____ Alpen

3. _____ zu Hause   _____ allein

4. _____ Ski fahren   _____ gehören

5. _____ Seite   _____ Auto

6. _____ fliegen   _____ zu Fuß gehen

E. Ein Interview. A journalist, Frau Berger, is conducting interviews about the traveling habits of Germans. You will hear an interview with Herr Kaiser. Listen, and then check the correct answers to the questions printed in your lab manual. You will hear the interview twice.

1. Welches Land ist Ferienland Nummer 1 für die Deutschen?

   _____ a. Die Schweiz.

   _____ b. Österreich.

   _____ c. Dänemark.

2. Warum fahren die Deutschen gern nach Österreich?

   _____ a. In Österreich scheint immer die Sonne.

   _____ b. In Österreich ist das Essen teuer.

   _____ c. Österreich ist ein sehr schönes Land.

3. Wie reist° man von Deutschland nach Österreich?   I travel

   _____ a. Viele Leute fahren mit dem Motorrad nach Österreich.

   _____ b. Man braucht nicht lange zu fahren.

   _____ c. Man kann mit dem Zug oder dem Auto fahren.

4. Was machen die Deutschen, wenn sie nach Österreich fahren?

   _____ a. Sie wandern und schwimmen.

   _____ b. Sie fahren viel mit dem Rad.

   _____ c. Sie spielen Tennis.

5. Mit wem fährt Herr Kaiser in die Ferien?

   _____ a. Mit Freunden.

   _____ b. Mit Deutschen.

   _____ c. Mit Frau Berger.

6. Wo schlafen die Freunde, wenn das Wetter gut ist?

   _____ a. In Jugendherbergen.

   _____ b. Im Auto.

   _____ c. Sie zelten.

F. Übungen zur Aussprache. Listen and repeat the word pairs. You may wish to review the pronunciation of **k, ck, ch,** and **sch,** and the suffix **-ig** in the Reference Section of your textbook, pages R-7 and R-8.

[k]	[x]	[ç]	[š]	[x]	[ç]
Flak	Flach	welche	Welsche	Bach	Bäche
nackt	Nacht	Fächer	fescher	Loch	Löcher
Akt	acht	Wicht	wischt	Bruch	Brüche
buk	Buch	Gicht	Gischt	sprach	spräche
Lack	Lachen	Löcher	Löscher	Buch	Bücher

[iç]	[ig]
Pfennig	Pfennige
König	Könige
schuldig	schuldige
billig	billiger

Now listen and repeat the sentences, paying special attention to the sounds [k], [x], [ç], and [š] in the boldfaced words.

1. Wir **können noch frischen Kuchen** beim **Bäcker kaufen.**
2. Unsere **Nachbarin** Frau **Gärstig kann wirklich keinen** guten **Kaffee kochen.**
3. **Christl spricht** sehr **wenig.**
4. Oft sagt sie die ganze **Woche nichts.**

Kapitel 7

A. Freizeitspläne. Listen to the reading of the *Lesestück* "Freizeitspläne."

B. Richtig oder falsch? You will hear ten statements based on the *Lesestück* "Freizeitspläne." Check **richtig** if the statement is correct. Check **falsch** if it is incorrect. You will hear one new word.

Kur   *spa*

	richtig	falsch		richtig	falsch
1.	_____	_____	6.	_____	_____
2.	_____	_____	7.	_____	_____
3.	_____	_____	8.	_____	_____
4.	_____	_____	9.	_____	_____
5.	_____	_____	10.	_____	_____

C. Das Gegenteil°. You will hear five questions containing an adjective or | the opposite
an adverb. Complete the answer printed in your lab manual by checking the
antonym of the adjective or adverb you hear.

▶ Nein, er ist ...   ✓ a. kalt   _____ b. toll

1. Nein, er hat ... Geld   _____ a. wenig   _____ b. schon

2. Nein, sie war ...   _____ a. fertig   _____ b. langweilig

3. Nein, es ist ...   _____ a. teuer   _____ b. frisch

4. Nein, ich gehe ... nach Hause.   _____ a. oft   _____ b. früh

5. Nein, sie ist ...   _____ a. gesund   _____ b. genau

D. Diktat. Tanja and Karla are packing for a trip to Hamburg. Complete their conversation by filling
in the blanks with the words you hear on the tape. You will hear the conversation twice. You will
hear one new word:

meinen   *to think, have an opinion*

Tanja: Glaubst du, wir brauchen sehr warme _____ ,

Karla?

Karla: Nein, ich glaube nicht. Eine _____ und der

_____ sind bestimmt genug.

Tanja: Gut. Du, _____ du mir deine rote

_____ ? Die _____ gut

_____ zu meinem schwarzen

_____ .

Karla: Ja, ja. Was meinst du—soll ich meinen grünen

_____ _____ ?

Tanja: Nein, bitte nicht!

Karla: Also gut. Aber den grünen _____

_____ ich.

Tanja: Und deine _____ _____

du auch mitbringen.

E. Im Restaurant. Anita and Paul are in a restaurant. They are looking at the menu and deciding what they want to eat. Listen to their conversation, then check the correct answers to the questions printed in your lab manual. You will hear the conversation twice. You will hear three new words:

dazu   *with it*
Nachtisch   *dessert*
Flasche   *bottle*

1. Was ißt Anita?

_____ a. Fisch und Gemüse.

_____ b. Kuchen.

_____ c. Brot und Käse.

2. Wie sind die Steaks in diesem Restaurant?

_____ a. Nicht besonders gut.

_____ b. Leider ziemlich klein.

_____ c. Sehr gut.

3. Hat Paul Hunger?

_____ a. Nein, er hat keinen Hunger.

_____ b. Er hat wirklich großen Hunger.

_____ c. Nein, er hat nur Durst.

4. Wie findet Anita den Käsekuchen?

_____ a. Sie weiß nicht.

_____ b. Nicht besonders gut.

_____ c. Sie findet, der schmeckt toll.

5. Was trinkt Paul?

_____ a. Rotwein.

_____ b. Erst Mineralwasser, dann Wein.

_____ c. Cola.

F. Übungen zur Aussprache.   Listen and repeat the words. You may wish to review the pronunciation of **s** (before and between vowels), **ß (ss)**, and **z** in the Reference Section of your textbook, page R-6.

[s̩]	[ts]	[s̩]	[s]	[ts]
so	Zoo	reisen	reißen	reizen
sehen	zehn	heiser	heißen	heizen
Seile	Zeile	Geisel	Geiß	Geiz
sog	zog	weisen	weißen	Weizen
Sohn	Zone	leise	beißen	beizen

Now listen and repeat the sentences, paying special attention to the way you pronounce **s, ß (ss)**, and **z** in the boldfaced words.

1. Warum haben **Sie zwei Gläser,** und **Sabine** hat nur ein **Glas?**
2. **Sie müssen** doch **wissen, was Sie essen sollen.**
3. Kann man wirklich **zu** viel **lesen?**
4. Wie **heißt** Ihr **Sohn,** Frau **Seidel?**
5. Wenn ich im **Sommer Zeit** habe, mache ich eine **Reise** in die **Schweiz.**

Kapitel 8

A. Andere Länder-Andere Sitten.   Listen to the reading of the *Lesestück* "Andere Länder—Andere Sitten."

B. Richtig oder falsch?   You will hear eight statements based on the *Lesestück* "Andere Länder—Andere Sitten." Check **richtig** if the statement is correct. Check **falsch** if it is incorrect.

	richtig	falsch		richtig	falsch		richtig	falsch
1.	_____	_____	4.	_____	_____	7.	_____	_____
2.	_____	_____	5.	_____	_____	8.	_____	_____
3.	_____	_____	6.	_____	_____			

C. Ist das logisch?   You will hear eight pairs of questions and responses. If the response is a logical reply to the question, check **logisch.** If the response is not logical, check **unlogisch.**

	logisch	unlogisch		logisch	unlogisch		logisch	unlogisch
1.	_____	_____	4.	_____	_____	7.	_____	_____
2.	_____	_____	5.	_____	_____	8.	_____	_____
3.	_____	_____	6.	_____	_____			

D. Der richtige Ort°.   You will hear six questions about locations. | place
Check the letter of the correct answer.

1. a. _____	b. _____	4. a. _____	b. _____		
2. a. _____	b. _____	5. a. _____	b. _____		
3. a. _____	b. _____	6. a. _____	b. _____		

E. Erlebnisse° in Deutschland. Thomas, an American student, takes his | experiences
first trip to Germany. He sees many things that are quite different from
what he is used to in the U.S. You will hear some of his impressions. Listen,
then check the correct answers to the questions printed in your lab manual.
A question may have more than one correct answer. You will hear the text
twice. You will hear two new words:

Balkon   *balcony*
Bäume   *trees*

1. Wo wohnt Thomas in Deutschland?

    _____ a. In einem Studentenheim.

    _____ b. Bei einer Gastfamilie.

    _____ c. In München.

2. Was macht Frau Schneider?

    _____ a. Sie geht jeden Tag in die Bibliothek.

    _____ b. Sie arbeitet an den Blumen auf dem Balkon.

    _____ c. Sie arbeitet auf dem Bahnhof.

3. Wie ißt man in Deutschland?

    _____ a. Man benutzt Messer und Gabel.

    _____ b. Man hat die Hände unter dem Tisch.

    _____ c. Beim Essen spricht man sehr wenig.

4. Was gibt es im Biergarten?

    _____ a. Es gibt große Gläser.

    _____ b. Es gibt sehr gutes Essen.

    _____ c. Es gibt Blumen und alte Bäume.

5. Was erzählt Thomas über das deutsche Bier?

    _____ a. Es schmeckt ziemlich bitter.

    _____ b. Die Deutschen trinken es sehr gern.

    _____ c. Es ist sehr teuer.

6. Kennt Thomas schon viele Leute?

    _____ a. Nein, er kennt nur Familie Schneider.

    _____ b. Ja, er hat schon viele Leute kennengelernt.

    _____ c. Nein, er kennt nur Stefan und Karin.

    _____ d. Nein, er kennt nur die Leute im Biergarten.

F.   Ein Telefongespräch.   Gabi has moved into a new apartment. An old friend telephones her. Listen to their conversation, then check the correct answers to the questions printed in your lab manual. You will hear the conversation twice. You will hear one new word:

Miete   *rent*

1.   Warum ruft Fred bei Gabi an?

_____ a.   Er will sie besuchen.

_____ b.   Er hört, sie hat eine neue Wohnung.

2.   Wie viele Zimmer hat Gabis Wohnung?

_____ a.   3 Zimmer, Küche und Bad.

_____ b.   6 Zimmer.

3.   Was gefällt Gabi sehr an der Wohnung?

_____ a.   Das große Badezimmer.

_____ b.   Der Balkon.

4.   Was denkt Fred über Gabis Miete?

_____ a.   Er findet sie ziemlich hoch.

_____ b.   Er denkt, daß sie recht niedrig° ist. | low

5.   Wann kann Fred Gabis Wohnung sehen?

_____ a.   Am Samstag, auf dem Fest.

_____ b.   Heute abend.

6.   Was macht Gabi, wenn am Samstag schönes Wetter ist?

_____ a.   Sie geht Bücherregale kaufen.

_____ b.   Sie macht das Fest auf dem Balkon.

G. Übungen zur Aussprache. Listen and repeat the word pairs. You may wish to review the pronunciation of long and short **i** and **e** in the Reference Section of your textbook, page R-4.

long ī	short i	long ē	short e
bieten	bitten	beten	Betten
vieler	Filter	Fehler	Felle
Wiege	Wicke	Weg	weg
stiehlt	stillt	stehlt	stellt
riet	ritt	Reeder	Retter
ihn	in	fehle	Fälle
		gähnt	Gent

Now listen and repeat the sentences, paying special attention to the way you pronounce long and short **i** and **e** in the boldfaced words.

1. Warum **sind sie nicht hier geblieben?**
2. Er **ist gestern gegen sechs** Uhr gegangen.
3. **Wie findest** du **dieses Winterwetter?**
4. **Diese Männer** haben doch **recht.**
5. **Niemand fliegt** nach **Wien.**
6. **Dieses Beispiel** habe **ich in** der **Zeitung gelesen.**
7. Jens **trinkt immer Milch.**

Kapitel 9

A. Zwei Frauenporträts. Listen to the reading of the *Lesestück* "Zwei Frauenporträts."

B. Richtig oder falsch? You will hear eight statements based on the *Lesestück* "Zwei Frauenporträts." Check **richtig** if the statement is correct. Check **falsch** if it is incorrect.

	richtig	**falsch**			**richtig**	**falsch**			**richtig**	**falsch**
1.	_____	_____		4.	_____	_____		7.	_____	_____
2.	_____	_____		5.	_____	_____		8.	_____	_____
3.	_____	_____		6.	_____	_____				

C. Ist das logisch? You will hear six short conversational exchanges. If the response is a logical reply to the question or statement, check **logisch.** If the response is not logical, check **unlogisch.**

	logisch	**unlogisch**			**logisch**	**unlogisch**
1.	_____	_____		4.	_____	_____
2.	_____	_____		5.	_____	_____
3.	_____	_____		6.	_____	_____

D. Die richtige Wortbedeutung. You will hear eight statements. For each statement, you will see two words or phrases printed in your lab manual. Check the word to which the recorded statement refers.

1.	_____ Karten	_____ Schreibmaschinen
2.	_____ Informatik	_____ Stelle
3.	_____ Kollegin	_____ Musikerin
4.	_____ Geschäftsmann	_____ Lehrer
5.	_____ Ärztin	_____ Informatikerin
6.	_____ Hausfrauen	_____ Rechtsanwälte
7.	_____ beim Zahnarzt	_____ auf der Bank
8.	_____ Wortprozessor	_____ Beruf

E. Ein Gespräch. Two friends, Renate Bär and Angela Kurz, haven't seen each other for awhile. Listen to the following conversation between them. Then check the correct answers to the questions printed in your lab manual. You will hear the dialogue twice. You will hear three new words:

Vorurteile	*prejudices*
leichter	*easier*
kämpfen	*to fight*

1. Welchen Beruf hat Renate Bär?

   _____ a. Informatikerin.

   _____ b. Personalchefin.

2. Warum gefällt ihr der neue Job?

   _____ a. Sie kommt viel mit Menschen zusammen.

   _____ b. Sie arbeitet gern mit dem Computer.

3. Welches Problem hat sie in ihrem neuen Job?

   _____ a. Sie verdient nicht gut.

   _____ b. Einige Männer in der Firma haben Vorurteile gegen sie.

4. Was ist Angela Kurz von Beruf?

   _____ a. Musikerin.

   _____ b. Lehrerin.

5. Wie ist die Atmosphäre unter Angelas Kollegen und Kolleginnen?

   _____ a. Ruhig und freundlich.

   _____ b. Unfreundlich.

6. Was gefällt Angela Kurz an ihrem Beruf?

   _____ a. Die meisten ihrer Kollegen sind Frauen.

   _____ b. Sie arbeitet gern mit jungen Leuten.

F. Übungen zur Aussprache.   Listen and repeat the words. You may wish to review the pronunciation of **r** and **l** in the Reference Section of your textbook, pages R-5 and R-6.

[r]	[l]	full [r]	full [r]	full [r]
wird	wild	fragt	ragt	warum
Schmerzen	schmelzen	kriechen	riechen	gierig
Karte	kalte	trugen	rufen	führen
Schurz	Schulz	Preis	Reis	Tiere
Worte	wollte	grünen	rühmen	schnüren

Now listen and repeat the sentences, paying special attention to the way you pronounce **r** and **l** in the boldfaced words.

1. Wer hat **Frau Kugel** das **gefragt?**
2. Es hat **Cornelia** nicht **gefallen,** daß wir so **schnell gefahren** sind.
3. Im **Juli wollen** wir im **Schwarzwald** wandern und **zelten.**
4. Im **Frühling fahre** ich mit **Freunden** nach **Österreich.**

Kapitel 10

A. Die Schweiz.   Listen to the reading of the *Lesestück* "Die Schweiz."

B. Richtig oder falsch?   You will hear eight statements based on the *Lesestück* "Die Schweiz." Check **richtig** if the statement is correct. Check **falsch** if it is incorrect.

	richtig	falsch		richtig	falsch		richtig	falsch
1.	_____	_____	4.	_____	_____	7.	_____	_____
2.	_____	_____	5.	_____	_____	8.	_____	_____
3.	_____	_____	6.	_____	_____			

C. Entgegnungen°.   You will hear five statements or questions about being | responses
ill. Check the answer in your lab manual that makes the most sense.

1. _____ a. Schade.

   _____ b. Du tust mir leid.

   _____ c. Nein, ich bin erkältet.

2. _____ a. Ich putze mir morgens die Zähne.

   _____ b. Ich fühle mich schwächer als gestern.

   _____ c. Ich freue mich darauf.

3. _____ a. Du hast recht, sonst kann ich nächste Woche nicht Ski fahren.

   _____ b. Hoffentlich bekomme ich diesen Herbst keine Erkältung!

   _____ c. Fühlst du dich auch krank?

4. _____ a. Das ist ja toll!

   _____ b. Ach, schade!

   _____ c. Geh doch zum Zahnarzt!

5. _____ a. Nein, ich glaube nicht.

   _____ b. Morgen gehe ich Ski fahren.

   _____ c. Nein, ich huste nicht.

D. Körperteile. You will hear five sentences describing parts of the body. Check the correct answer.

1. _____ a. Hände _____ b. Füße

2. _____ a. Ohren _____ b. Augen

3. _____ a. Hals _____ b. Nase

4. _____ a. Zähne _____ b. Beine

5. _____ a. Finger _____ b. Haare

E. Ein Interview. Herr Gruber, a journalist, is trying to find out what the Swiss think about their standard of living and the European Union. You will hear his interview with an older woman, Frau Beck. Listen, then check the correct answers to the questions printed in your lab manual. A question may have more than one correct answer. You will hear the interview twice. You will hear the following new word:

Europäische Union   *European Union*

1. Wie findet Frau Beck den Lebensstandard in der Schweiz?

    _____ a. Der Lebensstandard ist relativ hoch.

    _____ b. Die meisten Leute kaufen sich jedes Jahr ein neues Auto.

    _____ c. Vieles ist billiger geworden.

2. Haben die Leute jetzt ein einfacheres Leben?

    _____ a. Ja, viele haben keine Spülmaschine und keinen Fernseher.

    _____ b. Nein, aber sie sind sparsamer° geworden. | more thrifty

    _____ c. Ja, nur wenige können sich ein Auto kaufen.

3. Warum hat Frau Beck kein Auto?

    _____ a. Sie braucht es nicht.

    _____ b. Sie kann es sich nicht kaufen.

    _____ c. Sie fährt immer mit dem Rad oder mit dem Zug.

4. Was denkt Frau Beck über die Europäische Union?

    _____ a. Sie denkt nicht darüber nach.

    _____ b. Sie möchte, daß die Schweiz neutral bleibt.

    _____ c. Sie weiß nicht, was die Europäische Union ist.

5. Fürchtet Frau Beck, daß die Schweiz von der Welt isoliert ist?

    _____ a. Ja, sie fürchtet es.

    _____ b. Nein, sie glaubt, andere Länder kaufen ihre Qualitätsprodukte.

    _____ c. Nein, sie glaubt, daß andere Länder Schweizer Produkte wollen.

6. Was sagt Frau Beck über die Wirtschaft in der Schweiz?

_____ a. Sie hat Angst, daß sie jetzt weniger kaufen kann.

_____ b. Sie hat keine Angst, daß es der Schweiz wirtschaftlich schlechter geht.

_____ c. Sie meint, die Schweiz ist wirtschaftlich stark.

F. Übungen zur Aussprache.   Listen and repeat the words. You may wish to review the pronunciation of final **-en, -e,** and **-er** in the Reference Section of your textbook, page R-4.

[ən]	[ə]	[ər]
bitten	bitte	bitter
fahren	fahre	Fahrer
denken	denke	Denker
fehlen	fehle	Fehler
besten	beste	bester

Now listen and repeat the sentences, paying special attention to your pronunciation of final **-en, -e,** and **-er** in the boldfaced words.

1. **Fahren** Sie **bitte** etwas **schneller!**
2. **Viele Amerikaner fliegen** im **Sommer** nach Europa.
3. **Manche Länder brauchen** mehr Schulen.
4. Die **Tage werden kürzer** und **kälter.**
5. **Diese Männer arbeiten** wirklich schwer.
6. **Viele Wörter** sind relativ, zum Beispiel **länger, größer oder jünger.**

Kapitel 11

A. Deutschland: 1945 bis heute.   Listen to the reading of the *Lesestück* "Deutschland: 1945 bis heute."

B. Richtig oder falsch?   You will hear eight statements based on the *Lesestück* "Deutschland: 1945 bis heute." Check **richtig** if the statement is correct. Check **falsch** if it is incorrect.

	richtig	falsch		richtig	falsch		richtig	falsch
1.	_____	_____	4.	_____	_____	7.	_____	_____
2.	_____	_____	5.	_____	_____	8.	_____	_____
3.	_____	_____	6.	_____	_____			

C. Ist das logisch?   You will hear eight short conversational exchanges. If the response is a logical reply, check **logisch.** If the response is not logical, check **unlogisch.**

	logisch	unlogisch		logisch	unlogisch		logisch	unlogisch
1.	_____	_____	4.	_____	_____	7.	_____	_____
2.	_____	_____	5.	_____	_____	8.	_____	_____
3.	_____	_____	6.	_____	_____			

D. Die gleiche Bedeutung.   You will hear six sentences. For each one, you will see a second sentence printed in your lab manual. If the sentence you hear and the printed sentence have the same meaning, check **gleich.** If the meanings are different, check **nicht gleich.**

		gleich	nicht gleich
1.	Das Theater hat schon angefangen.	_____	_____
2.	Du solltest das Musical sehen. Es ist wirklich toll.	_____	_____
3.	Ich habe viel Geld auf der Bank.	_____	_____
4.	Meine Kusine schreibt für eine Zeitung.	_____	_____
5.	Nach dem Zweiten Weltkrieg hatte Europa Angst vor dem Kommunismus.	_____	_____
6.	Die Ostdeutschen haben die Mauer gebaut.	_____	_____

E. Ein Gespräch.   You will hear a short conversation between Georg and Ursel. Listen, then check the correct answers to the questions printed in your lab manual. You will hear their conversation twice. You will hear the following new word:

Reklame   *publicity*

1. Warum ist Georg so müde?

    _____ a. Er war gestern abend in der Oper.

    _____ b. Er jobbt auf dem Theaterfestival.

2. Was für eine Arbeit hat Georg?

    _____ a. Er macht Musik.

    _____ b. Er macht Reklame für das Theater.

3. Warum macht Georg diese Arbeit?

    _____ a. Alles, was mit dem Theater zu tun hat, interessiert ihn.

    _____ b. Weil er gut verdient.

4. Was macht Georg meistens mit den Freikarten?

    _____ a. Er benutzt sie selbst.

    _____ b. Er schenkt sie Freunden.

5. Warum geht Ursel mit ins Theater?

    _____ a. Sie hat heute abend nichts anderes zu tun.

    _____ b. Den *Faust* fand sie sehr interessant, als sie ihn in der Schule las.

6. Wo wollen sie sich treffen?

    _____ a. Sie treffen sich am Theater.

    _____ b. Georg holt Ursel ab.

F. Übungen zur Aussprache.   Listen and repeat the word pairs. You may wish to review the pronunciation of **sp** and **st** in the Reference Section of your textbook, page R-7.

[sp]	[šp]	[st]	[št]
lispeln	spielen	Listen	stehlen
knuspern	springen	Hengst	streng
Espen	spenden	Küste	Stücke
Knospe	Sprossen	kosten	stocken
Haspe	Spatz	Last	Stall

Now listen and repeat the sentences, paying special attention to the way you pronounce **sp** and **st** in the boldfaced words.

1. Die **Studentin spricht** die deutsche **Sprache** sehr schön.
2. Schweizer Deutsch **versteht Stefan** nicht.
3. In der **Stadt** müssen Kinder oft auf den **Straßen spielen.**
4. **Sport** treiben macht **Spaß.**
5. Es hat **gestern** am **späten** Nachmittag **stark** geregnet.

Kapitel 12

A. Probleme mit der Wirtschaft. Listen to the reading of the *Lesestück* "Probleme mit der Wirtschaft."

B. Richtig oder falsch? You will hear eight statements based on the *Lesestück* "Probleme mit der Wirtschaft." Check **richtig** if the statement is correct. Check **falsch** if it is incorrect.

	richtig	falsch		richtig	falsch		richtig	falsch
1.	_____	_____	4.	_____	_____	7.	_____	_____
2.	_____	_____	5.	_____	_____	8.	_____	_____
3.	_____	_____	6.	_____	_____			

C. Entgegnungen. You will hear five questions which might begin a conversation. In your lab manual you will see three possible responses to each question. Check the reply that makes sense.

1. _____ a. Tut mir leid, sie ist heute nicht da.

   _____ b. Ich hoffe, Sie hatten eine gute Reise.

   _____ c. Sie war ein Jahr in den USA.

2. _____ a. Ja, gehen Sie bitte gleich hinein.

   _____ b. Ja, ich habe drei Jahre in Frankreich gearbeitet.

   _____ c. Ja, ich habe einen Termin bei ihm.

3. _____ a. Ja bitte, er erwartet Sie schon.

   _____ b. Ich habe einige Fragen.

   _____ c. Nein, leider nicht.

4. _____ a. Ich möchte bei einer Exportfirma arbeiten.

   _____ b. Ich glaube ja.

   _____ c. Tut mir leid. Ich habe die Heiratsanzeigen durchgesehen.

5. _____ a. Nein, Ihre Preise sind zu hoch.

   _____ b. Oh ja, die Arbeit muß interessant sein.

   _____ c. Nein, sie telefoniert gerade.

D. Die gleiche Bedeutung. You will hear six pairs of sentences. If the meaning of both sentences is the same, check **gleich.** If their meaning is different, check **nicht gleich.**

	gleich	nicht gleich		gleich	nicht gleich
1.	_____	_____	4.	_____	_____
2.	_____	_____	5.	_____	_____
3.	_____	_____	6.	_____	_____

E. Zwei Gespräche. You will hear two short dialogues. Listen, then read the statements printed in your lab manual. Check **richtig** if the statement is correct, **falsch** if it is incorrect, or **man weiß es nicht** if the information was not in the dialogue. You will hear each dialogue twice.

		richtig	falsch	man weiß es nicht
1.	Frau Schulze erwartet Herrn Meier.	_____	_____	_____
2.	Frau Schulze kann ihn heute nicht sehen.	_____	_____	_____
3.	Die Sekretärin will Frau Schulze fragen, ob sie Zeit hat.	_____	_____	_____
4.	Frau Schulze hat jetzt einen Termin.	_____	_____	_____
1.	Frau Schulze findet Herrn Meiers Sachen billig.	_____	_____	_____
2.	Sie hat aber viele Fragen wegen der Qualität.	_____	_____	_____
3.	Frau Schulze ruft Herrn Meier am Montag an.	_____	_____	_____
4.	Sie will die Sachen von Herrn Meier kaufen.	_____	_____	_____

F. Übungen zur Aussprache. Listen and repeat the word pairs. You may wish to review the pronunciation of **ei, eu (äu), au,** and **ie** in the Reference Section of your textbook, page R-4.

[ai]	[oi]	[au]	[oi]	[ī]	[ai]
nein	neun	Maus	Mäuse	Miene	meine
heiser	Häuser	Haus	Häuser	Biene	Beine
Seile	Säule	Bauch	Bäuche	viele	Feile
Eile	Eule	Haufen	häufen	diene	deine
leite	Leute	Laute	Leute	Liebe	Leibe

Now listen and repeat the sentences, paying special attention to the way you pronounce **eu (äu), au, ei,** and **ie** in the boldfaced words.

1. Herr **Neumann** ist **heute** nicht **einkaufen** gegangen.
2. Hat **Paula** schon **einen Brief** an **euch geschrieben?**
3. **Eugen** hat **Deutsch studiert.**
4. Abends geht **Klaus** mit **seinen Freunden** in **eine Kneipe.**
5. **Heike läuft** jeden Tag zur **Arbeit.**
6. **Dieter** hat **seit** Ende **Mai sein eigenes Auto.**

Kapitel 13

A. Die multikulturelle Gesellschaft. Listen to the reading of the *Lesestück* "Die multitkulturelle Gesellschaft."

B. Richtig oder falsch? You will hear eight statements based on the *Lesestück* "Die multikulturelle Gesellschaft." Check **richtig** if the statement is correct. Check **falsch** if it is incorrect.

	richtig	**falsch**		**richtig**	**falsch**		**richtig**	**falsch**
1.	_____	_____	4.	_____	_____	7.	_____	_____
2.	_____	_____	5.	_____	_____	8.	_____	_____
3.	_____	_____	6.	_____	_____			

C. Ist das logisch? You will hear six short conversational exchanges. If the response is a logical reply, check **logisch.** If the response is not logical, check **unlogisch.**

	logisch	**unlogisch**		**logisch**	**unlogisch**
1.	_____	_____	4.	_____	_____
2.	_____	_____	5.	_____	_____
3.	_____	_____	6.	_____	_____

D. Der richtige Ort. You will hear six questions about locations. Below are two possible answers to each. Place a check mark beside the response that makes sense.

1. _____ a. in der Heimat

   _____ b. in der Industrie

2. _____ a. ins Kino

   _____ b. ins Konzert

3. _____ a. in der Zeitung

   _____ b. in der Literatur

4. _____ a. an der Mauer

   _____ b. in den Bergen

5. _____ a. in ein Lokal

   _____ b. auf eine Demonstration

6. _____ a. in der Bibliothek

   _____ b. auf der Bank

E. Ein Interview. Birgit, a staff member of the local **Jugendzeitung,** is interviewing Ali, a Turk who lives in Germany. Listen to their conversation, then check the correct answers to the questions printed in your lab manual. You will hear the interview twice. You will hear two new words:

Grund   *reason*
Viertel   *quarter, district*

1. Wann ist Ali nach Deutschland gekommen?

    _____ a. Als er sehr klein war.

    _____ b. Er ist dort geboren.

2. Warum sind Alis Eltern nach Deutschland gekommen?

    _____ a. Sein Vater fand in der Türkei keine Arbeit.

    _____ b. Aus politischen Gründen.

3. Warum spricht Ali so gut Deutsch?

    _____ a. Er geht auf eine deutsche Schule und hat ein paar deutsche Freunde.

    _____ b. Er spricht mit seinen Eltern oft Deutsch.

4. Was sind Alis Zukunftspläne?

    _____ a. Er will ein türkisches Lokal öffnen.

    _____ b. Er will Elektroingenieur werden.

5. Wo möchte Ali später mal leben?

    _____ a. Er möchte in der Türkei leben; dort ist seine Heimat.

    _____ b. Er möchte in Deutschland bleiben.

F. Übungen zur Aussprache. Listen and repeat the word pairs. You may wish to review the pronunciation of **d** and **t** in the Reference Section of your textbook, page R-5.

[d]	[t]
hindern	hintern
Sonde	sonnte
Seide	Seite
bieder	Bieter
Mieder	Mieter

Now listen and repeat the sentences, paying special attention to the way you pronounce **d** and **t** in the boldfaced words.

1. **Die Kinder trugen** ihre **beste Kleidung** zum **Fest.**
2. Im **Winter arbeitet Walter** in einem **Hotel.**
3. Sein **Vater hat** viele **Freunde eingeladen.**
4. **Dieters Bruder hat** ein **tolles Kassettendeck.**
5. **Der Bundespräsident redete** über **die** neuen **Länder.**

Kapitel 14

A. Die Umwelt. Listen to the reading of the *Lesestück* "Die Umwelt."

B. Richtig oder falsch? You will hear eight statements based on the *Lesestück* "Die Umwelt." Check **richtig** if the statement is correct. Check **falsch** if it is incorrect.

	richtig	falsch		richtig	falsch		richtig	falsch
1.	_____	_____	4.	_____	_____	7.	_____	_____
2.	_____	_____	5.	_____	_____	8.	_____	_____
3.	_____	_____	6.	_____	_____			

C. Ist das logisch? You will hear eight short conversational exchanges. If the response is a logical reply, check **logisch.** If the response is not logical, check **unlogisch.**

	logisch	unlogisch		logisch	unlogisch		logisch	unlogisch
1.	_____	_____	4.	_____	_____	7.	_____	_____
2.	_____	_____	5.	_____	_____	8.	_____	_____
3.	_____	_____	6.	_____	_____			

D. Die richtige Bedeutung. You will hear six sentences. For each one, you will see a second sentence printed in your lab manual. If the sentence you hear and the printed sentence have the same meaning, check **gleich.** If the meanings are different, check **nicht gleich.**

		gleich	nicht gleich
1.	Der Müll wird wieder verwertet.	_____	_____
2.	Wir verbrauchen zuviel Energie.	_____	_____
3.	Die Abgase der Autos sind weniger geworden.	_____	_____
4.	Die Glasflaschen wurden gestern abgeholt.	_____	_____
5.	Auf einem Picknick sollte man Plastikbestecke benutzen.	_____	_____
6.	Meine Familie sitzt viel auf dem Balkon.	_____	_____

E. Ein Gespräch. You will hear a short conversation between Markus und Sabrina. Markus tells about an article concerning a German-Brazilian agricultural chemist, José Lutzenberger. Listen, then check the correct answers to the questions printed in your lab manual. You will hear their conversation twice. You will hear four new words:

die Zerstörung	*destruction*
die Regenwälder	*rain forests*
kämpfen	*to fight*
der Bauer	*farmer*

1. Warum ist Markus so müde?

   _____ a. Er war gestern abend in einer Kneipe.

   _____ b. Er hat zu lange gelesen.

2. Wer ist José Lutzenberger?

   _____ a. Ein deutscher Bauer.

   _____ b. Ein Wissenschaftler, der für die Umwelt arbeitet.

3. Wo lebt Lutzenberger heute?

   _____ a. In Brasilien.

   _____ b. In Deutschland.

4. Warum ist Lutzenbergers Arbeit so wichtig?

   _____ a. Er kämpft gegen die Zerstörung der Regenwälder.

   _____ b. BASF ist ein wichtiger Chemie-Konzern.

5. Warum geht Markus oft zu Fuß?

   _____ a. Er meint, daß frische Luft sehr gesund ist.

   _____ b. Er möchte umweltfreundlicher leben.

6. Warum fährt Sabrina mit dem Auto zur Uni?

   _____ a. Sonst kommt sie zu spät in die Vorlesung.

   _____ b. Sie geht nicht gern zu Fuß.

7. Was machen die meisten Leute?

   _____ a. Sie sind oft faul und fahren deshalb mit dem Auto.

   _____ b. Sie gehen alle zu Fuß.

F. Übungen zur Aussprache.   Listen and repeat the word pairs. You may wish to review the pronunciation of **b, d,** and **g** in the Reference Section of your textbook, page R-5.

[b]	[p]	[d]	[t]	[g]	[k]
graben	Grab	finden	Fund	Tage	Tag
gaben	gab	Hunde	Hund	Wege	Weg
Staube	Staub	senden	Sand	Trugen	trug
hoben	hob	Bäder	Bad	Kriege	Krieg

Now listen and repeat the sentences, paying special attention to the way you pronounce **b, d,** and **g** in the boldfaced words.

1. **Haben** Sie das **Bild** meines **Bruders** und seiner **Freundin** gesehen?
2. Ich **habe über** ein **halbes** Jahr in **Freiburg gelebt.**
3. Es ist **gesund,** mit dem **Rad** aufs **Land** zu fahren.
4. Am **Montag habt** ihr **Probe** fürs Konzert, nicht?
5. Wie viele **Tage bleibt** ihr in **Hamburg?**

Listen and repeat the words and word pairs. You may wish to review the pronunciation of **ng, pf,** and **kn** in the Reference Section of your textbook, pages R-6–R-7.

[ŋ]	[f]	[pf]	[n]	[kn]
Finger	fand	Pfand	Nabe	Knabe
länger	feil	Pfeil	Narren	Knarren
Vorstellung	flogen	pflogen	nicken	knicken
Hunger	Flug	Pflug	nie	Knie
singen	Fund	Pfund	Noten	Knoten
Dinge				

Now listen and repeat the sentences, paying special attention to the way you pronounce **ng, pf,** and **kn** in the boldfaced words.

1. Im **Frühling** werden die Tage **länger.**
2. Während des Konzerts **sang** die große **Sängerin** Ilse **Lange.**
3. **Nach** dem Konzert **gingen** wir in eine **neue Kneipe.**
4. Zum Geburtstag hat **Inge fünf Pflanzen** bekommen.
5. Kostet ein **Pfund Kartoffeln fünfzig Pfennig?**
6. Frau **Bunge** und ihr Sohn hatten großen **Hunger.**

Self-Tests

Kapitel 1

A. How do you ask someone for personal information in German?
1. What is your name?
2. How old are you?
3. What is your address?
4. What is your telephone number?

B. Give the German equivalents of the following courtesy expressions.
1. thank you
2. you're welcome

C. 1. Give the days of the week in German.
2. Ask what day it is.
3. Say it is Thursday.

D. 1. Name five colors in German.
2. Ask what color the wall is.

E. 1. How can you tell what gender a German noun is?
2. Give the gender of the following nouns.
   a. Bleistift   d. Frau
   b. Tür   e. Mann
   c. Bett
3. Complete the sentences with the proper definite article.
   a. _____ Kugelschreiber ist neu.
   b. _____ Zimmer ist klein.
   c. _____ Lampe ist alt.
   d. Wie ist _____ Tisch? Groß oder klein?
   e. Wie alt ist _____ Uhr?
   f. _____ Kind da ist groß.

F. Complete each sentence with the pronoun that corresponds to the noun in parentheses.
1. _____ ist groß. (das Zimmer)
2. _____ ist neu. (die Adresse)
3. _____ ist zwanzig Jahre alt. (der Sekretär)
4. _____ ist zwei. (das Kind)
5. _____ ist klein. (der Stuhl)
6. _____ heißt Meyer. (die Sekretärin)

Kapitel 2

A. 1. How would you greet someone at the following times of day?
   a. in the morning
   b. in the afternoon
   c. in the evening
2. Someone asks how you are. Give one positive and one negative response.
   Wie geht's?

B. 1. Give antonyms for the following words.
   a. faul   d. gut
   b. freundlich   e. klein
   c. ernst
2. Give two ways to say good-bye in German.

C. 1. Write the German equivalent for each of the following sentences relating to time.
   a. What time is it?
   b. I'm going at one o'clock.
2. Write out the following clock times in German using conversational German (Method 1).
   a. 2:15   b. 3:45   c. 6:30
3. How is official time indicated, for example in train schedules?

D. 1. What are the three words for *you* in German?
2. Which form of *you* do you use in talking to the following people?
   a. a saleswoman   c. a friend
   b. two children   d. your mother
3. Give the German equivalents of the following English pronouns.
   a. he   b. she   c. we
   d. I   e. they
4. How can you tell whether **sie** means *she* or *they*?
5. Give the German equivalents of:
   a. She plays tennis well.
   b. They play tennis well.

E. 1. What are the German equivalents of the forms of the English verb *to be*?
   a. I am   d. they are
   b. we are   e. you are (*3 forms*)
   c. she is

F.
1. What is the basic form of a German verb?
2. What is the most common ending of the basic verb form?
3. Give the German infinitives for the following verbs:
   a. to believe b. to hike   c. to work
4. Give the stems of the verbs in 3 above.
5. What do you call the form of the verb that agrees with the subject?
6. What ending does the verb take when used with the following subjects?
   a. du   d. wir   f. sie (*sg.*)
   b. ihr   e. er   g. sie (*pl.*)
   c. ich
7. Complete the following sentences with the proper form of the verb in parentheses.
   a. _____ du heute Volleyball? (spielen)
   b. Ich _____ gern Musik. (hören)
   c. Er _____ viel. (arbeiten)
   d. Gabi _____ gern. (wandern)
   e. Wir _____ gern. (schwimmen)
   f. Das Mädchen _____ Lore. (heißen)
   g. Wie _____ du? (heißen)

G.
1. In German, one form of a verb in the present tense is used to express ideas that require several different forms in English. Give the German equivalents of the following sentences.
   a. You do play well.
   b. Frank is working today.
   c. Ute does work a lot.
2. The German present tense also expresses something intended or planned for the future. Give the German equivalents of the following sentences.
   a. I'm going to the movies this evening.
   b. What will you do?

H.
1. How do you say you like to do something in German?
2. Say that the following people like to do the things named.
   a. Ute spielt Schach.
   b. Ich wandere.
   c. Wir treiben Sport.

I.
1. Where does **nicht** come in relationship to the following:
   a. predicate adjectives and nouns
   b. prepositional phrases
   c. specific time expressions
   d. most other adverbs
   e. pronouns and nouns used as objects

2. Make the following sentences negative by adding **nicht** in the proper place.
   a. Wir schwimmen gern.
   b. Frank wandert viel.
   c. Ich gehe ins Kino.
   d. Wir arbeiten morgen.
   e. Heike ist nett.
   f. Ich glaube das.

J.
1. What is the first word in an informational question?
2. Where does the verb come? The subject?
3. Name three interrogative words.
4. Ask informational questions using the words in parentheses.
   a. Jürgen spielt gut Fußball. (wer)
   b. Veronika spielt gern Volleyball. (was)
   c. Wir gehen heute abend ins Kino. (wann)

K.
1. What is the first word in a yes/no question?
2. Convert the following statements into yes/no questions.
   a. Petra spielt oft Fußball.
   b. Kurt arbeitet viel.
   c. Du spielst gut Schach.

L.
1. What words are used to form tag questions in German?
2. Give the German equivalents of the following sentences:
   a. We're playing tennis tomorrow, aren't we?
   b. Paul is tired, isn't he?
   c. You like to dance, don't you? (Use **du.**)

Kapitel 3

A. Give three types of responses to the following statement about the weather:
Morgen ist es bestimmt schön.
1. Agree.
2. Disagree.
3. Express hope or expectation.

B. Write out the names of the months in German.

C.
1. What is the gender of the names of most countries in German?
2. Name one feminine country and one plural country in German.

D. Give the feminine and masculine forms of the following nouns.
1. student
2. Swiss (citizen)
3. neighbor

E. Replace the word **heute** with **auch gestern** and rewrite each of the following sentences in the simple past.
1. Ich bin heute müde.
2. Eva ist heute krank.
3. Du bist heute faul.
4. Sie sind heute fleißig.

F. Ask when the birthdays of the following people are:
1. du
2. Frank
3. ihr
4. Ulrike und Kathrin

G. 1. In what position is the finite verb in a German statement?
2. Rewrite the following sentences, beginning with the word(s) in bold type.
   a. Das Wetter war **am Sonntag** nicht gut.
   b. Die Sonne scheint **hoffentlich** morgen.

H. 1. How does English generally signal the grammatical function of nouns in a sentence?
2. What type of signal does German use to indicate the grammatical function of nouns?
3. What case is used for the subject of a sentence and a predicate noun?
4. Which verbs are often followed by predicate nouns?
5. Write out the subjects and any predicate nouns in the following sentences.
   a. Gestern war das Wetter schön.
   b. Frank Schmidt ist Student.
   c. Das Mädchen heißt Cornelia.

I. 1. What is the definite article used with all plural nouns?
2. Give the plural of the following nouns, including the article.
   a. das Fenster
   b. der Tisch
   c. das Buch
   d. die Uhr
   e. der Stuhl
   f. die Studentin

J. 1. Give the two forms of the indefinite article in German.
2. Give the English equivalents.

3. Complete the following sentences with an indefinite article.
   a. Ist das Kind _____ Mädchen oder _____ Junge?
   b. Ist die Frau _____ Nachbarin?
   c. Ist das wirklich _____ Kugelschreiber?

K. 1. What is the negative form of **ein**?
2. What are the English equivalents of the negative form of **ein**?
3. What negative do you use when the noun is preceded by a definite article?
4. Complete the following sentences with **kein** or **nicht,** as appropriate.
   a. Das ist _____ Uhr.
   b. Das ist _____ die Parkstraße.
   c. Warum ist _____ Stuhl hier?

L. 1. Give the German equivalents of the following English possessive adjectives and nouns.
   a. your (*fam. sg.*) radio
   b. their basketball
   c. her cards
   d. our country
   e. my address
2. Give the German equivalents of the following proper names and nouns.
   a. Klaus's room
   b. Tanja's watch

M. 1. Answer the following questions in the affirmative, using a personal pronoun.
   a. Ist der Tisch neu?
   b. Ist das Kind nett?
   c. Schwimmt die Frau gut?
   d. Ist die Uhr alt?
   e. Tanzen die Jungen gern?
2. Answer the following questions in the negative, using a demonstrative pronoun.
   a. Ist Dieter faul?
   b. Ist Karin ernst?
   c. Ist der Stuhl neu?
   d. Sind die Kinder nett?

Kapitel 4

A. What German word do you use to contradict the assumptions in the following sentences?
1. Monika ißt keinen Fisch. _____ !
2. Arbeitest du denn nicht? _____ !

B. How do you say in German that you like Andrea?

C. What advice would you give to a friend who said the following:
Ich brauche etwas gegen Kopfschmerzen.

D. Give three foods/beverages a German might have at each of the following meals.
1. Frühstück   3. Abendessen
2. Mittagessen

E. 1. Which noun in a compound determines the gender?
2. Make a compound of the following nouns.
   a. der Tisch + die Lampe
   b. die Butter + das Brot

F. 1. Which forms of the verbs **essen, geben,** and **nehmen** show stem vowel change?
2. Complete the following sentences with the proper form of the verb in parentheses.
   a. Was _____ du gegen Kopfschmerzen? (nehmen)
   b. Ich _____ Aspirin. (nehmen)
   c. Zum Frühstück _____ Monika immer frische Brötchen. (essen)
   d. Wir _____ oft Eier. (essen)
   e. _____ es hier keinen Kaffee? (geben)
   f. _____ du mir zwei Mark? (geben)

G. 1. When a sentence has both time and place expressions, which comes first in English? In German?
2. Write a sentence from the following cues.
   wann / du / kommen / nach Hause / heute abend / ?

H. 1. What verb form do you use to tell someone to do something?
2. What is the position of this verb in the sentence?
3. Complete the following commands with the verb form that corresponds to the people indicated.
   a. (Detlev) _____ mir bitte die Butter. (geben)
   b. (Gabi und Stefan) _____ gleich nach Hause. (kommen)
   c. (Herr Huber) _____ den Kaffee bei Messner. (kaufen)

I. 1. Which case is used for:
   a. nouns and pronouns that are subjects?
   b. nouns and pronouns that are direct objects?

2. Complete the following sentences with the possessive adjective that corresponds to the subject pronoun.
   a. Ich brauche _____ Heft wieder.
   b. Inge fragt _____ Freund Michael.
   c. Nehmt ihr _____ Bücher?
   d. Brauchst du _____ Lampe?

3. A few masculine nouns show a change in the accusative. Give the accusative form of:
   a. der Junge
   b. der Nachbar

4. Name the prepositions that take accusative case.

5. Complete the following sentences, using the cues in parentheses.
   a. _____ ist von gestern. (der Kuchen)
   b. Warum kaufst du _____ ? (der Kuchen)
   c. Gisela und Lars kennen _____ gut. (ihre Stadt)
   d. Uwe arbeitet für _____ . (sein Professor)
   e. Habt ihr denn _____ mehr? (kein Brot)
   f. Warum kaufst du nur _____ ? (ein Stuhl)
   g. _____ hast du gern? (wer)
   h. Kennst du _____ da? (der Student)
   i. Gibt es hier _____ ? (kein Supermarkt)

6. Complete the following sentences with demonstrative pronouns.
   a. Der Kaffee ist gut, nicht?—Nein, _____ finde ich nicht gut.
   b. Ich brauche Brot.—Kauf _____ aber bei Meier!
   c. Wer ist der Herr da?—_____ kenne ich nicht.

7. Give the accusative forms of the following pronouns.
   a. Wie findest du _____ ?(er)
   b. Brauchst du _____ ? (ich)
   c. Wir kennen _____ nicht. (sie, *pl.*)
   d. Die Kinder haben _____ gern. (du)
   e. Sie brauchen _____ heute nicht. (wir)
   f. Unsere Nachbarn finden _____ lustig. (ihr)

Kapitel 5

A. 1. Give three responses to the following question to indicate you are preparing class work or studying for a test.
Was machst du heute abend?

2. Give two expressions of agreement and two expressions of regret as a response to the following request:
Willst du jetzt Kaffee trinken gehen?

B. Tell how many members of your family and relatives you have.

C. Express the following sentences in German.
1. Alex is an American.
2. He is going to be a baker.
3. Andrea is a student.

D. 1. What vowel changes do the verbs **lesen, sehen,** and **werden** have?
2. Give the irregular forms of **werden.**
3. Complete the sentences with the correct form of the verb in parentheses.
a. Sabine _____ viel. (lesen)
b. _____ du gern lustige Filme? (sehen)
c. Erik _____ besser in Mathe. (werden)

E. 1. You have learned three German equivalents for *to know.* For each of the following definitions, write the appropriate German word.
a. to know a fact
b. to be acquainted with a person, place, or thing
c. to know a language

2. Complete the following sentences with a form of **wissen, kennen,** or **können.**
a. _____ du den Studenten da?
b. Ich _____ nicht, wie er heißt.
c. Rita _____ gut Deutsch.
d. _____ du, wie alt sie ist?

F. 1. What pattern of endings do the words **dieser, jeder, welcher, mancher,** and **solcher** follow?
2. Which **der**-word is used only in the singular? What does it mean?
3. Which two **der**-words are used mostly in the plural? What do they mean?
4. Complete the following sentences with the correct form of the cued **der**-word.
a. Ist _____ Bücherregal neu? (dieser)
b. _____ Computer hier ist teuer. (jeder)

c. _____ Film willst du sehen? (welcher)
d. _____ Bücher lese ich nicht. (solcher)
e. _____ Referate waren sehr gut. (mancher)

G. 1. Which kind of verb expresses an attitude about an action rather than the action itself?
2. Give the German infinitives that express the following ideas.
a. to want to   d. to be allowed to
b. to be supposed to   e. to be able to
c. to have to   f. to like

H. 1. German modals are irregular. Which forms lack endings?
2. What other irregularity do most modals show?
3. Give the proper forms of the verbs indicated.
a. ich _____ (können)
b. er _____ (dürfen)
c. du _____ (müssen)
d. wir _____ (sollen)
e. Erika _____ (wollen)
f. Ich _____ es (mögen)

I. The modal **mögen** and its subjunctive form **möchte** have two different meanings. Give the German equivalents of the following sentences.
1. Do you like Inge?
2. Would you like to work this evening?

J. 1. Modal auxiliaries are generally used with dependent infinitives. Where does the infinitive come in such a sentence?
2. Rewrite the following sentences, using the modal in parentheses.
a. Arbeitest du heute? (müssen)
b. Ich mache es nicht. (können)
c. Petra sagt etwas. (wollen)
3. When is the infinitive often omitted?
4. Give the German equivalent of the following English sentence.
I have to go home now.

K. 1. Which of the following verbs are separable-prefix verbs?
a. fernsehen   d. spazierengehen
b. bekommen   e. verdienen
c. einkaufen
2. In what position is the separable prefix in the present tense and the imperative?

3. Write sentences using the guidelines.
   a. Gerd / mitbringen / Bier
   b. du / spazierengehen / morgen / ?
   c. ich / müssen / vorbereiten / Abendessen
   d. du / oft / fernsehen / ?
   e. ich / sollen / meine Notizen / durcharbeiten

Kapitel 6

A. Name three things you would like to do during the summer vacation.

B. 1. What are two words for *where* in German?
2. Complete the following sentences with **wo** or **wohin.**
   a. _____ wohnt Cornelia?
   b. _____ fährst du in den Ferien?

C. Name in German three forms of private transportation and three forms of public transportation.

D. 1. What vowel change do the verbs **fahren, laufen,** and **schlafen** have?
2. Complete the sentences with the correct form of the verb in parentheses.
   a. Wann _____ Paula nach Hamburg? (fahren)
   b. _____ sie bei Freunden? (schlafen)
   c. Wann _____ Frank nach Hause? (laufen)
   d. _____ du morgen in die Stadt? (fahren)

E. 1. What are the five coordinating conjunctions you have learned?
2. What word means *but* in the sense of *on the contrary*?
3. What word means *but* in the sense of *nevertheless*?
4. Do coordinating conjunctions affect word order?
5. Choose the conjunction that makes sense and use it to combine the sentences.
   a. Gabi bleibt zu Hause. Sie ist krank. (denn, oder)
   b. Holger geht nicht schwimmen. Er spielt Tennis. (aber, sondern)
   c. Er schwimmt nicht gut. Er schwimmt gern. (aber, sondern)

F. 1. Where does the verb go in a dependent clause?
2. If there are both a modal auxiliary and an infinitive, which comes last?
3. If the sentence begins with a dependent clause, does the finite verb of the independent clause come before or after the subject?
4. Combine the following sentences with the conjunction indicated.
   a. Wir können nicht fahren. (weil) Unser Auto ist kaputt.
   b. (wenn) Es regnet morgen. Wir müssen zu Hause bleiben.
5. Rewrite the following direct statements as indirect statements, using **daß.**
   a. Sabine sagt: „Die Nachbarn kaufen oft im Supermarkt ein."
   b. Erik glaubt: „Das Obst ist nicht so frisch."

G. 1. What case is used in German to signal the indirect object?
2. What is the indirect object in the following sentence?
   Gerd schenkt seiner Schwester ein Poster.
3. Give the dative form of the following nouns:
   a. die Frau   d. die Berge
   b. das Büro   e. der Student
   c. das Auto
4. Name the verbs you know that take dative.
5. Which of the following prepositions are followed by dative case?
   aus, durch, für, mit, nach, ohne, seit, von
6. Complete the following sentences with the correct form of the cued words.
   a. Der Vater erzählt _____ eine Geschichte. (die Kinder)
   b. _____ gehören diese Wasserskier? (wer)
   c. Warum glaubst du _____ nicht? (mein Bruder)
   d. Fährst du oft mit _____ ? (der Zug)
   e. Kaufst du die Uhr für _____ ? (dein Vater)
   f. Frank wohnt bei _____ . (eine Familie)
   g. Erika schenkt ihrer Mutter _____ . (ein Kugelschreiber)
   h. Willst du mit _____ Straßenbahn fahren? (dieser)
   i. Von _____ Nachbarn sprecht ihr? (welche)

H. 1. Give the accusative and dative forms of the following pronouns.
    a. ich   c. du   e. sie
    b. er   d. wir   f. Sie

    2. Complete the following sentences with the proper form of the cued pronouns.
    a. Ich möchte mit _____ sprechen. (du)
    b. Was fragst du _____ ? (ich)
    c. Glaubst du _____ ? (er)
    d. Die CDs gehören _____ . (sie, *pl.*)
    e. Soll ich eine Pflanze für _____ kaufen. (sie, *sg.*)
    f. Wann holst du _____ ab? (wir)
    g. Von _____ erzählst du? (wer)

I. Show your understanding of the word order for direct and indirect objects by completing the sentences with the cued words.
    1. Kaufst du _____ _____ ? (dieses Buch / mir)
    2. Ich gebe _____ _____ . (meinen Eltern / diese Lampe)
    3. Der Pulli? Ich schenke _____ _____ . (meinem Bruder / ihn)

Kapitel 7

A. 1. Name three articles of clothing that both men and women wear.
    2. Name three articles of women's clothing.

B. 1. The infinitive of a verb may be used as a noun. What gender is such a noun?
    2. The English equivalent of such a noun is often a gerund. What ending does an English gerund have?
    3. Give the English equivalents of the following sentences, in which one of the infinitives is used as a noun and the other as a dependent infinitive.
    a. Wandern ist gesund.
    b. Mußt du heute arbeiten?

C. 1. When is the German present perfect tense used?
    2. Why is it often called the "conversational past"?

D. 1. The present perfect tense consists of two parts. What are the two parts of the verb?
    2. What verb is used as the auxiliary for most verbs in the present perfect tense?

    3. What other verb is used as an auxiliary for some verbs in the present perfect tense?
    4. What conditions must be met to use the auxiliary **sein** with a past participle?
    5. What two verbs are exceptions to the general rule about verbs requiring **sein**?
    6. Supply the auxiliaries.
    a. Er _____ viel gearbeitet.
    b. _____ du spät aufgestanden?
    c. Wir _____ bis elf geblieben.
    d. Ilse und Paul _____ mir geholfen.
    e. _____ ihr mit dem Zug gefahren?
    f. Ich _____ gut geschlafen.

E. 1. What ending is added to the stem of a regular weak verb like **spielen** to form the past participle?
    2. How is the ending different in a verb like **arbeiten,** which has a stem ending in **-t**?
    3. How does an irregular weak verb like **bringen** form the past participle differently from regular weak verbs?
    4. Give the past participles of the following verbs.
    bringen, kosten, machen, denken, haben, kennen, regnen, wandern, wissen, tanzen

F. 1. What is the ending of the past participle of a strong verb like **sehen**?
    2. What other change is characteristic for the past participle of many strong verbs?
    3. Give the past participles of the following verbs.
    finden, geben, helfen, lesen, nehmen, schreiben, trinken, tun

G. 1. What happens to the **ge-**prefix in the past participle of a separable-prefix verb like **einkaufen**?
    2. Give the past participles of the following verbs.
    anrufen, einladen, mitbringen

H. 1. How does the past participle of an inseparable-prefix verb like **bekommen** differ from that of most other verbs?
    2. What other type of verb adds no **ge-**prefix?
    3. Give the present perfect tense of the following verb phrases.
    a. Ich bezahle das Essen.
    b. Wir erzählen es ihm.
    c. Verstehst du das?
    d. Sie bekommen es.

e. Sie studiert in Bonn.

f. Das Buch interessiert mich nicht.

I. 1. In what position is the past participle in an independent clause?

   2. Where do the past participle and the auxiliary verb come in a dependent clause?

   3. Rewrite the following sentences in the present perfect tense.

     a. Ich stehe spät auf, denn ich arbeite bis elf.

     b. Frank ißt viel, weil das Essen so gut schmeckt.

J. Rewrite the following sentences in the present perfect tense.

   1. Wen rufst du an?

   2. Bringt ihr das Essen mit?

   3. Alles sieht wirklich gut aus.

   4. Wir diskutieren viele Probleme.

   5. Die Gäste bleiben bis zehn Uhr.

   6. Inge kommt nicht.

   7. Wir verstehen das nicht.

   8. Ich schenke Gerd ein Buch, weil er mir hilft.

   9. Was bekommst du zum Geburtstag?

Kapitel 8

A. A friend asks what house chores you do. Give three possible answers.

Welche Arbeiten machst du zu Hause?

B. 1. The words **hin** and **her** can be used alone or in combination with several parts of speech (for example **hierher, hinfahren**) to show direction. Which word indicates direction towards the speaker? Which indicates direction away from the speaker?

   2. What position do **hin** and **her** occupy in a sentence when they stand alone?

   3. Complete the following sentences with **hin, her, wo, woher,** or **wohin.**

     a. _____ wohnen Sie?

     b. _____ kommen Sie? Aus Österreich?

     c. _____ fahren Sie in den Ferien?

     d. Meine Tante wohnt in Hamburg. Ich fahre jedes Jahr _____ .

     e. Kommen Sie mal _____ .

C. 1. Indicate which of the following prepositions are always followed by

     a. the accusative

     b. the dative

     c. either dative or accusative

     an, auf, aus, bei, durch, für, gegen, in, nach, neben, ohne, seit, unter, über, von, vor, zu, zwischen

   2. List two contractions for each of the following prepositions:

     a. an

     b. in

D. Construct sentences from the guidelines.

   1. ich / fahren / in / Stadt

   2. wir / gehen / auf / Markt

   3. Sabine / studieren / an / Universität Hamburg

   4. du / denken / an / dein / Freund / ?

   5. warum / Tisch / stehen / zwischen / Stühle / ?

   6. Alex / arbeiten / in / ein / Buchhandlung

E. English uses *to put* and *to be* as all-purpose verbs to talk about position. German uses several different verbs. Complete the following sentences with an appropriate verb from the list.

legen, liegen, stellen, stehen, setzen, sitzen, hängen, stecken

   1. Lena _____ die Lampe auf den Tisch.

   2. Die Lampe _____ auf dem Tisch.

   3. Alex _____ die Uhr an die Wand.

   4. Lena _____ das Kind auf den Stuhl.

   5. Das Kind _____ auf dem Stuhl.

   6. Alex _____ das Heft auf den Tisch.

   7. Das Heft _____ auf dem Tisch.

   8. Er _____ das Buch in die Büchertasche.

F. 1. What case must be used for time expressions that indicate a definite time or period of time?

   2. What case is used with time expressions beginning with **an, in,** or **vor**?

   3. Complete the following sentences with the cued words.

     a. Wir bleiben _____ . (ein / Tag)

     b. Bernd hat vor _____ den Führerschein gemacht. (ein / Jahr)

     c. Susi arbeitet _____ . (jeder / Abend)

     d. Er kommt in _____ wieder. (eine / Woche)

G. 1. What construction is used in a German statement in place of a preposition + a pronoun that refers to things or ideas?

   2. In German questions, what construction is usually used to replace **was** as the object of a preposition?

3. When does **da-** expand to **dar-** and **wo-** expand to **wor-**?
4. Complete the following sentences using a **da**-compound or a preposition and pronoun, as appropriate.
   a. Spricht Anna oft von ihrer Reise?—Ja, sie spricht oft _____ .
   b. Machst du das für deine Freundin?—Ja, ich mache das _____ .
5. Complete the sentences using a **wo**-compound or a preposition and interrogative pronoun, as appropriate.
   a. _____ spielst du morgen Tennis?—Ich spiele mit Inge.
   b. _____ habt ihr geredet?—Wir haben über den Film geredet.

H. 1. What word do indirect questions begin with?
2. What conjunction do indirect yes/no questions begin with?
3. Rewrite the following direct questions as indirect questions:
   a. Paul fragt Birgit: „Fährst du morgen zur Uni?"
   b. Birgit fragt Paul, wann er zu Mittag ißt.

Kapitel 9

A. Name three professions that appeal to you and three that do not.

B. Give two responses to your friend's question: **Warum willst du deine Stelle wechseln?**

C. Form nouns by adding **-heit** or **-keit** to the following adjectives.
1. krank
2. freundlich
3. frei

D. Add at least two words related to:
1. studieren
2. Sonne
3. wandern

E. Give the German words for:
1. lawyer (male)
2. computer specialist (female)
3. architect (female)
4. dentist (male)

F. 1. In the genitive case, what ending is added to masculine (**der-**) and neuter (**das-**) nouns of the following kinds:
   a. one-syllable
   b. two or more syllables
   c. masculine N-nouns
2. Give the genitive of the following nouns.
   a. das Bild   d. ein Haus
   b. dieser Laden   e. ihr Bruder
   c. der Junge
3. What is the genitive form of **wer**?
4. Give the German equivalent of:
   Whose book bag is that?

G. 1. Do feminine (**die-**) nouns and plural nouns add a genitive ending?
2. Give the genitive form of the following:
   a. die Frau   c. diese Kinder
   b. eine Ausländerin d. meine Eltern

H. In German, does the genitive precede or follow the noun it modifies?

I. Give the English equivalents of the following phrases.
1. eines Tages   2. eines Abends

J. Name four prepositions that are followed by the genitive.

K. Complete the following sentences, using the cued words.
1. Wegen _____ kommt er nicht. (das Wetter)
2. Den Studenten gefällt die Vorlesung _____ . (der Professor)
3. Kennst du die Adresse _____ ? (mein Freund Michael)
4. Wir haben während _____ geschlafen. (die Reise)
5. Wie ist die Telefonnummer _____ ? (deine Freundin)
6. Kennst du die Namen _____ ? (die Geschäfte)

L. Complete the following sentences, using the cued words.
1. Das ist ein _____ Kind. (nett)
2. Thomas ist ein _____ Student. (gut)
3. Anni ist aber auch _____ . (gut)
4. Mark hat ein sehr _____ Fahrrad gekauft. (teuer)
5. Wegen des _____ Wetters bleiben wir zu Hause. (kalt)

6. Ich esse gern Brot mit _____ Butter. (frisch)
7. Ich habe _____ Durst. (groß)
8. _____ Bier schmeckt mir nicht. (warm)
9. Die Sonne ist heute richtig _____ . (heiß)
10. Sophie, ist das dein _____ Pulli? (neu)
11. Kennen Sie die Geschichte dieser _____ Häuser? (alt)
12. Das ist keine _____ Idee. (schlecht)

M. 1. How are the ordinal numbers from 2–19 formed in German?
2. Give the German words for:
   a. first   c. fifth
   b. third   d. sixteenth
3. What is added to numbers after 19 to form the ordinals?
4. Give the German words for:
   a. thirty-first   b. hundredth
5. Ordinals take adjective endings. Complete the following sentences with the cued ordinals.
   a. Am _____ November habe ich Geburtstag. (7.)
   b. Wir müssen leider ein _____ Auto kaufen. (2.)

N. 1. Ask the date in German.
2. Say it is June first.
3. Write the date, July 6, 1996, as it would appear in a letter heading.

Kapitel 10

A. Give two expressions of regret when your friend says:
Ich kann nicht mit zum Fest. Ich fühle mich nicht wohl.

B. Name three acts of hygiene that are part of your morning ritual.

C. Complete the German expressions for:
1. *something good*   etwas _____
2. *nothing special*   nichts _____
3. *a good acquaintance*   ein guter _____
4. *a German (female)*   eine _____

D. For each subject pronoun below, give the accusative and dative reflexive pronoun.
1. ich   3. sie (*sg. and pl.*)   5. er
2. du   4. wir

E. Some German verbs are called reflexive verbs because reflexive pronouns are regularly used with these verbs. Construct sentences using the following guidelines.
1. du / sich fühlen / heute / besser/ ?
2. Cornelia / sich erkälten / gestern

F. When referring to parts of the body, German usage differs from English in some constructions. Complete the following German sentences.
1. Ich habe mir _____ Hände gewaschen.
2. Tanja putzt sich _____ Zähne.

G. 1. What word precedes the dependent infinitive with most verbs in German?
2. When are dependent infinitives *not* preceded by that word?
3. Punctuate the following sentence.
   Hast du Zeit mir zu helfen?
4. What is the German construction equivalent to the English (*in order*) *to* + infinitive?
5. Complete the following sentences with the cued words.
   a. Es macht Spaß, _____ . (im Wald / wandern)
   b. Ich möchte mir _____ . (eine neue CD / kaufen)
   c. Vergiß nicht, _____ . (Blumen / mitbringen)
   d. Ich beginne _____ . (deine Ideen / verstehen)
   e. Ich bleibe heute zu Hause _____ . (um ... zu / machen / meine Arbeit)

H. 1. How are comparative adjectives and adverbs formed in German?
2. How do some one-syllable adjectives and adverbs change the stem vowel in the comparative?
3. Complete the following sentences using the comparative form of the cued adjective.
   a. Es ist heute _____ als gestern. (kalt)
   b. Mein neues Auto war _____ als mein altes. (teuer)
   c. Helmut wohnt jetzt in einem _____ Zimmer. (groß, schön)

I. 1. How are superlative adjectives and adverbs formed in German?
2. What is the ending for the superlative if the base form ends in **-d** (**wild**), **-t** (**leicht**), or a sibilant (**heiß**)?
3. How do some one-syllable adjectives and adverbs change the vowel in the superlative?

4. What form does an adverb or a predicate adjective have in the superlative?
5. Complete the following sentences using the superlative form of the cued adjective or adverb.
   a. Dieser Kassettenrecorder ist _____ . (teuer)
   b. Gabi arbeitet _____ . (schwer)
   c. Das ist mein _____ Pulli. (schön)
   d. Gestern war der _____ Tag dieses Jahres. (kalt)

J. Give the comparative and superlative forms of:
   1. gern   2. gut   3. viel

Kapitel 11

A. Give two logical responses to the question: **Wo warst du gestern abend?**

B. Give one example of
   1. giving an invitation to attend an event
   2. responding to an invitation

C. 1. When is the simple past tense used? What is it often called?
   2. When is the present perfect tense used? What is it often called?
   3. Which verbs occur more frequently in the simple past than in present perfect tense, even in conversation?

D. 1. What tense marker is added to modals in the simple past tense?
   2. What happens to modals with an umlaut in the simple past?
   3. Give the simple past tense forms of the following:
      a. ich darf   c. sie muß
      b. du kannst   d. wir mögen

E. 1. What is the tense marker for weak verbs in the simple past tense?
   2. What is the past tense marker for **regnen, öffnen,** and verbs with stems ending in **-d** or **-t**?
   3. Which forms add no endings in the simple past?
   4. Change each of the following present-tense forms to simple past.
      a. ich spiele   c. es regnet
      b. Dieter arbeitet   d. wir sagen

F. Irregular weak verbs have a vowel change in the simple past tense, and several of these verbs have consonant changes. Give the simple past form of the following sentences.
   1. Ich bringe den Wein.
   2. Sie denkt an Gerd.
   3. Sie wissen es schon.

G. 1. How do strong verbs show the simple past tense?
   2. Which forms add no endings?
   3. Give the simple past tense of the following verbs.
      a. er spricht   f. ich bin
      b. sie sieht   g. sie wird
      c. ich helfe   h. sie gehen
      d. wir bleiben   i. ich laufe
      e. er fährt   j. er trägt

H. 1. Where does the prefix of separable-prefix verbs go in the simple past tense?
   2. Construct sentences in the simple past, using the guidelines.
      a. das Konzert / anfangen / um sieben Uhr
      b. Kerstin / mitbringen / Blumen
      c. ich / aufstehen / immer / früh
      d. wir / einkaufen / in / Stadt

I. 1. When is the past perfect tense used?
   2. How is it formed?
   3. Give the English equivalents of the following sentences.
      a. Ich habe gut geschlafen, weil ich 20 Kilometer gelaufen war.
      b. Nachdem es den ganzen Tag geregnet hatte, schien die Sonne am Abend.

J. Restate the following sentences in the simple past and present perfect tenses.
   1. Stefan schreibt den Brief.
   2. Anna geht nach Hause.

K. **Als, wenn,** and **wann** are equivalent to English *when.*
   1. Which must be used for *when* to introduce direct or indirect questions?
   2. Which must be used for *when* in the sense of *whenever* (that is, for repeated events) in past time?
   3. Which must be used for *when* in clauses with events in the present or future?
   4. Which must be used for *when* in clauses concerned with a single past event?

5. Complete the following sentences with **als,** **wenn,** or **wann,** as appropriate.
   a. Wir haben viel Spaß, _____ Schmidts uns besuchen.
   b. Sie kamen mit, _____ wir gestern ins Café gingen.
   c. Immer, _____ wir schwimmen wollten, regnete es.
   d. Ich weiß nicht, _____ wir zurückgekommen sind.

Kapitel 12

A. You have an appointment. Give a possible response from the secretary to your question: **Ist Frau/Herr Neumann zu sprechen?**

B. Express two wishes using **wenn** and the subjunctive.

C. Form adjectives or adverbs from the following nouns by adding **-lich.** Give the English equivalents.
   1. Frage   2. Tag

D. Give two favorable answers and a negative answer to your friend's question. Use **würde-**constructions and/or the subjunctive of the main verb.
   Hättest du Lust, nach Deutschland zu fliegen?

E. 1. Give three uses of the **würde-**construction and the subjunctive of the main verb.
   2. Say that Trudi would also like to do the following. Use **würde.**
      Christoph faulenzt viel.
   3. Say that you wish the following situation were different. Use **würde.**
      Die Sonne scheint nicht.
      Wenn die Sonne nur ...
   4. Restate as a request, using **würde.**
      Bleib noch eine Stunde!

F. 1. What is the subjunctive form of the verb **sein?**
   2. What is the subjunctive form of the verb **haben?**
   3. Give the present-time subjunctive of the following verb forms.
      a. ich bin   c. wir sind
      b. du hast   d. sie hat

G. 1. How is the present-time subjunctive of modals formed?
   2. Give the subjunctive of the following verb forms.
      a. ich muß   b. du kannst

H. 1. How is the present-time subjunctive of strong verbs formed?
   2. Give the subjunctive of the following verb forms.
      a. es gibt   c. sie kommen
      b. sie tut es   d. du bleibst

I. 1. How is the present-time subjunctive of weak verbs formed?
   2. Give the subjunctive of the following verb forms.
      a. sie lernt   b. du arbeitest

J. 1. How is the present-time subjunctive of irregular weak verbs formed?
   2. Give the subjunctive of the following verb forms.
      a. sie bringt   c. wir wissen
      b. ich denke

K. 1. How is the past-time subjunctive formed?
   2. Give the past-time subjunctive of the following verb forms.
      a. wir sind   c. ich fahre mit
      b. er sieht

L. 1. When a modal is used in the past-time subjunctive with another verb, what form does the modal have? What is this construction called?
   2. Give the English equivalent.
      Ich hätte das allein machen können.

M. 1. What are the two clauses in a conditional sentence called?
   2. What word begins the condition clause?
   3. In what kind of conditional sentence is the indicative used?
   4. In what kind of conditional sentence are the **würde-**construction and the subjunctive of the main verb used?
   5. Restate as conditions contrary to fact, both in the present time and in the past time.
      a. Christine schläft länger, wenn sie Zeit hat.
      b. Wenn ich Geld habe, gehe ich ins Konzert.

N. Construct sentences using the guidelines.
   1. ich / tun / das / nicht (*present-time subj.*)

2. du / glauben / mir / nicht (*use* **würde**)
3. wir / können / fahren / morgen (*present-time subj.*)
4. Wenn sie Geld hätte, sie / kaufen / ein neues Auto (*use* **würde**)
5. Ich hätte das getan, wenn / ich / wissen / das (*past-time subj.*)
6. Ich wollte, du / können / bleiben / länger (*present-time subj.*)

Kapitel 13

A. 1. Which tense is generally used in German to express future time?
2. Construct a sentence using the guidelines: ich / anrufen / dich / heute abend (*present tense*)

B. 1. When is the future tense used in German?
2. How is the future tense formed in German?
3. In an independent clause where the future is used, what position is the infinitive in?
4. In a dependent clause where the future is used, what verb form is in the final position?
5. Restate in the future tense.
   a. Sandra hilft uns.
   b. Machst du das wirklich?
   c. Michael sagt, daß er einen neuen Job sucht. (*Do not change* **Michael sagt.**)

C. Express the idea of *assumption* or *probability* in the following sentences.
1. My parents are probably at home.
2. That's probably wrong.

D. Show your understanding of the various meanings of **lassen** by giving the English equivalents of the following sentences.
1. Laß mich heute abwaschen.
2. Wo hast du wieder deine Handschuhe gelassen?
3. Ich muß leider mein Kassettendeck reparieren lassen.
4. Laßt uns gehen.

E. 1. What form of **lassen** is used in the present perfect and past perfect tenses when a dependent infinitive is also used?
2. Give the English equivalents of the following sentences.
   a. Warum hast du Kurt dein Auto fahren lassen?

b. Ich habe meinen Führerschein zu Hause gelassen.

F. 1. What function does a relative pronoun serve?
2. Where does the finite verb come in a relative clause?

G. 1. With what forms are most of the relative pronoun forms identical?
2. Dative plural and genitive forms are exceptions. The genitive forms are **dessen** and **deren.** What is the relative pronoun in dative plural?

H. 1. How do you decide the gender and number of the relative pronoun you use?
2. How do you decide what case of a relative pronoun to use?
3. What case does a relative pronoun have when it follows a preposition?

I. Complete the following sentences with a relative pronoun.
1. Ist das der Mann, _____ soviel arbeitet?
2. Wie heißt die Frau, von _____ du gerade erzählt hast?
3. Wo ist das Restaurant, in _____ wir morgen essen?
4. Wie gefällt dir der Pulli, _____ du zum Geburtstag bekommen hast?
5. Die Freunde, mit _____ wir in den Ferien waren, sind wirklich nette Leute.
6. Ist das der Mann, _____ das rote Auto gehört?
7. Frank hat einen CD-Spieler gekauft, _____ nicht zu teuer war.
8. Mit dem wenigen Geld, _____ ich diese Woche verdient habe, kann ich nicht viel anfangen.

Kapitel 14

A. List three things we can do to help the environment.

B. 1. What is the role of the subject of a sentence in active voice?
2. What is the role of the subject in passive voice?

C. 1. How is passive voice formed in German?

2. In the perfect tenses of the passive voice what form of **werden** is used in place of **geworden**?
3. Complete the following sentence.
   Die Arbeit ist gemacht _____ .
4. Construct sentences using the guidelines, and then give the English equivalents.
   a. Müll / verwerten (*passive, present*)
   b. Geld / investieren / gerade (*passive, simple past*)
   c. Zeitungen recyceln (*passive, present perfect*)
   d. Fabrik / modernisieren (*passive, past perfect*)

D. 1. In English the agent in the passive voice is the object of the preposition *by: The work was done by our neighbors.* How is the agent expressed in German?
2. How is "means" expressed in passive in German?
3. Complete the following sentences.
   a. Das Haus wurde _____ den starken Wind zerstört.
   b. Die Arbeit wurde _____ unseren Nachbarn gemacht.

E. 1. Modals may be used with a passive infinitive. How is the passive infinitive formed?

2. Give the English equivalents of the following sentences.
   a. Wann muß die Arbeit gemacht werden?
   b. Die Probleme können nicht gelöst werden.

F. 1. What are three uses of **werden**?
2. Identify the use of **werden** and give the English equivalents for the following sentences.
   a. Eine Reise nach Dresden wurde geplant.
   b. Es wird endlich wärmer.
   c. Er wird an uns schreiben.

G. 1. Give three alternatives to the passive voice.
2. Restate the following sentences, using the alternative to the passive in parentheses.
   a. Das darf nicht vergessen werden. (man)
   b. Wie kann man das erklären? (sein ... zu)
   c. Mit der Chefin kann man gut reden. (sich lassen)
   d. Da kann man nichts machen. (sein ... zu)
   e. Die Umwelt muß geschützt werden. (man)
   f. Eine Lösung kann nicht so leicht gefunden werden. (sich lassen)
   g. Man kann das Auto leicht reparieren. (sich lassen)

Answer Key to Self-Tests

Kapitel 1

A. 1. Wie heißt du [heißen Sie]?
2. Wie alt bist du [sind Sie]?
3. Wie ist deine [Ihre] Adresse?
4. Wie ist deine [Ihre] Telefonnummer?

B. 1. danke   2. bitte

C. 1. Montag, Dienstag, Mittwoch, Donnerstag, Freitag, Samstag [Sonnabend], Sonntag
2. Welcher Tag ist heute?
3. Heute ist Donnerstag.

D. 1. *Answers may vary.*
2. Welche Farbe hat die Wand?

E. 1. By the article and the pronoun that refer to the noun.
2. a. *masculine,* der Bleistift
   b. *feminine,* die Tür
   c. *neuter,* das Bett
   d. *feminine,* die Frau
   e. *masculine,* der Mann
3. a. der Kugelschreiber
   b. das Zimmer
   c. die Lampe
   d. der Tisch
   e. die Uhr
   f. das Kind

F. 1. Es   3. Er   5. Er
2. Sie   4. Es   6. Sie

Kapitel 2

A. 1. a. Guten Morgen!
   b. Guten Tag!
   c. Guten Abend!
2. *Answers will vary. Possibilities are:*
Positive: Gut, danke. / Danke, ganz gut.
Negative: Nicht so gut. / Schlecht. / Ich bin krank.

B. 1. a. fleißig   d. schlecht
   b. unfreundlich   e. groß
   c. lustig
2. Auf Wiedersehen; Tschüs

C. 1. a. Wieviel Uhr [Wie spät] ist es?
   b. Ich gehe um ein Uhr [um eins].
2. a. Viertel nach zwei
   b. Viertel vor vier
   c. halb sieben
3. Official time uses a 24-hour clock.

D. 1. du, ihr, Sie
2. a. Sie   c. du
   b. ihr   d. du
3. a. er   c. wir   e. sie
   b. sie   d. ich
4. By the verb: **sie** + singular verb = *she;* **sie** + plural verb = *they*
5. a. Sie spielt gut Tennis.
   b. Sie spielen gut Tennis.

E. 1. a. ich bin   d. sie sind
   b. wir sind   e. du bist; ihr seid; Sie sind
   c. sie ist

F. 1. the infinitive
2. -en
3. a. glauben   b. wandern   c. arbeiten
4. a. glaub-   b. wander-   c. arbeit-
5. the finite verb
6. a. -st   d. -en   f. -t
   b. -t   e. -t   g. -en
   c. -e
7. a. Spielst   e. schwimmen
   b. höre   f. heißt
   c. arbeitet   g. heißt
   d. wandert

G. 1. a. Du spielst gut.
   b. Frank arbeitet heute.
   c. Ute arbeitet viel.
2. a. Ich gehe heute abend ins Kino.
   b. Was machst du? [macht ihr? machen Sie?]

H. 1. Use **gern** + verb.
2. a. Ute spielt gern Schach.
   b. Ich wandere gern.
   c. Wir treiben gern Sport.

I. 1. a. before predicate adjectives and nouns
   b. before prepositional phrases
   c. after specific time expressions
   d. before most other adverbs
   e. after pronouns and nouns used as objects

2. a. Wir schwimmen nicht gern.
   b. Frank wandert nicht viel.
   c. Ich gehe nicht ins Kino.
   d. Wir arbeiten morgen nicht.
   e. Heike ist nicht nett.
   f. Ich glaube das nicht.

J. 1. the interrogative expression
   2. The verb comes second, after the interrogative. The subject comes after the verb.
   3. wann, was, wer, wie, wieviel, welch-, was für ein
   4. a. Wer spielt gut Fußball?
      b. Was spielt Veronika gern?
      c. Wann gehen wir ins Kino?

K. 1. the verb
   2. a. Spielt Petra oft Fußball?
      b. Arbeitet Kurt viel?
      c. Spielst du gut Schach?

L. 1. nicht, nicht wahr
   2. a. Wir spielen morgen Tennis, nicht (wahr)?
      b. Paul ist müde, nicht (wahr)?
      c. Du tanzt gern, nicht (wahr)?

Kapitel 3

A. *Answers will vary. Possible ones are:*
   1. Ja, morgen ist es bestimmt schön.
   2. Ich glaube nicht.
   3. Hoffentlich. / Ja, vielleicht.

B. Januar, Februar, März, April, Mai, Juni, Juli, August, September, Oktober, November, Dezember

C. 1. neuter (das)
   2. die Schweiz, die Tschechische Republik, die USA, die Niederlande

D. 1. die Studentin; der Student
   2. die Schweizerin; der Schweizer
   3. die Nachbarin; der Nachbar

E. 1. Ich war auch gestern müde.
   2. Eva war auch gestern krank.
   3. Du warst auch gestern faul.
   4. Sie waren auch gestern fleißig.

F. 1. Wann hast du Geburtstag?
   2. Wann hat Frank Geburtstag?
   3. Wann habt ihr Geburtstag?
   4. Wann haben Ulrike und Kathrin Geburtstag?

G. 1. second position
   2. a. Am Sonntag war das Wetter nicht gut.
      b. Hoffentlich scheint die Sonne morgen.

H. 1. by word order
   2. case
   3. the nominative case
   4. sein; heißen
   5. a. subject = das Wetter
      b. subject = Frank Schmidt; pred. noun = Student
      c. subject = das Mädchen; pred. noun = Cornelia

I. 1. die
   2. a. die Fenster
      b. die Tische
      c. die Bücher
      d. die Uhren
      e. die Stühle
      f. die Studentinnen

J. 1. ein; eine
   2. a, an
   3. a. ein Mädchen; ein Junge
      b. eine Nachbarin
      c. ein Kugelschreiber

K. 1. kein
   2. not a; not any; no
   3. nicht
   4. a. keine   b. nicht   c. kein

L. 1. a. dein Radio
      b. ihr Basketball
      c. ihre Karten
      d. unser Land
      e. meine Adresse
   2. a. Klaus' Zimmer
      b. Tanjas Uhr

M. 1. a. Ja, er ist neu.
      b. Ja, es ist nett.
      c. Ja, sie schwimmt gut.
      d. Ja, sie ist alt.
      e. Ja, sie tanzen gern.
   2. a. Nein, der ist nicht faul.
      b. Nein, die ist nicht ernst.
      c. Nein, der ist nicht neu.
      d. Nein, die sind nicht nett.

Kapitel 4

A. 1. Doch!   2. Doch!

B. Ich habe Andrea gern.

C. *Answers will vary:* Nimmst du Aspirin? Das habe ich. / Nimm doch Aspirin! / Geh doch in die Apotheke!

D. *Answers may vary.*
1. Frühstück: Brötchen, Butter, Eier, Kaffee, Tee
2. Mittagessen: Fisch, Gemüse, Fleisch, Kartoffeln, Obst
3. Abendessen: Käse, Brot, Wurst, Bier, Mineralwasser, Tee

E. 1. the last noun
2. a. die Tischlampe   b. das Butterbrot

F. 1. **du** and **er/es/sie**-forms
2. a. nimmst   c. ißt   e. Gibt
     b. nehme   d. essen   f. Gibst

G. 1. Time follows place in English. Time precedes place in German.
2. Wann kommst du heute abend nach Hause?

H. 1. the imperative
2. first position
3. a. Gib   b. Kommt   c. Kaufen Sie

I. 1. a. nominative case   b. accusative case
2. a. mein   c. eure
     b. ihren   d. deine
3. a. den Jungen   b. den Nachbarn
4. durch, für, gegen, ohne, um
5. a. Der Kuchen   f. einen Stuhl
     b. den Kuchen   g. Wen
     c. ihre Stadt   h. den Studenten
     d. seinen Professor   i. keinen Supermarkt
     e. kein Brot
6. a. den   b. das   c. Den
7. a. ihn   c. sie   e. uns
     b. mich   d. dich   f. euch

Kapitel 5

A. *Answers will vary. Possible ones are:*
1. Ich bereite mein Referat vor. / Ich schreibe meine Seminararbeit. / Ich mache Deutsch. /

Ich lese einen Artikel über ... / Ich arbeite für die Klausur.
2. Agreement: Ja, gern. / Klar. / Natürlich. Regret: Ich kann leider nicht. / Es tut mir leid. / Ich habe kein Geld. / Ich muß lesen.

B. *Answers will vary.* Ich habe einen Bruder, eine Schwester, vier Tanten, usw.

C. 1. Alex ist Amerikaner.
2. Er wird Bäcker.
3. Andrea ist Studentin.

D. 1. **lesen** and **sehen** change **e** to **ie**; **werden** changes **e** to **i**
2. du wirst, er/es/sie wird
3. a. liest   b. Siehst   c. wird

E. 1. a. wissen   b. kennen   c. können
2. a. Kennst   c. kann
     b. weiß   d. Weißt

F. 1. the same as the definite articles
2. **jeder**; it means *each, every*
3. **manche, solche; manche** means *some*, **solche** means *such*
4. a. dieses Bücherregal   d. Solche Bücher
     b. Jeder Computer   e. Manche Referate
     c. Welchen Film

G. 1. modal auxiliary
2. a. wollen   d. dürfen
     b. sollen   e. können
     c. müssen   f. mögen

H. 1. **ich** and **er/es/sie**-forms
2. a stem-vowel change
3. a. ich kann   d. wir sollen
     b. er darf   e. Erika will
     c. du mußt   f. Ich mag es

I. 1. Magst du [Mögen Sie] Inge?
2. Möchtest du [Möchten Sie] heute abend arbeiten?

J. 1. in last position
2. a. Mußt du heute arbeiten?
     b. Ich kann es nicht machen.
     c. Petra will etwas sagen.
3. If a verb of motion or the idea of *to do* is clear from the context.
4. Ich muß jetzt nach Hause.

K. 1. The separable-prefix verbs are **fernsehen, einkaufen, spazierengehen.**
2. in last position
3. a. Gerd bringt Bier mit.
   b. Gehst du morgen spazieren?
   c. Ich muß das Abendessen vorbereiten.
   d. Siehst du oft fern?
   e. Ich soll meine Notizen durcharbeiten.

Kapitel 6

A. *Answers will vary:* Ich möchte wandern, viel schwimmen, Tennis spielen, schlafen, usw.

B. 1. wo; wohin
2. a. wo   b. Wohin

C. Private: das Auto/der Wagen, das Fahrrad/das Rad, das Flugzeug, das Motorrad
Public: der Bus, das Flugzeug, das Schiff, die Straßenbahn, die U-Bahn, der Zug

D. 1. **a** to **ä** for **du** and **er/es/sie**-forms
2. a. fährt   c. läuft
   b. Schläft   d. fährst

E. 1. aber, denn, oder, sondern, und
2. sondern
3. aber
4. no
5. a. Gabi bleibt zu Hause, denn sie ist krank.
   b. Holger geht nicht schwimmen, sondern er spielt Tennis.
   c. Er schwimmt nicht gut, aber er schwimmt gern.

F. 1. in last position
2. modal auxiliary comes last
3. The finite verb comes before the subject.
4. a. Wir können nicht fahren, weil unser Auto kaputt ist.
   b. Wenn es morgen regnet, müssen wir zu Hause bleiben.
5. a. Sabine sagt, daß die Nachbarn oft im Supermarkt einkaufen.
   b. Erik glaubt, daß das Obst nicht so frisch ist.

G. 1. dative
2. seiner Schwester

3. a. der Frau   d. den Bergen
   b. dem Büro   e. dem Studenten
   c. dem Auto
4. gehören, glauben
5. aus, mit, nach, seit, von
6. a. den Kindern   f. einer Familie
   b. Wem   g. einen Kugelschreiber
   c. meinem Bruder   h. dieser Straßenbahn
   d. dem Zug   i. welchen
   e. deinen Vater

H. 1.   *acc.*   *dat.*
   a. mich   mir
   b. ihn   ihm
   c. dich   dir
   d. uns   uns
   e. sie   ihr
   f. Sie   Ihnen
2. a. dir   d. ihnen   f. uns
   b. mich   e. sie   g. wem
   c. ihm

I. 1. mir dieses Buch
2. meinen Eltern diese Lampe
3. ihn meinem Bruder

Kapitel 7

A. 1. der Handschuh, der Hut, der Pulli, der Stiefel, der Regenmantel, der Schuh, der Sportschuh, das Hemd, das T-Shirt, die Hose, die Jacke, die Jeans, die Shorts, die Socke, die Mütze
2. der Rock, das Kleid, die Bluse, die Strumpfhose

B. 1. neuter   2. -ing
3. a. Hiking is healthy.
   b. Do you have to work today?

C. 1. To refer to past actions or states.
2. It is used especially in conversation.

D. 1. an auxiliary and the past participle of the verb
2. haben
3. sein
4. The verb must (1) be intransitive and (2) indicate change of condition or motion to or from a place.
5. bleiben; sein
6. a. hat   c. sind   e. Seid
   b. Bist   d. haben   f. habe

E. 1. -t
    2. adds -et instead of -t
    3. There is a stem vowel change and sometimes a consonant change: **gebracht**
    4. gebracht, gekostet, gemacht, gedacht, gehabt, gekannt, geregnet, gewandert, gewußt, getanzt

F. 1. -en
    2. Many past participles have a stem vowel change; some also have consonant changes.
    3. gefunden, gegeben, geholfen, gelesen, genommen, geschrieben, getrunken, getan

G. 1. The prefix **ge-** comes between the prefix and the stem of the past participle: **eingekauft.**
    2. angerufen, eingeladen, mitgebracht

H. 1. It adds no **ge-**prefix.
    2. verbs ending in **-ieren**
    3. a. Ich habe das Essen bezahlt.
       b. Wir haben es ihm erzählt.
       c. Hast du das verstanden?
       d. Sie haben es bekommen.
       e. Sie hat in Bonn studiert.
       f. Das Buch hat mich nicht interessiert.

I. 1. in final position
    2. The auxiliary follows the past participle and is in final position.
    3. a. Ich bin spät aufgestanden, denn ich habe bis elf gearbeitet.
       b. Frank hat viel gegessen, weil das Essen so gut geschmeckt hat.

J. 1. Wen hast du angerufen?
    2. Habt ihr das Essen mitgebracht?
    3. Alles hat wirklich gut ausgesehen.
    4. Wir haben viele Probleme diskutiert.
    5. Die Gäste sind bis zehn Uhr geblieben.
    6. Inge ist nicht gekommen.
    7. Wir haben das nicht verstanden.
    8. Ich habe Gerd ein Buch geschenkt, weil er mir geholfen hat.
    9. Was hast du zum Geburtstag bekommen?

Kapitel 8

A. *Answers will vary. Possible ones are:* Ich mache die Wohnung sauber. / Ich wische Staub. / Ich wasche die Wäsche. / Ich staubsauge. / Ich putze das Bad.

B. 1. **Her** indicates direction towards the speaker; **hin** indicates direction away from the speaker.
    2. last position
    3. a. Wo   c. Wohin   e. her
       b. Woher   d. hin

C. 1. accusative: durch, für, gegen, ohne
       b. dative: aus, bei, nach, seit, von, zu
       c. two-way prepositions: an, auf, in, neben, über, unter, vor, zwischen
    2. a. ans, am   b. ins, im

D. 1. Ich fahre in die Stadt.
    2. Wir gehen auf den Markt.
    3. Sabine studiert an der Universität Hamburg.
    4. Denkst du an deinen Freund?
    5. Warum steht der Tisch zwischen den Stühlen?
    6. Alex arbeitet in einer Buchhandlung.

E. 1. stellt   5. sitzt
    2. steht   6. legt
    3. hängt   7. liegt
    4. setzt   8. steckt

F. 1. accusative
    2. dative
    3. a. einen Tag   c. jeden Abend
       b. einem Jahr   d. einer Woche

G. 1. **da**-compound   2. **wo**-compound
    3. When the preposition begins with a vowel.
    4. a. davon   b. für sie
    5. a. Mit wem   b. Worüber

H. 1. with the question word
    2. with **ob**
    3. a. Paul fragt Birgit, ob sie morgen zur Uni fährt.
       b. Birgit fragt Paul, wann er zu Mittag ißt.

Kapitel 9

A. *Answers will vary.*

B. *Answers will vary. Possible ones are:* Ich möchte [will] eine Stelle mit mehr [viel] Verantwortung. / Ich finde die Arbeit nicht mehr interessant. Ich möchte mehr verdienen. / Ich möchte [will] bei einer kleinen [großen] Firma arbeiten.

C. 1. die Krankheit   3. die Freiheit
    2. die Freundlichkeit

D. *Answers will vary. Possible answers are:*
1. Studium, Student, Studentin, Studentenheim
2. sonnig, die Sonnenbrille, Sonntag, Sonnabend
3. Wanderer, Wanderin, Wanderung

E. 1. der Rechtsanwalt   3. die Architektin
     2. die Informatikerin   4. der Zahnarzt

F. 1. a. -es   b. -s   c. -(e)n
     2. a. des Bildes   d. eines Hauses
        b. dieses Ladens   e. ihres Bruders
        c. des Jungen
     3. wessen
     4. Wessen Büchertasche ist das?

G. 1. no
     2. a. der Frau   c. dieser Kinder
        b. einer Ausländerin   d. meiner Eltern

H. The genitive follows the noun it modifies.

I. 1. one day; some day   2. one evening

J. (an)statt, trotz, während, wegen

K. 1. des Wetters   4. der Reise
     2. des Professors   5. deiner Freundin
     3. meines Freundes   6. der Geschäfte
        Michael

L. 1. nettes   5. kalten   9. heiß
     2. guter   6. frischer   10. neue
     3. gut   7. großen   11. alten
     4. teures   8. Warmes   12. schlechte

M. 1. By adding -t to the numbers.
     2. a. erst-   c. fünft-
        b. dritt-   d. sechzehnt-
     3. -st is added.
     4. a. einunddreißigst-   b. hundertst-
     5. a. siebten   b. zweites

N. 1. Der wievielte ist heute? / Den wievielten haben wir heute?
     2. Heute ist der erste Juni. / Heute haben wir den ersten Juni.
     3. den 6. Juli l996 / 6.7.96

Kapitel 10

A. *Answers will vary. Possible ones are:*
Das tut mir leid. / Hoffentlich fühlst du dich morgen besser. / Schade.

B. *Possible answers:*
Ich dusche (mich). / Ich putze mir die Zähne. / Ich rasiere mich. / Ich kämme mich. / Ich wasche mir Gesicht und Hände.

C. 1. etwas Gutes
     2. nichts Besonderes
     3. ein guter Bekannter
     4. eine Deutsche

D. 1. mich, mir   4. uns, uns
     2. dich, dir   5. sich, sich
     3. sich, sich

E. 1. Fühlst du dich heute besser?
     2. Cornelia hat sich gestern erkältet.

F. 1. die   2. die

G. 1. zu
     2. when used with modals
     3. Hast du Zeit, mir zu helfen?
     4. um ... zu + infinitive
     5. a. Es macht Spaß, *im Wald zu wandern.*
        b. *Ich möchte mir eine neue CD kaufen.*
        c. Vergiß nicht, *Blumen mitzubringen.*
        d. Ich beginne, *deine Ideen zu verstehen.*
        e. Ich bleibe heute zu Hause, *um meine Arbeit zu machen.*

H. 1. -er is added to the base form.
     2. The vowel a, o, or u adds umlaut.
     3. a. kälter   c. größeren, schöneren
        b. teurer

I. 1. -st is added to the base form
     2. -est
     3. The vowel a, o, or u adds umlaut.
     4. am + (e)sten
     5. a. am teuersten   c. schönster
        b. am schwersten   d. kälteste

J. 1. lieber, am liebsten
     2. besser, am besten
     3. mehr, am meisten

Kapitel 11

A. *Answers will vary. Possible ones are:* Ich war im Theater [Kino, Konzert] / Ich war in der Kneipe, Bibliothek. / Ich war zu Hause.

B. 1. Hast [Hättest] du Lust ins Kino [Theater, Konzert] zu gehen? / Möchtest du ins Kino [Theater, Konzert] gehen?
   2. *Answers will vary. Possible ones are:* Ja, gern. / Wenn du mich einlädst, schon. / Nein, ich habe keine Lust. / Nein, ich habe keine Zeit.

C. 1. to narrate a series of connected events in the past; often called narrative past
   2. in a two-way exchange to talk about events in the past; often called conversational past
   3. modals, **sein, haben**

D. 1. -te
   2. They lose the umlaut.
   3. a. ich durfte   c. sie mußte
      b. du konntest   d. wir mochten

E. 1. -te   2. -ete
   3. **ich** and **er/es/sie**-forms
   4. a. ich spielte   c. es regnete
      b. Dieter arbeitete d. wir sagten

F. 1. Ich brachte den Wein.
   2. Sie dachte an Gerd.
   3. Sie wußten es schon.

G. 1. They undergo a stem change.
   2. **ich** and **er/es/sie**-forms
   3. a. er sprach   e. er fuhr   h. sie gingen
      b. sie sah   f. ich war   i. ich lief
      c. ich half   g. sie wurde j. er trug
      d. wir blieben

H. 1. in final position
   2. a. Das Konzert fing um sieben Uhr an.
      b. Kerstin brachte Blumen mit.
      c. Ich stand immer früh auf.
      d. Wir kauften in der Stadt ein.

I. 1. It is used to report an event or action that took place before another event or action in the past.
   2. It consists of the simple past of the auxiliaries **haben** or **sein** and the past participle of the verb.

3. a. I slept well because I had run 20 kilometers.
   b. After it had rained all day the sun shone [shined] in the evening.

J. 1. Stefan schrieb den Brief. Stefan hat den Brief geschrieben.
   2. Anna ging nach Hause. Anna ist nach Hause gegangen.

K. 1. wann   2. wenn
   3. wenn   4. als
   5. a. wenn   c. wenn
      b. als   d. wann

Kapitel 12

A. *Answers will vary. Possible ones are:* Es tut mir leid. Sie/Er ist im Moment beschäftigt [nicht zu sprechen]. Sie/Er telefoniert gerade. / Sie/Er hat einen Termin. // Gehen Sie bitte gleich hinein. Sie/Er erwartet Sie.

B. *Answers will vary. Possible ones are:* Wenn ich nur mehr Geld hätte. / Wenn ich nur keine Hausaufgaben hätte. / Wenn ich nur fleißiger wäre.

C. 1. **fraglich** = questionable
   2. **täglich** = daily

D. *Answers will vary:* Ja, das wäre schön. / Wenn ich nur Geld [Zeit] hätte. / Das würde ich gern machen. / Das würde Spaß machen. // Dazu hätte ich keine Lust [Zeit].

E. 1. hypothetical statements (conditions contrary to fact), wishes, polite requests
   2. Trudi würde auch gern faulenzen.
   3. Wenn die Sonne nur scheinen würde.
   4. Würdest du noch eine Stunde bleiben?

F. 1. wäre
   2. hätte
   3. a. ich wäre   c. wir wären
      b. du hättest d. sie hätte

G. 1. The subjunctive of modals is identical to the simple past, except that where there is an umlaut in the infinitive there is also an umlaut in the subjunctive (**wollen** and **sollen** do not have umlaut).

2. a. ich müßte   b. du könntest

H. 1. Add subjunctive endings to the simple past stem. (An umlaut is added to the vowels **a, o,** or **u.**)

2. a. es gäbe   c. sie kämen
    b. sie täte es   d. du bliebest

I. 1. The subjunctive is identical to the simple past forms.

2. a. sie lernte   b. du arbeitetest

J. 1. An umlaut is added to the simple past stem.

2. a. sie brächte   c. wir wüßten
    b. ich dächte

K. 1. It consists of the subjunctive forms **hätte** or **wäre** + past participle.

2. a. wir wären gewesen
    b. er hätte gesehen
    c. ich wäre mitgefahren

L. 1. The infinitive; the double infinitive.

2. I could have done that alone.

M. 1. the condition (**wenn**-clause) and the conclusion

2. wenn

3. conditions of fact

4. conditions contrary to fact

5. a. *present time:* Christine würde länger schlafen, wenn sie Zeit hätte. *or* Christine schliefe länger, wenn sie Zeit hätte.
    past time: Christine hätte länger geschlafen, wenn sie Zeit gehabt hätte.

    b. *present time:* Wenn ich Geld hätte, würde ich ins Konzert gehen. *or* Wenn ich Geld hätte, ginge ich ins Konzert.
    past time: Wenn ich Geld gehabt hätte, wäre ich ins Konzert gegangen.

N. 1. Ich täte das nicht.

2. Du würdest mir nicht glauben.

3. Wir könnten morgen fahren.

4. ... würde sie ein neues Auto kaufen.

5. ... wenn ich das gewußt hätte.

6. ... du könntest länger bleiben.

Kapitel 13

A. 1. present tense

2. Ich rufe dich heute abend an.

B. 1. When it is not clear from the context that the event will occur in the future, or to express an assumption.

2. a form of **werden** plus an infinitive

3. final position

4. the auxiliary (**werden**), just after the infinitive

5. a. Sandra wird uns helfen.
    b. Wirst du das wirklich machen?
    c. Michael sagt, daß er einen neuen Job suchen wird.

C. 1. Meine Eltern werden wohl [schon / sicher] zu Hause sein.

2. Das wird wohl [schon / sicher] falsch sein.

D. 1. Let me do the dishes today.

2. Where did you leave your gloves again?

3. Unfortunately I have to have my cassette player/deck repaired.

4. Let's go.

E. 1. the infinitive

2. a. Why did you let Kurt drive your car?
    b. I left my driver's license at home.

F. 1. It introduces a relative clause. It refers back to a noun or pronoun in the preceding clause.

2. in last position. (The auxiliary follows the infinitive or the past participle.)

G. 1. Most forms are identical with the definite article forms.

2. denen

H. 1. It depends on the gender and number of the noun to which it refers, its antecedent.

2. It depends on the relative pronoun's grammatical function in the clause (subject, direct object, etc.).

3. It depends on what case that preposition takes.

I. 1. der   4. den   7. der
2. der   5. denen   8. das
3. dem   6. dem

Kapitel 14

A. *Answers will vary. Possible answers are:* Wir sollten / könnten langsamer fahren. / Wir sollten keine Pappteller benutzen. / Wir sollten Zeitungen recyceln. / Wir sollten nicht rauchen. / Wir sollten weniger Wasser verbrauchen.

B. 1. The subject is the agent and performs the action expressed by the verb.
   2. The subject is acted upon by an expressed or unexpressed agent.

C. 1. a form of the auxiliary **werden** + past participle of the main verb
   2. worden
   3. worden
   4. a. Der Müll wird verwertet.
      The trash is (being) made use of.
      b. Das Geld wurde gerade investiert.
      The money was just (being) invested.
      c. Die Zeitungen sind recycelt worden.
      The newspapers have been [were] recycled.
      d. Die Fabrik war modernisiert worden.
      The factory had been modernized.

D. 1. It is the object of the preposition **von.**
   2. It is the object of the preposition **durch.**
   3. a. durch   b. von

E. 1. the past participle of the main verb + the infinitive **werden**
   2. a. When does the work have to be done?
      b. The problems can't be solved.

F. 1. (1) main verb (*to grow, get, become*) in the active voice
      (2) auxiliary verb in the future tense (a form of **werden** + dependent infinitive)
      (3) auxiliary verb in the passive voice (a form of **werden** + past participle)
   2. a. A trip to Dresden was / was being planned. (*passive voice, simple past tense*)
      b. It's finally getting warmer. (*active voice—main verb, present tense*)
      c. He'll write to us. (*active voice—auxiliary verb, future tense*)

G. 1. (a) **man** as subject
      (b) **sein** ... **zu** + infinitive
      (c) **sich lassen** + infinitive
   2. a. Man darf das nicht vergessen.
      b. Wie ist das zu erklären?
      c. Mit der Chefin läßt sich gut reden.
      d. Da ist nichts zu machen.
      e. Man muß die Umwelt schützen.
      f. Eine Lösung läßt sich nicht so leicht finden.
      g. Das Auto läßt sich leicht reparieren.

Video Workbook

Einfach toll!

Name _____ Date _____

Einführung: Wir stellen uns vor.

EINLEITUNG

A. Besondere Ausdrücke. Here are some words and expressions that you will hear in the Introduction. Read through the list to get acquainted with the words and listen for them as you view the video. Try memorizing the ones that you think would be most useful to you.

das Abitur	*comprehensive exam taken in high school to qualify for university study*
die Bildhauerin	*female sculptor*
die Kunst	*art*
der Kunstlehrer	*art teacher*
alt	*old*
jung	*young*
schüchtern	*shy*
erst vor kurzem	*just a short while ago*
nach Mainz gezogen	*moved to Mainz*
sitzengeblieben	*said of a student who has had to repeat a grade in school (literally: remained seated)*

B. Wer macht was? You will hear two people, Alex and Erika, introduce themselves and talk about their friends and family. As you are watching the video, put a check in the appropriate boxes, based on what you hear. You may need to watch the segment more than once to get it all.

Descriptions	Alex	Erika	Dagmar	Uwe	Karl	Susanne
1. studies art						
2. is in the 13th grade						
3. failed a year						
4. acts in a theater group						
5. Erika's cousin						
6. Alex's oldest sister						
7. is shy						
8. father is an art teacher						
9. is taking a dancing course						
10. Erika's boyfriend						

C. Wie alt sind sie? Listen to Alex and Erika introducing themselves, their friends, and their family. Based on what you hear, match the people with the correct ages. More than one person may be the same age. Some ages you may have to guess based on other information about the characters.

1. _____ Alex

2. _____ Dagmar

3. _____ Dennis

4. _____ Erika

5. _____ Karl

6. _____ Nadine

7. _____ Susanne

8. _____ Uwe

a. jünger als 16 Jahre alt

b. 16 Jahre alt

c. 18 Jahre alt

d. 19 Jahre alt

e. 21 Jahre alt

D. Stimmt's? Read through the following statements. Then watch the *Einführung* again. Put a check mark before the statements which are true.

Alex

1. _____ Alex studiert Kunst in Heidelberg.

2. _____ Seine Eltern haben vier Kinder.

3. _____ Sein Vater ist Kunstlehrer.

4. _____ Seine Mutter ist Lehrerin.

5. _____ Sein Freund, Karl, ist sitzengeblieben.

6. _____ Alex kennt Erika seit einem Jahr.

Erika

7. _____ Erika geht in die 13. Klasse.

8. _____ Im Sommer fährt sie nach Italien.

9. _____ Ihre Kusine, Dagmar, ist sehr schüchtern.

10. _____ Dagmar mag Karl.

11. _____ Erikas beste Freundin heißt Nicole.

12. _____ Ihr Freund, Uwe, geht auf die Universität.

E. Familie und Freunde. The following charts are to help you get to know the characters in this video. In the space near the pictures, write one characteristic of each person based on what Alex and Erika say. You may have to watch the video more than once to do this.

Alex und seine Familie

Herr Lipp

Frau Lipp

Susanne   **Alex**   **Dennis**   **Nadine**

Erika und ihre Freunde

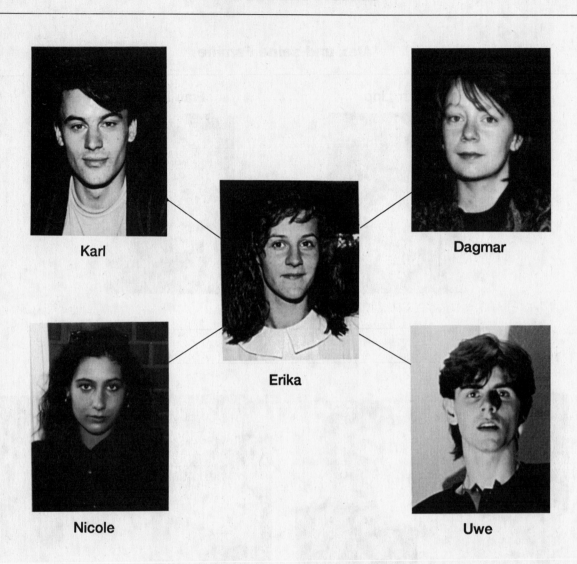

Karl

Dagmar

Erika

Nicole

Uwe

1. Schule: Neue Bekanntschaften

EINLEITUNG

A. Vorschau. This segment takes place in a **Gymnasium,** which is a college preparatory high school. Erika's cousin, Dagmar, has just moved to Mainz, and Erika introduces her to her friends. Notice that in colloquial German it is common to use the article with proper names. As you watch the video, look for answers to the following questions:

- How does the school look compared to the high school you attended?
- How is the school yard different or similar to the school yards you know?
- How is the room equipped and decorated?
- How similar or different is the atmosphere in the classroom compared to your experience?
- Do you notice a difference in the door handles?
- How do Erika's friends respond to her cousin Dagmar who has just moved to Mainz?
- What do the students think of the new teacher?

B. Besondere Ausdrücke. Here are some words and idiomatic expressions that you will hear in this segment of the video. Read through the list to get acquainted with the expressions and listen for them as you view the video. Try memorizing the ones that you think would be most useful to you. The items are listed in order of appearance.

vor·stellen	*to introduce*
(Das) kann passieren.	*That can happen.*
in der Nähe von	*near*
das Lieblingsfach	*favorite course*
Echt?	*Really?*
Es geht gleich los.	*It's about to start.*
gleich jetzt	*right now*
toll	*great*
Das hätte ich gar nicht geglaubt.	*I never would have believed it.*
ich nehme an (an·nehmen)	*I assume (to assume)*
schlagt sie auf (auf·schlagen)	*open them [the books] (to open)*

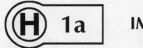 **IM FLUR**

C. Landeskunde. The students you see in this segment attend a **Gymnasium** and are preparing to go on to college. Those in their last year, like Erika, will have to take the **Abitur** at the end of the year to determine their eligibility for further studies. The **Abitur** covers many of the major subject areas studied. It actually consists of both oral and written exams taken over a period of several days. The scores often determine when, where, and what the student will be eligible to study. After completion of the **Abitur,** students celebrate and may even parade through the town in cars, honking their horns.

D. Ich hab's gesehen. Watch the video segment with the sound off. Write in English the name of each article of clothing which you see, but write the color of that article of clothing in German.

_____   _____

_____   _____

_____   _____

_____   _____

_____   _____

_____   _____

E. Schauen Sie genau. Watch the video segment again with the sound off and watch for information to help you complete the statements below. Circle the best choice based on what you see. You may consult the glossary at the end of the video workbook section of the *Arbeitsheft* for the meanings of any words you do not understand.

1. Die Schule ist ...
   a. alt.   b. modern.   c. sehr klein.

2. Vor der Schule stehen viele ...
   a. Fahrräder.   b. Autos.   c. Busse.

3. Die Freunde treffen sich ...
   a. vor der Schule.   b. in der Schule.   c. im Klassenzimmer.

4. Die Schüler sind ...
   a. nervös.   b. freundlich.   c. müde.

F. Hören Sie zu. Read the following list of German remarks. You will find the meaning of unfamiliar words in the glossary at the end of the workbook. Then view *Haltestelle 1a.* Mark each question, statement, or fragment you hear.

1. _____ ... die neue Lehrerin ...

2. _____ ... meine Kusine vorstellen.

3. _____ Sie ist jetzt neu in Mainz.

4. _____ Setz dich neben ihn.

5. _____ Das wär' toll.

6. _____ Wie alt ist sie?

7. _____ Mein Vater hat die Arbeitsstelle gewechselt.

8. _____ Wir sind vor einem Monat umgezogen.

9. _____ Das ist mein Lieblingsfach.

10. _____ Ich hab' einen negativen Eindruck.

11. _____ Es geht gleich los.

G. Stimmt's? Read through the following statements. Then watch *Haltestelle 1a* again. Put a check mark before the statements that are true according to the video.

1. _____ Dagmar ist neu in Mainz.

2. _____ Ihr Vater arbeitet in Hamburg.

3. _____ Sie ist siebzehn Jahre alt.

4. _____ Sie wohnt ganz in der Nähe von Erika.

5. _____ Die neue Lehrerin unterrichtet Englisch.

6. _____ Karl ist älter als die anderen in seiner Klasse.

7. _____ Dagmars Lieblingsfach ist Mathematik.

8. _____ Karl lernt gern Mathematik.

9. _____ Mascha hat einen positiven Eindruck von der neuen Lehrerin.

 **IM KLASSENRAUM**

H. Landeskunde. When you listen to the teacher speaking you will hear her refer to **Mathematik** as **Mathe**. It is common to shorten subject names in school slang. Can you guess what the following subjects are: **Bio, Reli**?

 I. Ich hab's gesehen. Watch *Haltestelle 1b* with the sound off and write in German the names of the school objects you see. Include the gender if you know it.

_____   _____

_____   _____

_____   _____

_____   _____

J. Schauen Sie genau. Watch the video segment again with the sound off and watch for information to help you complete the statements below. Circle the best choice based on what you see.

1. Die Lehrerin heißt ...
   a. Brunner.   b. Blum.   c. Tengler.

2. Sie hat ... Haare.
   a. kurze, dunkle   b. kurze, blonde   c. lange, blonde

3. Sie ...
   a. sitzt auf dem Tisch.   b. steht auf dem Tisch.   c. steht vor der Klasse.

4. Sie unterrichtet ...
   a. Mathematik.   b. Gymnastik.   c. Musik.

K. Hören Sie zu.   Read the following list of German remarks. Then view *Haltestelle 1b*. Mark each question, statement, or fragment you hear.

1. _____ ... Mathelehrerin ...

2. _____ ... dieses Schuljahr ...

3. _____ ... wirklich gut ...

4. _____ Ich finde sie auch ganz toll.

5. _____ Ich habe kein Mathebuch dabei.

6. _____ Schlagt sie dann bitte mal auf.

NOCH EINMAL

L.   Land und Leute.   In this segment you will see some students writing with a fountain pen. This is still common in Germany. Most school children carry their books and materials in a book bag (**Schultasche**) that is usually worn on their backs. Many have reflectors on them so that children can be seen more easily on dark winter mornings.

M. Ich hab's gesehen.   Watch the *Noch einmal* section with the sound off. Write in German the name of the objects which you see in the video. Concentrate on the items you didn't see during the first two segments.

_____   _____

_____   _____

_____   _____

_____   _____

N. Wer macht was?   Watch this segment without sound and check who is doing what. A few items might be debatable. Be prepared to defend your opinion.

Wer ...	Dagmar	Erika	Karl	Mascha	Frau Tengler
1. schüttelt (*shakes*) die Hand?					
2. hat die Hand in der Tasche?					
3. kommt die Treppe herauf (*up*)?					
4. hält ein Buch in der Hand?					
5. sitzt neben Karl im Klassenraum?					
6. trägt eine Hose?					
7. trägt eine Schultasche?					
8. ist nervös?					
9. ist entspannt (*relaxed*)?					

P
1

Bilder aus Deutschland

A. Landeskunde. In this *Parkplatz* segment you will view scenes of the Rhineland countryside and village life. The Rhine Valley is famous for its vineyards. Notice the wine corking machine. The Rhine River is not only a tourist attraction but also a major transportation route for cargo of all kinds. Many major cities in Germany are found on the Rhine or one of its tributaries. Compare the layout of the village you see in this segment to small towns you are familiar with. Notice that bread in Germany is usually not sliced and comes in a variety of shapes and sizes.

B. Was gibt's? Check off the objects which you see in this segment.

1. _____ Kinderwagen

2. _____ Kirche

3. _____ Haus

4. _____ Auto

5. _____ Großvater

6. _____ Blumen

7. _____ Baum

8. _____ Hund

9. _____ Schiff

10. _____ Schild

11. _____ Garten

12. _____ Fluß

C. Stimmt's? Read through the following statements. Then watch *Parkplatz 1.* Put a check mark before the statements that you think are true.

1. _____ Drei Frauen sitzen auf einer Bank.

2. _____ Die Kirche steht auf einem Berg.

3. _____ Ein Auto steht vor der Kirche.

4. _____ In diesem Dorf werden Weintrauben° angebaut°. | wine grapes / cultivated

5. _____ Diese Stadt ist eine große Industriestadt.

6. _____ Das Dorf ist in der Nähe von Bacharach.

7. _____ Das Dorf liegt an einem Fluß.

8. _____ Das Schiff ist ein Öltanker.

2. Geburtstagsfeier: Wie alt bist du?

EINLEITUNG

A. Vorschau. Alex visits his relatives to attend the birthday party of his cousin, Ruth. The majority of Germans live in apartments. Alex's uncle and aunt live in a single-family home, which is not as common in Germany. (Why do you suppose this is so?)

- Listen to the birthday song. Is the melody familiar to you?
- Alex is the only member of his family at the party. Where are the others?
- Do you think Ruth's parents spent a lot of money on her birthday party?
- How would you describe Ruth's personality?
- What role does the grandmother play in the birthday party?
- Who else has a birthday today?

B. Besondere Ausdrücke. Here are some words and idiomatic expressions that you will hear in this segment of the video. Read through the list to get acquainted with the expressions and listen for them as you view the video. Try memorizing the ones that you think would be most useful to you. The items are listed in order of appearance.

leider	*unfortunately*
Ich hoffe, es gefällt ihr.	*I hope she likes it (it pleases her).*
Wollen 'mer reingehen?	*Shall we go in? ('mer is dialect for wir.)*
Sechs mal hoch.	*Six cheers for . . .*
Was machen eigentlich deine Geschwister?	*What are your brother and sister doing actually?*
die Klassenfahrt	*class trip*
die Ludwigschlösser	*famous castles built by King Ludwig II of Bavaria*
das Geschenk	*gift*
Stell dir das mal vor.	*Imagine that.*
vergessen	*to forget*
Anscheinend nicht.	*Apparently not.*

 **AN DER TÜR**

C. Landeskunde. This is a single-family home in a residential part of the city. Do you note differences from your experience where you live? Listen to how Peter and his uncle greet each other. Relatives address each other with the informal **du.** It is also common to shake hands when greeting others. Even young children may shake hands when they meet for play.

D. Ich hab's gesehen. Watch the video segment *Haltestelle 2a* with the sound off and write in German the names of the objects you see. Include the gender if you know it.

_____   _____

_____   _____

_____   _____

_____   _____

 E. Schauen Sie genau. Watch *Haltestelle 2a* again with the sound off and watch for information to help you complete the statements below. Circle the choices that you think are best based on what you see.

1. Das Haus von Onkel Peter ist ...
   a. ziemlich alt.　　　　　b. neu.　　　　　c. sehr klein.

2. Onkel Peter ist ...
   a. sehr alt.　　　　　b. jünger als Alex.　　　　　c. jung, aber älter als Alex.

3. Das Wetter ist ...
   a. warm und sonnig.　　　　　b. kalt und regnerisch.　　　　　c. kalt und sonnig.

4. Alex gibt Onkel Peter ...
   a. einen Brief.　　　　　b. ein Paket.　　　　　c. Blumen.

5. Alex ...
   a. geht zurück nach Hause.　　　b. geht ins Haus.　　　c. bleibt vor der Tür stehen.

 F. Hören Sie zu. Read the following list of German remarks. Then view *Haltestelle 2a* with the sound on. Mark each question, statement, or fragment you hear.

1. _____ Wie geht's dir?

2. _____ ... in Südamerika.

3. _____ ... dieses Paket ...

4. _____ ... es gefällt ihm ...

5. _____ Vielen Dank.

 G. Stimmt's? Read through the following statements. Then watch *Haltestelle 2a* again. Put a check mark before the statements that are true, based on the information in the video.

1. _____ Alex' Onkel raucht eine Zigarette.

2. _____ Alex' Eltern konnten nicht mitkommen.

3. _____ Seine Eltern sind in Japan.

4. _____ Das Paket ist für Ruth.

5. _____ Alex bleibt draußen.

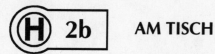 **2b**   **AM TISCH**

H. Landeskunde. You may notice some differences between German birthday celebrations and those where you live. What is the same? What is different? Would you have grandparents and parents at the same table with the children? Are there any differences in the way candles are placed on the cake?

 I. Ich hab's gesehen. Watch *Haltestelle 2b* with the sound off and write in German the names of the objects you see that are part of a birthday celebration. Include the gender if you know it.

_____   _____

_____   _____

_____   _____

 J. Schauen Sie genau. Watch the video segment again with the sound off and watch for information to help you complete the statements below. Circle the choices that you think are best based on what you see. More than one response may be possible in some cases.

1. Am Tisch sitzen ...
   a. viele Kinder.
   b. Kinder und eine Katze.
   c. nur Ruth und ihre Eltern.

2. Ruths Großmutter ...
   a. schneidet° den Kuchen.
   b. gibt Ruth ein Geschenk.
   c. ißt keinen Kuchen. | cuts

3. Die Kinder ...
   a. spielen mit Ruths Geschenken.
   b. essen Kuchen und Eis.
   c. wollen lieber spielen als essen.

4. Der Großvater gibt Ruth ...
   a. ein Geschenk.
   b. Blumen.
   c. einen Kuß°. | kiss

5. Ruths Großeltern ...
   a. sitzen nebeneinander°.
   b. sprechen wenig.
   c. sprechen nur mit Alex. | next to each other

6. Ruth setzt sich ...
   a. zum Großvater.
   b. zu Alex.
   c. zur Großmutter.

7. Ruth spricht ...
   a. mit Alex.
   b. mit dem Großvater.
   c. mit der Großmutter.

K. Hören Sie zu. Read the following list of German remarks. Then view *Haltestelle 2b*. Mark each question, statement, or fragment you hear.

1. _____ Ruthchen hat Geburtstag heut' ...

2. _____ Wer ist das?

3. _____ Sie sind in Heidelberg ...

4. _____ Das wär' schön.

5. _____ Direkt von Amerika.

6. _____ Stell dir das mal vor.

7. _____ ein Stück Kuchen ...

L. Fragen. Read through the following questions. Then watch *Haltestelle 2b* again. Answer the questions by circling the letter of the best choices.

1. Welches Mädchen trägt eine gelbe Blume im Haar?
   a. Ruth.   b. Vera.   c. Sonja.

2. Welches Mädchen trägt ein gestreiftes° Hemd? | striped
   a. Ruth.   b. Vera.   c. Sonja.

3. Warum sind Dennis und Nadine nicht mitgekommen?
   a. Sie sind auf Klassenfahrt.   b. Sie sind in Amerika.   c. Sie haben Ruths Geburtstag vergessen.

4. Wann kommen Alex' Eltern zurück?
   a. Nächsten Monat.   b. Nächstes Jahr.   c. Nächste Woche.

   **IM GARTEN**

M. Landeskunde. An American children's game similar to **Der Fuchs geht rum** is "Duck, duck, goose." Compare the house and yard to the ones you know in your home town. Any differences? What is the same?

N. Ich hab's gesehen. Watch *Haltestelle 2c* with the sound off and write in German the names of the objects you see. Include the gender if you know it.

_____   _____

_____   _____

_____   _____

_____   _____

O. Schauen Sie genau. Watch the video segment again with the sound off and watch for information to help you complete the statements below. Circle the choices that you think are best based on what you see. More than one response may be possible in some cases.

1. Die Kinder ...
   a. singen.   b. spielen ein Kinderspiel.   c. tanzen.

2. Zwei ... sind dabei.
   a. Zauberer°   b. Polizisten   c. Clowns | magicians

3. Alex ist ...
   a. sehr glücklich.   b. einsam°.   c. traurig. | lonely

4. Alex bekommt ...
   a. einen Walkman.   b. ein Buch.   c. einen Kassettenrecorder.

P. Hören Sie zu. Read the following list of German remarks. Then view *Haltestelle 2c* with sound. Mark each question, statement, or fragment you hear.

1. _____ Der Fuchs geht rum.

2. _____ Ich weiß nicht.

3. _____ Das ist für dich.

4. _____ ... nicht gegessen ...

5. _____ Anscheinend nicht.

Q. Stimmt's? Read through the following statements. Then watch *Haltestelle 2c* again. Put a check mark before the statements that are true.

1. _____ Die Kinder singen ein Lied über einen Wolf.

2. _____ Die Kinder tanzen mit den Clowns.

3. _____ Ein Clown spielt die Gitarre.

4. _____ Ein Clown hat einen Kassettenrecorder.

5. _____ Ein Clown hat ein Paket für Alex.

6. _____ Alex schläft im Garten.

7. _____ Das Paket ist ein Geschenk für Ruth.

8. _____ Das Paket ist ein Geschenk für Alex.

9. _____ Alex hat heute auch Geburtstag.

10. _____ Im Paket ist ein Walkman.

11. _____ Im Paket ist ein Buch.

NOCH EINMAL

R. Landeskunde. King Ludwig II built several castles in Bavaria which are popular tourist attractions today. His best-known castle, Neuschwanstein, is shown in this segment and was constructed between 1869 and 1886. The castle in Disneyland was modeled after Neuschwanstein.

S. Ich hab's gesehen. Watch the video segment *Noch einmal* with the sound off. Write in German the names of the objects which you see. Include the gender if you know it. Concentrate on the items you didn't see during the first three segments.

_____   _____

_____   _____

_____   _____

_____   _____

T. Stimmt's? Read through the following statements. Then watch *Noch einmal*. Put a check mark before the statements that are true.

1. _____ Ruth ist 6 Jahre alt.

2. _____ Auf dem Tisch gibt es nur einen großen Kuchen.

3. _____ Dennis und Nadine sind mit dem Bus nach München gefahren.

4. _____ Dennis und Nadine schauen sich einige Schlösser an.

5. _____ Zum Geburtstag hat Ruth ein Geschenk bekommen.

6. _____ Beim Kinderspiel spielt Alex mit.

U. Wunschliste. Your rich Onkel Otto has given you DM 3500 for your birthday. You have already prepared a wish list of items you would like to buy if you ever had the money. You may check items from the list below, but don't go over DM 3500! Otherwise you might have to go begging to Onkel Otto for more money.

_____	Mercedes Benz	DM	60.000
_____	Radio	DM	300
_____	Wörterbuch	DM	35
_____	Kleidung	DM	250
_____	Moped	DM	2.200
_____	*Deutsch heute*	DM	60
_____	Video-Recorder	DM	800
_____	Fahrrad	DM	450
_____	Computer	DM	1.800
_____	Reise nach Italien	DM	2.500
_____	Fernseher	DM	1.200
_____	Gitarre	DM	750
	Total	DM	

P 2   Einkaufen in der Innenstadt

A. Landeskunde. In this *Parkplatz* segment you will view scenes of Mainz. All the German states and many German cities have their own coats of arms (**Wappen**). Here you will see the **Mainzer Wappen.** Notice the pedestrian zone radiating out from the cathedral. You will find this arrangement in many cities in the German-speaking countries. Heidelberg or Vienna, for example, also have large pedestrian zones. Stores often display their wares outside. Many more traditional shops, such as the book store in this segment, have beautiful trade signs (**Zunftschilder**) displayed over the entrance. You should also take note of the half-timbered (**Fachwerk**) architecture which is typical for this region.

B. Was gibt's? Check off the objects you see in this segment.

1. _____ Blumen

2. _____ Kirche

3. _____ Haus

4. _____ Fahrrad

5. _____ Baum

6. _____ Laterne

7. _____ Fußgänger

8. _____ Schokolade

C. Stimmt's? Read through the following statements. Then watch *Parkplatz 2* again. Put a check mark before the statements that you think are true.

1. _____ In der Innenstadt sind Autos verboten°. | prohibited

2. _____ Das Schokoladenhaus verkauft Süßigkeiten° draußen. | sweets, candy

3. _____ Vor dem Blumenladen stehen ein Mann, eine Frau und ein Kind.

4. _____ Der Blumenladen ist in einem alten Haus.

5. _____ Im Blumenladen kann man Edelweiß° kaufen. | Alpine flower

6. _____ Edelweiß kostet DM 15.

7. _____ Die meisten Häuser in der Innenstadt sind modern.

D. Sie sind dran. Pick any scene in this *Parkplatz* and describe it in three short German sentences. You can describe objects, actions, or impressions. Use your imagination.

_____

_____

_____

E. Schilder. Read the descriptions below and match them with the corresponding sign by writing the number of the sign next to the appropriate description.

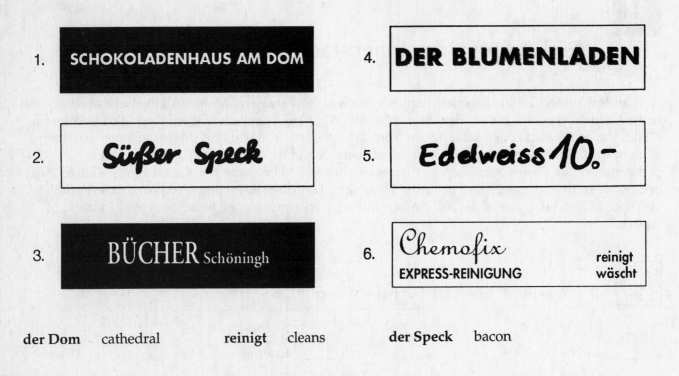

1. SCHOKOLADENHAUS AM DOM

2. *Süßer Speck*

3. BÜCHER Schöningh

4. **DER BLUMENLADEN**

5. *Edelweiss 10.–*

6. *Chemofix* EXPRESS-REINIGUNG — reinigt wäscht

der Dom cathedral   **reinigt** cleans   **der Speck** bacon

a. _____ Alpine flowers are for sale here.

b. _____ This sign is a favorite of book worms (**Bücherwürmer**).

c. _____ This sign shows you where you can buy flowers.

d. _____ This sign advertises a peculiar treat.

e. _____ Anyone with a sweet tooth will love it when this sign appears.

f. _____ You can have your clothes dry-cleaned where you see this sign.

3. Einkaufsbummel: In der Fußgängerzone

EINLEITUNG

A. Vorschau. The friends plan a get-together in the evening including a meal with stuffed peppers and tossed salad. Erika decides she needs a new dress for the party. Here you will see grocery and clothes shopping German style. Many German shops are closed between 12 noon and 2 p.m. They then close again around 6 p.m. On Thursday evenings many remain open until 8:30. On most Saturdays, shops close no later than 2:00; they are not open on Sunday.

- How do the friends greet each other compared to what is common where you live?
- What part of town are they in?
- How do the streets and stores differ from your hometown?
- How do Karl and Dagmar determine whether the fruit is fresh and firm?
- What does Karl say when he takes leave of the **Marktfrau**? Do you do the same?
- What do you think of the clothing styles at Cavallino?

B. Besondere Ausdrücke. Here are some words and idiomatic expressions that you will hear in this segment of the video. Read through the list to get acquainted with the expressions and listen for them as you view the video. Try memorizing the ones that you think would be most useful to you.

Sag mal, wo wart ihr gestern abend?	*Say, where were you last evening?*
Es ist wirklich zu empfehlen.	*I can highly recommend it.*
alles mögliche	*all sorts of things*
Das wär' toll.	*That would be great.*
Wie wär's mit gefülltem Paprika?	*How about stuffed peppers?*
der Kopfsalat	*lettuce*
süß und fest	*sweet and firm*
Warte mal.	*Wait.*
Welche Größe brauchst du denn?	*What size do you need?*
Das müßte dir wahrscheinlich unheimlich gut stehen.	*That would probably look really great on you.*
Probier das mal an.	*Try this on.*
Das sieht echt gut aus.	*That really looks good.*

 **3a** BEGRÜSSUNGEN

C. Landeskunde. In this segment the friends meet in a pedestrian zone (**Fußgängerzone**). Many cities have turned the downtown shopping district into pedestrian zones. There are very few shopping malls outside the cities.

 D. Schauen Sie genau. Watch *Haltestelle 3a* with the sound off and watch for information to help you complete the statements below. Circle the choices that you think are best based on what you see. More than one response may be possible in some cases.

1. Dagmar kennt ...
   a. nur Karl.   b. Karl und Erika.   c. alle drei.

2. Die vier Freunde treffen sich ...
   a. im Park.   b. vor einem Geschäft.   c. vor einem Hotel.

3. Nicole geht mit ... ins Geschäft.
   a. Karl   b. Erika   c. Dagmar

4. Die zwei anderen Freunde gehen ... kaufen.
   a. Blumen   b. Obst   c. Gemüse

 E. Hören Sie zu. Read the following list of German remarks. Then view *Haltestelle 3a* with sound. Mark each question, statement, or fragment you hear.

1. _____ ... es hat gar nicht geschmeckt.

2. _____ ... alles mögliche ...

3. _____ ... mit Salami und Sardellen ...

4. _____ ... gute Idee ...

5. _____ Sie muß noch ins Cavallino.

6. _____ ... gehen wir Gemüse kaufen ...

7. _____ Alles klar.

Name _____ Date _____

F. Stimmt's? Read through the following statements. Then watch *Haltestelle 3a* again. Put a check mark before the statements that are true.

1. _____ Erika war gestern abend im Theater.

2. _____ Karl war gestern abend im Kino.

3. _____ Dagmar hat eine große Pizza gegessen.

4. _____ Heute abend essen die Freunde gemeinsam.

5. _____ Dagmar und Karl wollen Gemüse kaufen.

6. _____ Erika hat ihr Geld vergessen.

7. _____ Erika braucht ein Kleid für die Party.

8. _____ Karl braucht eine Hose für die Party.

9. _____ Die vier Freunde treffen sich nach dem Einkaufen.

(H) 3b   **BEIM GEMÜSEHÄNDLER**

G. Landeskunde. Shopping at open-air markets for fresh vegetables and fruits is common in Germany. The selection and quality are usually better than what can be found in large grocery stores. Customers do not touch the fruit and vegetables; instead they ask the vendor about quality (**süß, fest**). Once they have made their selection, the vendor puts items in a bag and weighs them. The produce comes from many different locations: **belgische Tomaten, griechische Aprikosen, italienische Nektarinen,** etc.

H. Ich hab's gesehen. Watch *Haltestelle 3b* with the sound off and write in German the names of the fruits and vegetables which you see. Include the gender if you know it.

_____   _____

_____   _____

_____   _____

_____   _____

I. Schauen Sie genau. Watch the video segment again with the sound off and watch for information to help you complete the statements below. Circle the choices that you think are best based on what you see. More than one response may be possible.

1. Die Gemüsehändlerin ist ...
   a. freundlich.   b. ungeduldig°.   c. traurig.   **| impatient**

2. Das Gemüse ist ...
   a. frisch.   b. nicht frisch.

3. Die Gemüsehändlerin verkauft ...
   a. Gemüse und Obst.   b. nur Gemüse.   c. Gemüse und Käse.

J. Hören Sie zu. Read the following list of German remarks. Then view *Haltestelle 3b* with sound on. Mark each question, statement, or fragment you hear.

1. _____ ... eine schlechte Idee.

2. _____ Wieviel kosten ...

3. _____ ... das Kilo 9,70 DM.

4. _____ Machen wir Obstsalat.

5. _____ ... Kopfsalat und Bananen ...

6. _____ Sind sie noch frisch?

7. _____ ... fest und süß ...

8. _____ ... nehmen wir ein Kilo ...

9. _____ Warte mal.

K. Ich hab's verstanden. Read through the following items. Then watch *Haltestelle 3b* again. Circle the letter of the choices that you think best complete the sentence.

1. Dagmar und Karl wollen ... kochen.
   a. gefüllten Paprika   b. Schnitzel   c. Suppe

2. Was meinen Sie? Die Gemüsehändlerin spricht ...
   a. schnell.   b. langsam.   c. gerade richtig°.   **| just right**

3. Dagmar ißt lieber ... als Pfirsiche.
   a. Tomaten   b. Nektarinen   c. Bananen

4. Zum Abendessen essen die Freunde ...
   a. Schnitzel, Tomatensalat, Obstsalat.   b. gefüllten Paprika, Tomatensalat, Suppe.   c. gefüllten Paprika, Nektarinen, gemischten Salat.

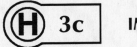 **3c**   **IM CAVALLINO**

L. Landeskunde. German clothing sizes are measured differently from American sizes. For example, a size 36 in dresses is equivalent to a size 8 in the American system.

     M. Ich hab's gesehen. Watch *Haltestelle 3c* with the sound off and write in German the names of the articles of clothing which you see in the store. Include the gender if you know it.

_____   _____

_____   _____

_____   _____

     N. Schauen Sie genau. Watch the video segment again with the sound off and watch for information to help you complete the statements below. Circle the choices that you think are best based on what you see.

1. Die Kleidung im Cavallino ist ...
    a. teuer.   b. billig.   c. nur für Mädchen.

2. Nicole und Erika suchen ...
    a. eine Bluse.   b. ein Kleid.   c. einen Pulli.

3. Der Spiegel° im Geschäft ist ... | mirror
    a. kaputt.   b. rund.   c. groß.

4. Der Computer im Cavallino sagt ...
    a. *DM 45, —.*   b. *Guten Tag.*   c. *Auf Wiedersehen.*

O. Hören Sie zu. Read the following list of German remarks. Then view *Haltestelle 3c* with sound. Mark each question, statement, or fragment you hear.

1. _____ Wie findest du denn das?

2. _____ Ich weiß nicht.

3. _____ Probier' das mal an.

4. _____ ... zu groß.

5. _____ Ich mag kein Blau.

6. _____ ... nicht zu teuer.

7. _____ ... echt süß.

8. _____ Ich kauf' mir das.

9. _____ Ich habe nichts gefunden.

10. _____ Gehen wir.

P. Stimmt's? Read through the following statements. Then watch *Haltestelle 3c* with sound. Put a check mark before the statements that are true.

1. _____ Nicole und Erika treffen Karl im Cavallino.

2. _____ Nicole will heute nichts kaufen.

3. _____ Erika braucht Größe 36.

4. _____ Erika will alles kaufen.

5. _____ Erika mag kein Grün.

6. _____ Das grüne Kleid ist viel zu teuer.

7. _____ Im Cavallino kann man auch Schuhe kaufen.

8. _____ Zwei Kinder sind im Cavallino.

9. _____ Nicole kauft einen Hut.

10. _____ Nicole hat kein Geld dabei.

11. _____ Nicole kauft eine Bluse.

12. _____ Nicole und Erika finden Karl und Dagmar beim Gemüsehändler.

NOCH EINMAL

Q. Landeskunde. The art of preparing and eating pizza may differ between Germany and your country. In Germany one doesn't usually order individual toppings. The pizzas are given Italian names and are sold as is. Pizzas are not cut into slices and eaten with the hands. Instead, they are served on a plate and are eaten with knife and fork. In Germany it is important to know your pepperoni. If you order just **Peperoni** you will get very hot green peppers. Be sure to specify **Peperoniwurst** if you want the spicy sausage slices many people like. If you don't like **Sardellen** (*anchovies*), be sure to watch what you order—they seem to appear on German pizzas when you least expect it.

R. Ich hab's gesehen. Watch the video segment with the sound off and write in German the names of any objects which you see. Include the gender if you know it. Concentrate on items that were not shown in the first three segments.

_____   _____

_____   _____

_____   _____

_____   _____

S. Schilder. While watching the segment *Noch einmal*, circle the numbers of the signs below which you see.

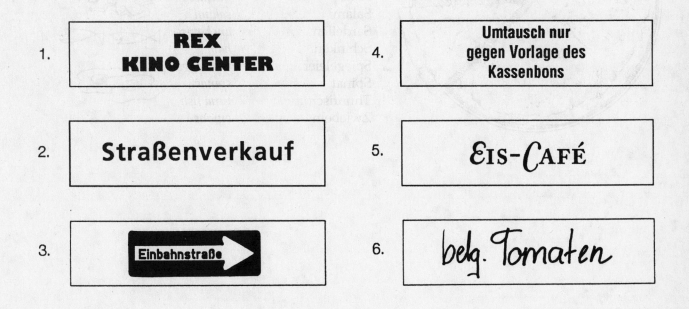

1. **REX KINO CENTER**

2. **Straßenverkauf**

3. Einbahnstraße

4. **Umtausch nur gegen Vorlage des Kassenbons**

5. **Eis-Café**

6. belg. Tomaten

Now read each description below and match it to its corresponding sign on page 191 by writing the letter of the sign next to the appropriate description.

a. _____ You'll find this sign at a vegetable stand which imports some of its produce.

b. _____ This sign tells you where you might find something that tastes good and cools you off on a hot day.

c. _____ This sign tells you you're at the cinema.

d. _____ This sign tells you that exchanges are possible only if you have the cash register receipt.

e. _____ You'll find this sign on a one-way street.

f. _____ This sign might be seen near a street vendor.

T. Pizza selbstgemacht. Now it's time to fantasize about your dream pizza. Below you see a life-like pizza shell with tomato sauce and cheese. Choose toppings by drawing lines from the selected topping to the pizza shell. Compare your choices with your classmates' selections. Did anybody pick anchovies? Who likes it hot (**scharf**)? Are there any vegetarians (**Vegetarier**) in the class?

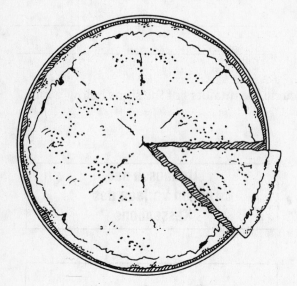

Artischocken	*artichokes*
grüne Peperoni	*hot green peppers*
Knoblauch	*garlic*
Meeresfrüchte	*seafood*
Oliven	*olives*
Paprika	*peppers*
Peperoniwurst	*pepperoni sausage*
Pilze	*mushrooms*
Salami	*salami*
Sardellen	*anchovies*
Schinken	*ham*
Spiegeleier	*fried eggs*
Spinat	*spinach*
Thunfisch	*tuna fish*
Zwiebeln	*onions*

P

3   ## Auf dem Markt

A. Landeskunde. The open-air market is a centuries old tradition in Europe. Farmers rent stands, often near a cathedral or church and sell their goods directly to the public. This usually occurs once or twice a week, especially on Saturday mornings. The vendor selects the produce and weighs it. The produce is often put into a paper cone (**Tüte**) and carried in a reusable shopping bag. You may notice some newer buildings among the older buildings in this segment. Many buildings were destroyed during World War II. Some were replaced with more modern-looking buildings. Other buildings were repaired and often have signs on the outside wall marking the day when the building was bombed.

   B. Was gibt's? Check off the objects which you see in this segment.

1. _____ Blumen
2. _____ Kirche
3. _____ Waage
4. _____ Geldtasche
5. _____ Kirschen
6. _____ Zwiebeln
7. _____ Huhn

8. _____ Baum
9. _____ Laterne
10. _____ Eier
11. _____ Gemüse
12. _____ Armbanduhr
13. _____ Bananen
14. _____ Karotten

C. Stimmt's? Read through the following statements. Then watch *Parkplatz 1.* Put a check mark before the statements that you think are true.

1. _____ Die Zwiebeln kommen aus Deutschland.

2. _____ Eine Frau schneidet Gemüse.

3. _____ Eine Frau hält ihre Geldtasche in der Hand.

4. _____ Die Kirschen kommen aus Spanien.

5. _____ Die Kirschen kosten DM 9,80 das Kilo.

6. _____ Das Obst ist frisch.

7. _____ Das Wetter ist schön.

8. _____ Viele Kinder spielen auf dem Marktplatz°.

| market square

D. Sie sind dran. Pick any scene in this *Parkplatz* and describe it in four short German sentences. You can describe objects, actions, or impressions. Use your imagination.

_____

_____

_____

_____

4. Hausarbeit: Wer macht was?

EINLEITUNG

A. Vorschau. Alex is sitting at the breakfast table with his family. His grandparents are coming for a visit and there is a discussion about who should do what chores.

- How do the individual family members feel about doing chores around the house?
- Does Susanne strike you as a **Faulpelz** (*lazy bones*) or did she just not get enough sleep?
- Are the chores assigned democratically?
- Are Alex' parents liberal or strict with their children?
- How does a German breakfast differ from an American one? Note the cold cuts and coffee pot.
- Do you notice anything different about German bread?

B. Besondere Ausdrücke. Here are some words and idiomatic expressions that you will hear in this segment. Read through the list to get acquainted with the expressions and listen for them as you watch the video. Try memorizing the ones that you think would be most useful to you. The items are listed in order of appearance.

Hauspflichten erledigen	*to do house chores*
zum Beispiel	*for example*
das Bad putzen	*to clean the bathroom*
Staub wischen	*to dust*
staubsaugen	*to vacuum*
das Geschirr spülen	*to wash dishes*
den Tisch abräumen	*to clear the table*
nee	*no (slang)*
überhaupt nicht	*not at all*
als Belohnung	*as a reward*

 **HAUSARBEIT**

C. Ich hab's gesehen. Watch *Haltestelle 4a* with the sound off and write in German the names of any objects you see which are *not* edible. Include the gender if you know it.

_____ _____

_____ _____

_____ _____

D. Schauen Sie genau. Watch the video segment again with the sound off and watch for information to help you complete the statements below. Circle the choices that you think are correct based on what you see. More than one response may be possible in some cases.

1. Die Familie sitzt ...
   a. im Wohnzimmer.
   b. im Eßzimmer.
   c. in der Küche.

2. Der Hund ...
   a. bellt°.
   b. liegt unter dem Tisch.
   c. steht neben dem Tisch.
   ° barks

3. Alle trinken ...
   a. Limonade.
   b. Wein.
   c. Kaffee.

4. Die Eltern ...
   a. essen.
   b. streiten°.
   c. machen das Frühstück.
   ° argue

5. Die Kinder ...
   a. essen.
   b. streiten.
   c. geben dem Hund etwas zu fressen°.
   ° eat (*animal*)

E. Hören Sie zu. Read the following list of German remarks. Then view *Haltestelle 4a* with sound. Mark each question, statement, or fragment you hear.

1. _____ Wir bekommen Besuch.

2. _____ Wer kommt denn?

3. _____ ... das Bad putzen ...

4. _____ ... keine Zeit ...

5. _____ ... das sagt sie immer ...

6. _____ ... schnell erledigen ...

7. _____ ... eine Arbeit in Geometrie ...

F. Stimmt's? Read through the following statements. Then watch *Haltestelle 4a* again. Put a check mark before the statements that are true.

1. _____ Onkel Peter kommt heute abend.

2. _____ Die Kinder müssen das Haus putzen.

3. _____ Alex hat keine Zeit.

4. _____ Er muß morgen eine Arbeit in Physik schreiben.

5. _____ Die Großeltern sind in Amerika.

6. _____ Der Vater trinkt keinen Kaffee.

7. _____ Die Mutter trinkt einen Kaffee.

8. _____ Susanne ißt nur Brot.

(H) 4b   **VATER HAT'S GESAGT**

 G. Hören Sie zu.   Read the following list of German remarks. Then view *Haltestelle 4b*. Mark each question, statement, or fragment you hear.

1. _____ ... staubsaugen und Staub wischen ...

2. _____ Das muß überhaupt nicht sein.

3. _____ ... keine Diskussion.

4. _____ ... um vier Uhr nachts ...

5. _____ Das ist keine gute Idee.

6. _____ ... eine tolle Aufgabe ...

7. _____ Jeden Freitag das gleiche.

8. _____ Das ist wirklich unfair.

H. Ich hab's verstanden.   Read through the following items. Then watch *Haltestelle 4b* again. Circle the number of the choices that you think best complete the sentence.

1. Susanne...
   a. schläft noch.
   b. arbeitet jetzt.
   c. ist bei den Großeltern.

2. Sie ist um ... Uhr nachts nach Hause gekommen.
   a. ein
   b. zwei
   c. drei

3. Alex ist um ... Uhr nachts nach Hause gekommen.
   a. ein
   b. zwei
   c. drei

4. Jeden Samstag muß Susanne ...
   a. das Bad putzen.
   b. das Geschirr spülen.
   c. staubsaugen.

I. Wer macht was? In this segment there is a family discussion about who does what. Based on your viewing of *Haltestelle 4b*, check off who does or did what on the chart below. You may want to listen to the segment several times as you fill in the chart.

Arbeitsgang	Alex	Dennis	Nadine	Susanne	Hund
1. Auto putzen					
2. Bad putzen					
3. Geschirr spülen					
4. mit dem Hund gehen					
5. schlafen					
6. staubsaugen					
7. Staub wischen					
8. Tisch abräumen					

NOCH EINMAL

J. Landeskunde. You may notice a few differences in the kitchen and foods shown in *Noch einmal*. Notice the difference in the light switches. Bread is usually bought at a bakery unsliced. The bread slicer you see in this segment is a common kitchen implement in Germany. German bakeries offer several different kinds of breads and rolls. **H-Milch (Haltbar-Milch)** is a kind of milk that doesn't need to be refrigerated until you open the container. German children are especially fond of bread spreads made of chocolate and hazelnut. These spreads have the texture of cake frosting and are very sweet. The spread is generally eaten the way many people eat peanut butter.

K. Ich hab's gesehen. Watch *Noch einmal* with the sound off and write in German the names of the objects which you see. Include the gender if you know it.

_____   _____

_____   _____

_____   _____

_____   _____

L. Was gibt's zum Frühstück? Check off the food items that you see on the breakfast table in *Noch einmal.*

1. _____ Äpfel

2. _____ Apfelsinensaft (Orangensaft)

3. _____ Bananen

4. _____ Brot

5. _____ Brötchen° | rolls

6. _____ Butter

7. _____ Joghurt

8. _____ Kaffee

9. _____ Käse

10. _____ Marmelade

11. _____ Reis Krispies

12. _____ Wurst

M. Ihre Meinung.   In this video segment there seems to be some controversy about who should do what chores. Put check marks next to the statements below that you agree with. Do your classmates share your opinions?

1. _____ Es ist unfair, daß Susanne jeden Samstag das Bad putzen muß.

2. _____ Dennis arbeitet zu wenig im Haus.

3. _____ Auch die Eltern sollten einige Hauspflichten erledigen.

4. _____ Mit dem Hund gehen ist wirklich keine Arbeit.

5. _____ Die Kinder sollten den Samstag frei haben.

6. _____ Die Eltern brauchen eine Putzfrau°. | cleaning lady

7. _____ Staubsaugen ist leichter° als Staub wischen. | easier

8. _____ Die Eltern sind zu streng°. | strict

P

4   **Jung und alt**

A. Landeskunde.   In this segment you will see window boxes on some of the houses. Flowers are very important in the German tradition and fresh flowers can be purchased year round. Notice the blue overalls on the workers. This is a trademark of the profession. The construction in the background is a preparation for a festival. You will see some sidewalks with separate lanes for bicycles. Bicycles are a common mode of transportation in Germany and bicyclists are expected to follow traffic regulations the same as motorists. Market places have always attracted street performers and traveling theatrical groups. Here you will see performers drawing on the Medieval tradition.

B. Was gibt's?   Check off the objects and people you see in this segment.

1. _____ Kinderwagen   7. _____ Ball

2. _____ Arbeiter   8. _____ Schauspieler

3. _____ Obst   9. _____ Junge

4. _____ Mutter   10. _____ Korb° | basket

5. _____ alter Mann   11. _____ Mädchen

6. _____ Fahrrad   12. _____ Bus

C. Wer macht was?   Below you will see a chart listing people and activities. Put check marks on the chart to indicate who is doing what.

Wer ...	Mann	Frau	Kind
1. geht mit zwei Hunden?			
2. spielt Ball?			
3. baut etwas?			
4. schiebt (*pushes*) ein Baby im Kinderwagen?			
5. läuft einem Ball nach?			
6. spielt Theater?			
7. hält eine Blume in der Hand?			
8. tanzt?			
9. trägt altmodische (*old fashioned*) Kleidung?			

5. Freizeit: Was machen wir?

EINLEITUNG

A. Vorschau. In this segment the friends discuss what they would like to do in the evening and on the coming weekend.

- Who has the most/best suggestions for something to do?
- Who is the **Spielverderber** (*party pooper*)?
- What kinds of movies are playing at the cinema?
- Where do the friends want to go on the weekend? Will all of them be able to go?
- What is the weather forecast for the weekend?

B. Besondere Ausdrücke. Here are some words and idiomatic expressions that you will hear in this segment. Read through the list to get acquainted with the expressions and listen for them as you watch the video. Try memorizing the ones that you think would be most useful to you.

Keine Ahnung.	*No idea.*
Ich habe keine Lust.	*I don't feel like it.*
Was ist heute in der Stadt los?	*What's going on in town today?*
Schade.	*Too bad.*
ausverkauft	*sold out*
Wie wär's denn mit Kino?	*How about (going to the) movies?*
Prima!, Super!, Klasse!	*Great!*
Das klappt nicht.	*That won't work.*
die Rheinfahrt	*trip on the Rhine river*
Es geht leider nicht.	*Unfortunately, that won't work (I can't).*
Paß auf.	*Listen. Pay attention.*
Die Vorhersage war sehr positiv.	*The (weather) forecast was very positive.*

 **WAS MACHEN WIR AM WOCHENENDE?**

 C. Ich hab's gesehen. Watch *Haltestelle 5a* with the sound off and write in German the names of the pieces of furniture, entertainment equipment, and other accessories which you see. Include the gender if you know it.

_____   _____

_____   _____

_____   _____

D. Schauen Sie genau. Watch the video segment again with the sound off and watch for information to help you complete the statements below. Circle the choice that you think is correct based on what you see.

1. Karl, Alex und Dennis sind ...
   a. im Schlafzimmer.
   b. im Garten.
   c. in der Küche.

2. Alex liest ...
   a. ein Buch.
   b. eine Zeitung.
   c. eine Zeitschrift°. | magazine

3. Dennis ...
   a. sieht fern.
   b. spielt ein Videospiel.
   c. hört sich Musik an.

4. ... kommt ins Zimmer.
   a. Susanne
   b. Nicole
   c. Erika

 E. Hören Sie zu. Read the following list of German remarks. Then view *Haltestelle 5a* with sound. Mark each question, statement, or fragment you hear.

1. _____ Was machen wir denn am Mittwoch?

2. _____ ... das interessiert mich nicht.

3. _____ Das wär' doch super.

4. _____ ... Was macht ihr heute nacht?

5. _____ ... ich habe keine Lust.

6. _____ ... ins Theater.

7. _____ ... drei Karten reservieren.

 F. Stimmt's? Read through the following statements. Then watch *Haltestelle 5a* again. Put a check mark before the statements that you think are true.

1. _____ Alex will ins Rockkonzert.

2. _____ Die Rockgruppe *The Cure* spielt heute abend in der Disco.

3. _____ Susanne will lieber tanzen gehen.

4. _____ Karl will auch tanzen gehen.

5. _____ Dennis geht lieber in die Disco.

6. _____ Die Freunde kaufen vier Karten zum Konzert.

7. _____ Andreas arbeitet im Kino.

8. _____ Andreas kann die Karten billiger kriegen°. | get

H 5b   **WAS MACHEN WIR DENN JETZT?**

G. Landeskunde. In this segment Alex makes a reference to the Ballplatzcafé. Cafés are very popular in Germany, even among young people. The atmosphere is usually cozy or **gemütlich,** as the Germans say. Besides coffee, you can order other drinks such as hot chocolate with whipped cream. You can also order pastries, read a newspaper, and just relax with friends. Many cafés have outdoor seating, which is great on a warm, sunny day.

H. Ich hab's gesehen. Watch *Haltestelle 5b* with the sound off and write in German the names of the articles of clothing and anything that has writing on it. Include the gender if you know it.

_____   _____

_____   _____

I. Hören Sie zu. Read the following list of German remarks. Then view *Haltestelle 5b* again. Mark each question, statement, or fragment you hear.

1. _____ Was ist denn los?

2. _____ Wo ist das?

3. _____ ... geh' ich mal schauen.

4. _____ Was machen wir denn jetzt?

5. _____ Wie wär's denn mit Theater?

6. _____ Guck doch mal ...

7. _____ ... Liebesfilm ...

8. _____ Das ist interessant.

J. Ich hab's verstanden. Read through the following items. Then watch *Haltestelle 5b* with sound. Circle the letter of the choices that you think best complete the sentence.

1. Erika, Nicole und Uwe sind im ...
   a. Altstadtcafé.
   b. Ballplatzcafé.
   c. Café Winkler.

2. Es gibt ... zum Konzert.
   a. noch zwei Karten
   b. noch viele Karten
   c. keine Karten

3. Es klappt nicht mit dem ...
   a. Konzert.
   b. Kino.
   c. Theater.

4. Karl und Alex wollen ...
   a. ins Theater.
   b. ins Kino.
   c. fernsehen.

5. Im Kino kommen heute ...
   a. Liebesfilme.
   b. Action-Krimis.
   c. Gruselfilme°. | horror films

6. Der Action-Film im Kino Royal beginnt um ...
   a. 7 Uhr.
   b. 19 Uhr.
   c. 20 Uhr 30.

7. Susanne...
   a. hat Lust, ins Kino zu gehen.
   b. findet den Film uninteressant.
   c. geht mit den Freunden tanzen.

 **5c** **AUSFLUGSPLÄNE**

 K. Ich hab's gesehen. Watch *Haltestelle 5c* with the sound off and write in German the names of the objects on the wall which you see. Include the gender if you know it.

_____   _____

_____   _____

_____   _____

L. Schauen Sie genau. Read through the following list and then watch the video segment again with the sound off. Check the statements that you think are true based on what you see.

1. _____ Susanne ist böse auf Alex.

2. _____ Alex liest.

3. _____ Dennis hört sich Musik an.

4. _____ Alex schläft.

5. _____ Erika und Susanne sprechen miteinander.

6. _____ Karl liest ein Buch.

7. _____ Susanne tanzt im Zimmer.

8. _____ Es ist spät am Abend.

9. _____ Dennis macht die Stereoanlage kaputt.

10. _____ Susanne sitzt auf dem Fußboden.

 M. Hören Sie zu. Read the following list of German remarks. Then view *Haltestelle 5c* with sound. Mark each question, statement, or fragment you hear.

1. _____ Ich auch nicht.

2. _____ ... nächste Woche ...

3. _____ Moment mal.

4. _____ Das ist doch Freitag!

5. _____ Hast du am Mittwoch Zeit?

6. _____ Ach schade.

7. _____ ... am Wochenende ...

8. _____ ... total super.

9. _____ Das Wetter ist bestimmt gut am Freitag.

N. Stimmt's? Read through the following statements. Then watch *Haltestelle 5c* again. Put a check mark before the statements that you think are true.

1. _____ Susanne will morgen etwas mit den anderen machen.

2. _____ Die anderen Freunde haben morgen keine Zeit.

3. _____ Nächsten Donnerstag haben sie Zeit.

4. _____ Mittwoch ist Feiertag.

5. _____ Dennis ist am Mittwoch frei.

6. _____ Dennis und Nadine fahren nach Paris.

7. _____ Susanne geht ins Ballplatzcafé.

8. _____ Sie fragt die anderen dort, ob sie mitkommen.

9. _____ Die anderen wollen nicht mitkommen.

10. _____ Die Wettervorhersage ist sehr positiv.

NOCH EINMAL

O. Landeskunde. In Germany, cinema prices vary depending on where you sit. Generally, the closer you are to the screen, the cheaper it is. The rating system is not listed G, PG, etc. Instead, the statement appears „**Freigegeben ab 18 Jahre"**. The age restriction varies depending on the content and explicitness of the film. Many films shown in German cinemas come from other countries, such as France, Italy, Japan, and, of course, the U.S. Most Hollywood blockbusters appear in Germany with dubbed German voices about six months after they open in the U.S. Germans are famous for the lip-synch precision of their film dubbing. Some German-speaking actors who have "made it" in Hollywood are Peter Lorre, Senta Berger, Marlene Dietrich, Billy Wilder, Klaus Maria Brandauer, and Arnold Schwarzenegger.

P. Was gibt's? Read through the following list and then watch the *Noch einmal* segment. Check off the objects you see. Put a **D** for **Deutschland** next to those items which can be readily identified as being German.

1. _____ Radio

2. _____ Telefonapparat

3. _____ Computer

4. _____ Sportgeschäft

5. _____ Telefonbuch

6. _____ Kinoprogramm

7. _____ Fernseher

8. _____ Lebensmittelgeschäft

9. _____ Fahrrad

10. _____ Berge

11. _____ Burg

12. _____ Fluß

Q. Ihre Meinung. In this video segment there is a discussion about leisure activities. What do you think about the following statements regarding leisure activities? Put check marks next to the statements below that you agree with. Then compare your answers with those of your classmates. How many prefer action films to romantic films? How many would rather go to a rock concert than take a trip on the Rhine? Try to explain your preferences.

1. _____ Action-Filme sind besser als Liebesfilme.

2. _____ Rockkonzerte sind zu teuer.

3. _____ Fernsehen ist langweilig°. | boring

4. _____ Country-Western-Musik ist toll.

5. _____ Ich gehe lieber ins Rockkonzert als auf eine Rheinfahrt.

6. _____ Fußgängerzonen sind nicht notwendig°. | necessary

7. _____ Ich gehe lieber ins Kino als ins Theater.

Name _____ Date _____

R. Schilder. While watching the segment *Noch einmal* circle the numbers of the signs below which you see.

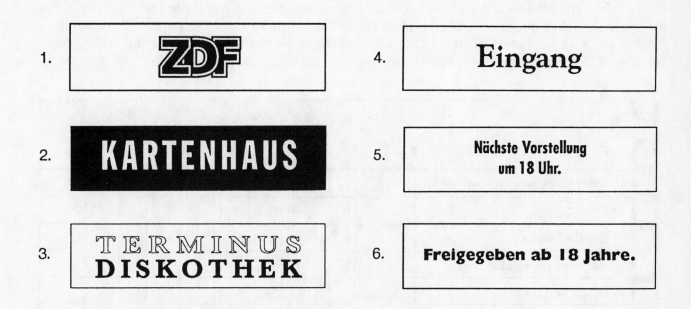

1. ZDF

4. Eingang

2. KARTENHAUS

5. Nächste Vorstellung um 18 Uhr.

3. TERMINUS DISKOTHEK

6. Freigegeben ab 18 Jahre.

Now read the descriptions below and match them with the signs above by writing the number of the sign next to the appropriate description.

a. _____ This sign tells you how old you have to be to get into the movie.

b. _____ This sign shows you where to buy tickets.

c. _____ This sign tells you where the entrance is.

d. _____ This sign shows you a place where you can dance.

e. _____ This sign tells you when the next movie showing is.

f. _____ This is the sign of the German TV station **Zweites Deutsches Fernsehen.**

g. _____ This sign tells you the name of an Italian rock group.

S. Gehen wir ins Kino. In this video segment you will see a listing of movies at the various cinemas in the area. Put the machine on pause when you get to the right spot and check off what's playing where on the chart below. Some of the titles are translations from English. Try to find them and write the original English title next to them. Discuss the following questions with a partner: Which of the films would you like to see? What kind of films are being shown? Do the titles sound like they might be violent? What countries do the films come from?

Filme	Kinos	Ambo 1	Ambo 2	Atelier 1	Atelier 2	Atrium	Kleines Haus	Bambi 1	Bambi 2	Cinema	City
Akira Kurosawas Träume											
Big											
Camille Claudel											
Die fabelhaften Baker-Boys											
Drugstore-Cowboy											
Eine Wahnsinnsfamilie											
Eine Welt ohne Mitleid											
Einstein junior											
Kuck mal, wer da spricht											
9 1/2 Wochen											
Pretty Woman											
Sea of Love											
Spiel mir das Lied vom Tod											

P
5

Schilder und Zeichen

Parkplatz 5 shows you several of the signs that must be heeded by drivers, cyclists, and pedestrians in Germany. Watch the segment and then try to match the signs with the descriptions below.

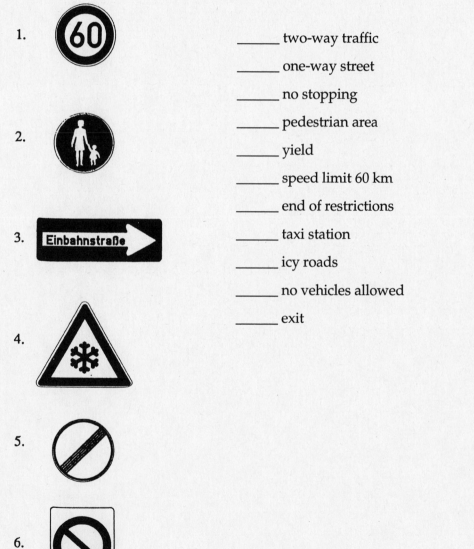

1.

2.

3. Einbahnstraße

4.

5.

6. TAXI

_____ two-way traffic

_____ one-way street

_____ no stopping

_____ pedestrian area

_____ yield

_____ speed limit 60 km

_____ end of restrictions

_____ taxi station

_____ icy roads

_____ no vehicles allowed

_____ exit

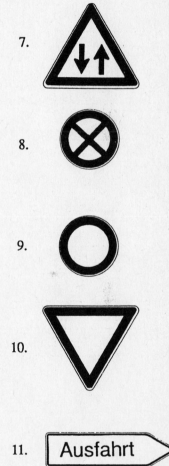

7.

8.

9.

10.

11. Ausfahrt

6. Treffpunkt: Café am Ballplatz

EINLEITUNG

A. Vorschau. In this segment Susanne finds Erika, Uwe, and Nicole in the Café am Ballplatz and invites them on the excursion to Bacharach. Uwe gets too friendly with Nicole for Erika's taste, which leads Erika to take drastic measures. Finally, there is a reconciliation between the two. Meanwhile, Nicole is left sitting with Susanne wondering how she is going to get to her driving lesson.

- What looks different in the opening scene outside the café?
- How does the café compare to hangouts for the young in your area?
- Why does Erika look at Susanne's arm?
- What kinds of drinks do the friends order in the café?
- What kind of relationship do Uwe and Erika have?
- Does Erika's and Uwe's relationship seem to be going well?
- Nicole has a problem. What kind of problem might that be?
- How does Nicole get to her driving lesson?

B. Besondere Ausdrücke. Here are some words and idiomatic expressions that you will hear in this segment. Read through the list to get acquainted with the expressions and listen for them as you watch the video. Try memorizing the ones that you think would be most useful to you.

Wieso?	*How come?*
Wir haben einen Ausflug vor.	*We're planning an excursion.*
Na gut, da kann man nichts machen.	*Oh, well. There's nothing you can do about that.*
Alles klar.	*OK.*
Was für ein schöner Armreif.	*What a nice bracelet!*
eifersüchtig	*jealous*
Die spinnt doch.	*She's crazy!*
Was hast du denn?	*What's the matter with you?*
Laß' mich in Ruhe.	*Leave me alone.*
Du nimmst dir allerhand heraus.	*You really take the cake.*
Sei doch nicht böse.	*Don't be angry.*
Was ist denn los?	*What's the matter?*
So ein Pech.	*What rotten luck. What a bummer.*

AM TISCH

C. Ich hab's gesehen. Watch *Haltestelle 6a* with the sound off and write in German the names of the objects on the table, on the chairs, or on the floor. Also, include verbs describing actions taking place in this scene.

_____   _____

_____   _____

_____   _____

_____   _____

_____   _____

D. Schauen Sie genau. Watch the video segment again with the sound off and watch for information to help you complete the statements below. Circle the choices that you think are correct based on what you see. If you don't remember who's who, refer to the portrait gallery in the *Einführung* section.

1. Susanne ist ...
    a. am Ballplatz.   b. im Park.   c. am Fluß.

2. Sie geht in ein ...
    a. Hotel.   b. Café.   c. Restaurant.

3. Am Tisch sitzen ...
    a. Erika und Uwe.   b. Nicole und Erika.   c. Erika und Karl.

4. ... gehen zusammen an die Bar.
    a. Erika und Susanne   b. Uwe und Erika   c. Uwe und Nicole

E. Hören Sie zu. Read the following list of German remarks. Then view *Haltestelle 6a* with sound. Mark each question, statement, or fragment you hear.

1. _____ ... total lustig.

2. _____ ... bei mir in der Klasse.

3. _____ ... in der Schule gesehen.

4. _____ ... nächste Woche Donnerstag ...

5. _____ Kommst du auch mit?

6. _____ ... leider keine Zeit.

7. _____ ... mit meinen Eltern wegfahren.

8. _____ ... heiße Schokolade.

F. Stimmt's? Read through the following statements. Then watch *Haltestelle 6a* again. Put a check mark before the statements that you think are true.

1. _____ Susanne findet Nicole, Uwe und Alex im Café am Ballplatz.

2. _____ Susanne findet Erikas Bluse total lustig.

3. _____ Erika und Susanne kennen sich nicht.

4. _____ Susanne hat Erika im Kino gesehen.

5. _____ Erika war schon mal in Bacharach.

6. _____ Auf Burg Stahleck ist eine Jugendherberge°. | youth hostel

7. _____ Erika hat nächste Woche Mittwoch keine Zeit.

8. _____ Nicole fährt mit nach Bacharach.

9. _____ Uwe hat am Mittwoch Bandprobe.

10. _____ Susanne nimmt einen Eiskaffee.

11. _____ Erika nimmt eine heiße Schokolade.

12. _____ Uwe holt die Getränke.

13. _____ Susanne hat einen schönen Armreif.

14. _____ Der Armreif hat DM 100 gekostet.

(H) 6b   DER STREIT

G. Landeskunde. One interesting expression found in this segment is **Die spinnt doch,** meaning she is crazy. In German, there are several different ways of expressing this idea. Uwe could have also said **Sie ist verrückt, Sie hat nicht alle Tassen im Schrank, Bei ihr stimmt 'was nicht im Oberstübchen** (*She's not quite right upstairs.*), **Sie hat einen Vogel, Sie hat eine Meise** (*titmouse*). Also, tapping your forehead or temple with your index finger expresses the same idea. However, if you do this on the road in Germany as a commentary on someone else's driving, you could be fined . . . even if you're right.

H. Ich hab's gesehen. Watch *Haltestelle 6b* with the sound off and write in German the names of any objects which can be consumed or worn. Include the gender if you know it.

_____   _____

_____   _____

_____   _____

I. Schauen Sie genau. Watch the video segment again with the sound off and watch for information to help you complete the statements below. Circle the choices that you think are correct based on what you see.

1. Nicole und Uwe stehen an der Bar und ...
    a. reden.
    b. trinken.
    c. lesen.

2. Erika ist ...
    a. böse.
    b. froh.
    c. müde.

3. Uwe gibt Erika ...
    a. einen Kuß.
    b. einen Armreif.
    c. eine Halskette°. | necklace

 J. Hören Sie zu. Read the following list of German remarks. Then view *Haltestelle 6b* with sound. Mark each question, statement, or fragment you hear.

1. _____ ... gerade 'rausgegangen.

2. _____ ... die ganze Zeit ...

3. _____ Die spinnt doch.

4. _____ Wo ist sie denn?

5. _____ Laß' mich in Ruhe.

6. _____ ... eine ganze Stunde ...

7. _____ Sei doch nicht böse.

8. _____ ... nichts Wichtiges ...

9. _____ ... auf den Ausflug ...

K. Ich hab's verstanden. Read through the following items. Then watch *Haltestelle 6b* again. Circle the letter of the choices that you think best complete the sentence.

1. Susanne sagt Uwe, Erika ...
   a. ist aus dem Café 'rausgegangen.
   b. ist nach Hause gegangen.
   c. ist mit Karl ins Kino gegangen.

2. Susanne sagt, Erika ist ...
   a. verliebt in Alex.
   b. eifersüchtig auf Nicole.
   c. böse auf Uwe.

3. Uwe hat ...
   a. die ganze Zeit nichts gesagt.
   b. Erika die ganze Zeit warten lassen.
   c. die ganze Zeit mit Nicole geredet.

4. Erika sagt, sie hat ... auf Uwe gewartet.
   a. eine halbe Stunde
   b. mehr als eine halbe Stunde
   c. weniger als eine halbe Stunde

5. Uwe geht mit Erika ...
   a. ins Café.
   b. auf den Ausflug.
   c. nach Italien.

6. Uwe ...
   a. holt Erika am Mittwoch ab.
   b. wartet auf Erika am Mittwoch im Café.
   c. geht am Mittwoch mit Nicole auf den Ausflug.

7. Erika ist auf Uwe ... böse.
   a. noch
   b. nicht mehr

(H) 6c **WIEDER AM TISCH**

L. Landeskunde. Nicole is learning how to drive. In Germany you must be at least 18 years old to get a driver's license. Everyone is required to take driving lessons, which are very intensive and very expensive. Part of the program includes taking a first aid course. Cars with automatic transmissions are not as common in Germany as in the U.S. Therefore, the driving lessons and the road test are taken in a manual shift car.

M. Ich hab's gesehen! Watch *Haltestelle 6c* with the sound off and write in German the names of the objects outside the café. Include the gender if you know it.

_____   _____

_____   _____

_____   _____

_____   _____

N. Schauen Sie genau. Watch the video segment again with the sound off. Check the statements that you think are true based on what you see.

1. _____ Niemand sitzt draußen vor dem Café.

2. _____ Uwe und Erika gehen zurück ins Café.

3. _____ Susanne spricht mit Nicole.

4. _____ Susanne und Nicole essen Kuchen.

5. _____ Susanne und Nicole trinken heiße Schokolade.

6. _____ Susanne hält einen Löffel in der Hand.

7. _____ Nicole hält eine Gabel in der Hand.

8. _____ Auf der Straße stehen zwei Autos.

9. _____ Es ist Abend.

10. _____ An der Bar sitzen zwei Männer und drei Frauen.

11. _____ Am Ende dieser Szene ist Nicole wieder froh.

O. Hören Sie zu. Read the following list of German remarks. Then view *Haltestelle 6c* with sound. Mark each question, statement, or fragment you hear.

1. _____ ... so etwas passieren.

2. _____ Was ist mit Uwe los?

3. _____ ... jetzt sind die beiden weg.

4. _____ Schade.

5. _____ So ein Pech.

6. _____ ... ganz dringend ...

7. _____ Das ist kein Problem.

8. _____ ... ganz schnell ...

9. _____ ... den Tee zu Ende trinken.

10. _____ Alles klar.

P. Stimmt's? Read through the following statements. Then watch *Haltestelle 6c* again. Put a check mark before the statements that you think are true.

1. _____ Nicole hat ein Problem.

2. _____ Susanne will weggehen.

3. _____ Nicole spricht mit Susanne über ihr Problem.

4. _____ Erika und Uwe sind weg.

5. _____ Erika und Uwe holen sich etwas zu trinken.

6. _____ Nicole hat es eilig°. | is in a hurry

7. _____ Sie hat in einer Stunde Klavierunterricht°. | piano lesson

8. _____ Sie hat bald eine Fahrstunde.

9. _____ Susanne hat auch eine Fahrstunde.

10. _____ Susanne ist mit dem Auto da.

11. _____ Nicole möchte ihren Eiskaffee zu Ende trinken.

12. _____ Nicole fährt mit Susanne zur Fahrstunde.

NOCH EINMAL

Q. Was gibt's? Check off the objects which you see in this segment. Watch out for the tricky ones.

1. _____ Bluse

2. _____ altes Haus

3. _____ Computer

4. _____ Blumen

5. _____ Burg

6. _____ Jugendherberge

7. _____ Fernseher

8. _____ Speisekarte

9. _____ Armreif

10. _____ Telefon

11. _____ Straßenkarte

12. _____ Fahrschule

R. Ihre Meinung. Based on your observation of Erika's and Uwe's relationship, put check marks next to the statements below that you agree with. Discuss your responses with a partner or with the class. Try to justify your opinions based on what the characters said or did.

1. _____ Erika und Uwe gehören zusammen.

2. _____ Erika ist leichtgläubig°. | gullible

3. _____ Uwe ist unverläßlich°. | unreliable

4. _____ Uwe ist unverläßlich, aber nett.

5. _____ Erika hat keinen Grund, eifersüchtig zu sein.

6. _____ Nicole will mit Uwe ausgehen.

S. Streit im Café Olé. Here you see Johann and Marie in the Café Olé. Marie is angry that Johann was seen with the niece of her boss' secretary's sister, who is currently married to her cousin's gardener's son, Egbert. Try putting yourself in Johann's and Marie's shoes and write a short dialog based on the situation at hand. On the other hand, if all these relationships seem too confusing to you, make up your own soap opera situation and write an excerpt from the conversation.

P

6 **Öffentliche Verkehrsmittel**

A. Landeskunde. You will notice in this segment that vehicles for public transportation are used for advertising. Sometimes the entire vehicle is painted. On the streetcar shown here the sign reads **Erdgas, denn saubere Luft geht alle an.** (*Natural gas, because clean air is everybody's concern.*) Pollution is a major concern in Germany and in all of Europe. The thick population density and close proximity of countries make the matter particularly critical. Germany is experiencing widespread destruction of its forests (**Waldsterben**). Also, the pollution of its rivers and north coast are issues being addressed by many interested parties, especially the Greens political party (**Die Grünen**). German cities are compact and public transportation is often preferred over private transportation for the sake of convenience. Streetcars and busses are found in most cities, and larger cities like Berlin and Munich also have subway systems. Payment for public transportation is usually based on the honor system. After entering a public transportation vehicle, the passenger is expected to insert the ticket into a machine (**Entwerter**) which stamps the date and time on the ticket. Those who try to ride for free (**schwarzfahren**) run the risk of being caught during random inspections resulting in hefty fines.

 B. Was gibt's? Check off the objects and people you see in this segment.

1. _____ Haltestelle

2. _____ Straßenbahn

3. _____ Taxi

4. _____ Fahrrad

5. _____ Telefon

6. _____ Bus

7. _____ Schulkind

8. _____ Uhr

9. _____ Restaurant

10. _____ Geschäftsmann

C. Sie sind dran. Pick any scene in this *Parkplatz* and describe differences you see in public transportation compared to your area. You can describe objects, actions, or impressions. Use your imagination.

_____

_____

_____

7. Wohnungssuche: Ist das Zimmer noch frei?

EINLEITUNG

A. Vorschau.   In this segment Alex decides to strike out on his own and get a room in the city. He starts out by responding to an ad. Then he checks out the room and talks with the landlady about rearranging the room and lowering the rent.

- How are Alex's telephone manners? Is he polite? Is he pushy?
- Does he find a room on the first call?
- Does the landlady want Alex to take the room?
- What part of the house is the room in?
- What arrangements are there for showering?
- Where is the bathroom?

B. Besondere Ausdrücke.   Here are some words and idiomatic expressions that you will hear in this segment. Read through the list to get acquainted with the expressions and listen for them as you watch the video. Try memorizing the ones that you think would be most useful to you.

die Wohnungsanzeige	*apartment ad*
Ist das Zimmer noch zu haben?	*Is the room still available?*
Auf Wiederhören.	*Good-bye (on the phone).*
Bis dahin.	*Until then.*
Ich hab's noch nicht nachgemessen.	*I haven't measured it yet.*
sich den Kopf stoßen	*to hit one's head*
bequem	*comfortable*
Über den Preis werden wir uns einig.	*We'll come to an agreement on the price.*
Wann könnte ich einziehen?	*When could I move in?*
Jetzt ist das Zimmer noch bewohnt.	*The room is still occupied.*
Anfang nächster Woche	*at the beginning of next week*
Ich überlege es mir mal.	*I'll think about it.*

 **ALEX SUCHT EIN ZIMMER**

C. Landeskunde.   Finding student housing is often difficult in Germany. Universities generally cannot provide housing for all their students. Many dormitories (**Studentenheime**) are privately operated. Students sometimes rent rooms within apartments or they find private rooms. Rooms usually have a sink but the bathroom is often outside the room and shared with several residents of the building. Universities have bulletin boards where students can hang up announcements for rooms or roommates.

D. Ich hab's gesehen. Watch *Haltestelle 7a* with the sound off and write in German the names of the objects you see. Include the gender if you know it.

_____   _____

_____   _____

_____   _____

 E. Schauen Sie genau. Watch the video segment again with the sound off and watch for information to help you complete the statements below. Circle the choices that you think are correct based on what you see.

1. Alex findet eine Wohnungsanzeige ...
   a. in der Zeitung.   b. an einer Tafel.   c. an einer Litfaßsäule° | column for advertisements

2. Er ruft ... an.
   a. einmal   b. zweimal   c. dreimal

3. Er fährt mit ... zur Wohnung.
   a. dem Taxi   b. dem Bus   c. der Straßenbahn

4. Die Telefonzelle ist ...
   a. blau.   b. gelb.   c. rot.

F. Hören Sie zu. Read the following list of German remarks. Then view *Haltestelle 7a* with sound. Mark each question, statement, or fragment you hear.

1. _____ ... Wohnungsanzeige.

2. _____ Kann man nichts machen.

3. _____ Ich suche ein Zimmer.

4. _____ Auf Wiedersehen.

5. _____ ... noch einmal wiederholen ...

6. _____ In der Nähe des Hauptbahnhofs.

7. _____ ... leider nicht ...

8. _____ Bis dahin.

Name _____ Date _____

G. Stimmt's? Read through the following statements. Then watch *Haltestelle 7a* again. Put a check mark before the statements that you think are true.

1. _____ Alex hat die Wohnung in einer Anzeige gefunden.

2. _____ Alex hat nicht genug Geld fürs Telefon.

3. _____ Das Telefon ist kaputt.

4. _____ Das erste Zimmer ist noch zu haben.

5. _____ Alex findet ein Zimmer, das noch zu haben ist.

6. _____ Alex will sich das Zimmer ansehen.

7. _____ Eine Frau will das Telefon benützen.

8. _____ Das Zimmer ist in der Nähe des Hauptbahnhofs.

9. _____ Die Frau am Telefon sagt Alex, wie er zu der Wohnung hinkommt.

(H) 7b UNTEN AN DER TÜR

H. Landeskunde. In Germany the bathroom situation can be quite different from what Americans are used to. Instead of a bathroom, there is often a WC (*water closet*) with the toilet and a separate room with the sink and bathtub. The washroom may also have a washing machine and a water heater. In a rental situation it is common for landlords and landladies to share their showers and kitchens with the renters.

 I. Ich hab's gesehen. Watch *Haltestelle 7b* with the sound off and write in German the names of the objects which you see. Include the gender if you know it.

_____   _____

_____   _____

_____   _____

 J. Schauen Sie genau. Watch the video segment again with the sound off and watch for information to help you complete the statements below. Circle the choices that you think are correct based on what you see.

1. Die Frau hat ... Haare.
   a. blonde   b. braune   c. rote

2. An der Wand hinter der Frau hängt ein Foto von ...
   a. einer Katze.   b. einem Haus.   c. einem Kind.

3. Die Frau spricht mit ...
   a. Alex.   b. Alex und ihrem Mann.   c. Alex und ihrer Tochter.

4. Die Frau und Alex ...
   a. gehen nach oben.   b. bleiben vor der Tür stehen.   c. gehen nach unten.

K. Hören Sie zu. Read the following list of German remarks. Then view *Haltestelle 7b* with the sound on. Mark each question, statement, or fragment you hear.

1. _____ ... wegen des Zimmers.

2. _____ Ist es noch frei?

3. _____ Es ist unten.

4. _____ ... die Treppe hochgehen ...

5. _____ ... neben dem Zimmer ...

6. _____ ... in der Wohnung ...

7. _____ ... in der Küche ...

8. _____ ... wie groß ...

9. _____ Ich mache die Tür auf.

10. _____ Gehen wir hoch.

L. Ich hab's verstanden. Read through the following items. Then watch *Haltestelle 7b* again. Circle the letter of the choices that you think best complete the sentence.

1. Das Zimmer ist ...
   a. noch frei.
   b. noch nicht frei.
   c. nicht mehr frei.

2. Es ist ...
   a. im Keller.
   b. oben.
   c. im 1. Stock.

3. Die Toilette ist ...
   a. neben dem Zimmer.
   b. im Keller.
   c. in der Wohnung von Frau Drost.

4. Die Dusche ist ...
   a. neben dem Zimmer.
   b. im Keller.
   c. in der Wohnung von Frau Drost.

5. Frau Drost sagt, das Zimmer ist ...
   a. schön.
   b. bequem.
   c. groß.

6. Alex ...
   a. möchte das Zimmer sehen.
   b. will ein anderes Zimmer suchen.
   c. will später zurückkommen.

7. Frau Drost holt ...
   a. ihren Mann.
   b. die Schlüssel.
   c. ihre Schuhe.

 **7c** **OBEN IM DACHZIMMER**

 M. Ich hab's gesehen! Watch *Haltestelle 7c* with the sound off and write in German the names of the objects in the room which you can identify. Include the gender if you know it.

_____   _____

_____   _____

_____   _____

_____   _____

_____   _____

 N. Schauen Sie genau. Watch the video segment again with the sound off. Check the statements that you think are true based on what you see. Some items might be subjective. Be prepared to justify your answer if your instructor calls upon you to do so.

1. _____ Das Zimmer hat ein Fenster.

2. _____ Das Zimmer hat eine Heizanlage°. | heating system

3. _____ Die Kommode ist alt.

4. _____ An der Wand hängt ein Bild von einem See und Bergen.

5. _____ Das Bett sieht modern aus.

6. _____ Das Bett ist zu kurz für Alex.

7. _____ Das Bett hat eine Decke°. | blanket

8. _____ Die Wände sind rot.

9. _____ Das Zimmer ist sehr groß.

10. _____ Das Zimmer ist hell.

11. _____ Die Frau wird plötzlich sehr unfreundlich zu Alex.

12. _____ Alex fährt mit der Straßenbahn zurück.

O. Hören Sie zu. Read the following list of German remarks. Then view *Haltestelle 7c* with sound. Mark each question, statement, or fragment you hear.

1. _____ ... unter dem Dach.

2. _____ ... es gefällt mir.

3. _____ ... ein sehr schönes Bett.

4. _____ ... sehr bequem.

5. _____ ... an die Wand stellen.

6. _____ Machen wir das.

7. _____ ... eine Frage zum Preis.

8. _____ Es ist etwas zu teuer.

9. _____ ... bis zum Ende der Woche.

P. Stimmt's? Read through the following statements. Then watch *Haltestelle 7c* again. Put a check mark before the statements that are true.

1. _____ Alex denkt, die Decke° ist zu niedrig. | ceiling

2. _____ Alex findet das Bett schön.

3. _____ Das Bett ist nicht sehr lang, aber sehr bequem.

4. _____ Im Zimmer gibt es eine Kommode, einen Schrank und einen Schreibtisch.

5. _____ Frau Drost hat einen Schreibtisch im Keller.

6. _____ Der Schreibtisch ist klein.

7. _____ Alex will den Schreibtisch unter das Fenster stellen.

8. _____ Frau Drost will das Bett unter das Fenster stellen.

9. _____ Alex findet den Preis zu hoch.

10. _____ Das Zimmer ist noch bewohnt.

11. _____ Am Montag kann Alex einziehen°. | move in

12. _____ Alex nimmt das Zimmer.

Q. Ihr Zimmer. You are a student at the Universität Heidelberg and have just found a room in the old city. You would like to rearrange the room to suit your taste. Draw arrows from the furniture pieces listed on the right to the desired part of the room. Then describe in short sentences where each item is located.

► *Der Schreibtisch ist am Fenster.*

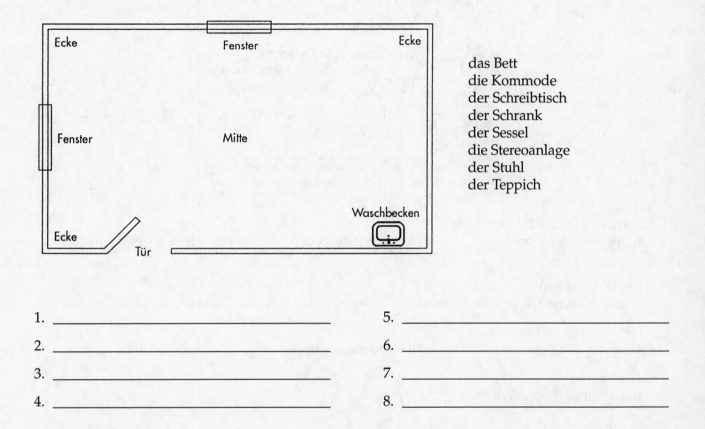

das Bett
die Kommode
der Schreibtisch
der Schrank
der Sessel
die Stereoanlage
der Stuhl
der Teppich

1. _____   5. _____

2. _____   6. _____

3. _____   7. _____

4. _____   8. _____

NOCH EINMAL

R. Landeskunde. In this scene, notice the light switch in the stairwell. It's on a timer which gives a person enough time to get to the door and enter the apartment before turning itself off.

S. Was gibt's? Check off the objects which you see in this segment. Watch out for the tricky ones.

1. _____ Wohnungsanzeige

2. _____ Telefonbuch

3. _____ Haltestelle

4. _____ Sportgeschäft

5. _____ Straßenbahn

6. _____ Klingel°

7. _____ Fernseher

8. _____ Türklinke° | door handle

9. _____ Fahrrad

10. _____ WC

11. _____ Schlüssel

12. _____ Radio | bell

T. Wohnungsanzeige. Here you see two apartment ads. One is for the apartment that Alex looked at. The other is an ad from some people looking for a roommate. Read the ads carefully and circle the statements that you think are correct based on what you read.

> Wir bieten
> für Student/in
> Zimmer mit Bad, separat unter
> dem Dach,
> bei Familie Drost, Mainz-
> Innenstadt
> DM 500,- incl.
>
> Telefon 06131/17302

1. The Drost family is looking for . . .
   a. male students only.   b. female students only.   c. either male or female students.

2. The DM 500 rent . . .
   a. does not include heat and utilities.   b. includes heat and utilities.

3. The Drost's apartment is . . .
   a. near a bus stop.   b. hard to reach without a car.   c. in the downtown area.

4. The room is . . .
   a. part of a larger apartment.   b. separate.

> Suchen zum 07. 08.
> Mitbewohner/-in für 3er WG.
> 15 m² - 300.- DM + Strom
> in Nieder-Olm/Essenheim
> auf dem Lande... Ohne Auto nur mit
> Strapazen zu erreichen

| der Strom electricity

| die Strapaze hardship

5. This apartment is . . .
   a. near a bus stop.   b. hard to reach without a car.   c. in the downtown area.

6. There is room for . . . occupants.
   a. two   b. three   c. four

7. There is/are already . . . people in the apartment.
   a. one   b. two   c. three

236   Video Workbook / 7. Wohnungssuche

| 7 | **Am Bahnhof** |

A. Landeskunde.   Here you will see a typical German train station. Trains are still a very common mode of transportation in Europe. Even school children may take the commuter train to school. German trains offer first and second class accommodations which differ in the number of passengers per compartment and the comfort of the seats. Signs are placed at each track showing the destination and main stops along the way. All major cities and most villages are accessible by train. Students can get major discounts on the **Bundesbahn.** Do you think the people depicted here are long-distance travelers or commuters?

You will notice people shaking hands in this segment. Germans shake hands at virtually every opportunity whether they are strangers or good friends. The custom of shaking hands originated as a means of displaying that you were not carrying any weapons. In the final scene of this segment you will see a panoramic view of a village on the Rhine. Notice the layout of the houses with vineyards in the back.

B. Schilder.   While watching the segment **Am Bahnhof,** circle the numbers of the signs below which you see. Although you may not know what the words on the signs mean, try to guess the meaning by the context shown in the video. The signs may be on buildings or vehicles.

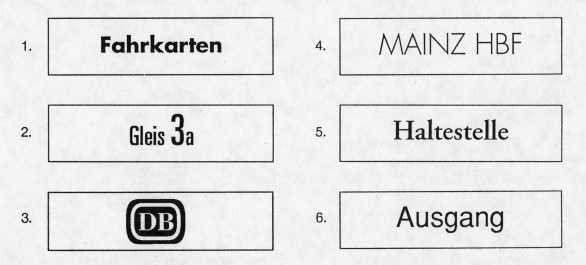

Now read the descriptions below and match them with the corresponding sign above by writing the number of the sign next to the appropriate description.

a. _____ This sign shows you the way out.

b. _____ This sign tells you which track you are on.

c. _____ This sign shows you where to buy tickets.

d. _____ This sign tells you that you are at the main train station of the city.

e. _____ This is the sign of the German Railway (**Deutsche Bahn**).

f. _____ This sign tells you that you are at a bus stop.

C. Was sehen Sie? Write four short sentences in German describing individuals you see and what they are doing.

_____

_____

_____

_____

8. Rheinfahrt: Ausflug nach Bacharach

EINLEITUNG

A. Vorschau. Many Germans of all ages are avid hiking enthusiasts. Hiking offers a good opportunity to get away from it all and enjoy the beauty of the countryside. Students also like to go on excursions during holidays and semester breaks. In the following segments you will see Erika, Samia, Uwe, Susanne, Karl, and Alex going on an overnight trip to Bacharach on the Rhine River. While you are watching, look for answers to the following questions:

- How do the friends travel?
- Where do they spend the night?
- Who are the optimists/pessimists in the group?
- Is there any friction between any members of the group?
- What kind of relationship do Uwe and Erika have?
- How is the weather and what role does it play in the story?

B. Besondere Ausdrücke. Here are some idiomatic expressions that you will hear in this segment of the video. Read through the list to get acquainted with the expressions and listen for them as you view the video. Try memorizing the ones that you think would be most useful to you. The items are listed in order of appearance.

Grüßt euch.	*Greetings (to you all).*
Ach, was.	*Go on!*
ein bißchen	*a (little) bit*
Keine Ahnung.	*No idea.*
Tut mir leid.	*I'm sorry.*
Ich mach's wieder gut.	*I'll make it up to you.*
Na, klar.	*Of course.*
Guck mal!	*Look!*
Wartet mal.	*Wait.*
Ist gut.	*OK.*
Ich bin hundemüde.	*I'm dog tired.*
Oh, je.	*Oh, no!*
Tja.	*Oh, well.*
Sag bloß.	*You don't say.*
Mensch.	*Man!*
Ach toll.	*Great!*
hin und zurück	*round trip*
einfach	*one-way*

 **8a** **AM UFER**

C. Landeskunde. Originally, a **Kirmes** was a fair held to celebrate a church dedication. Now, the term is used for fairs in general. In Mainz the **Kirmes** is called **Johannisnächte** and begins around June 24, the name day of St. John the Baptist. It continues for several days and is the largest festival in Mainz after Carnival (**Fasching**).

 D. Schauen Sie genau. Watch *Haltestelle 8a* with the sound off and write in German the names of the objects you see.

_____   _____

_____   _____

_____   _____

_____   _____

 E. Ihre Meinung. Watch the video segment again with the sound off and watch for information to help you complete the statements below. Circle the best choice based on what you see.

1. Die Stadt ist ...
   a. alt.   b. modern.   c. alt und modern.

2. Das Wetter ist ...
   a. sonnig.   b. regnerisch.   c. zu heiß.

3. Die Freunde treffen sich ...
   a. am Bahnhof.   b. am Ufer°.   c. am Flughafen. | shore

4. Auf dem Fluß sieht man ein ...
   a. Schiff.   b. U-Boot.   c. Segelboot°. | sailboat

5. Zwei Personen tragen einen ... Regenschirm.
   a. gelben   b. roten   c. bunten

F. Hören Sie zu. Read the following list of German remarks. Then view *Haltestelle 8a* with sound. Mark each question, statement, or fragment you hear.

1. _____ Grüß euch.

2. _____ Guten Tag.

3. _____ ... es gießt in Strömen.

4. _____ ... nur ein bißchen.

5. _____ Außerdem wurde im Radio Sonne angesagt°. | forecast

6. _____ ... immer am Freitag regnet's.

7. _____ ... das Wetter wird noch schlechter.

8. _____ ... wo ist denn Susanne?

9. _____ Keine Ahnung.

10. _____ Oh, je!

11. _____ Er kommt schon wieder zu spät.

G. Ich hab's verstanden. Read through the following items. Then watch *Haltestelle 8a* again. Complete the items by circling the letter of the correct choice.

1. Susanne hat versprochen, daß ...
   a. die Sonne scheint.
   b. das Schiff pünktlich ankommt.
   c. sie Schokolade kauft.

2. Im Radio wurde ...
   a. Schnee angesagt.
   b. Sonne angesagt.
   c. Regen angesagt.

3. Am Ufer wird ... gefeiert.
   a. Weihnachten
   b. das Oktoberfest
   c. eine Kirmes

4. Karl ...
   a. ist schon in Bacharach.
   b. hat sich wieder verspätet°.
   c. wartet schon auf dem Schiff. | was late

AN BORD

H. Landeskunde. Burg Rheinstein, across the river from Assmannshausen, is one of the most beautiful castles on the Rhine. It was originally used in the 14th century by the Archbishop of Mainz for collecting customs taxes and was reconstructed in 1825 by Prince Frederick of Prussia. Also, notice the heavy barge traffic that can be seen through the windows of the boat. The Rhine and its tributaries have been a major means for transporting cargo for centuries. It is possible to go from Holland to Switzerland on the Rhine.

I. Schauen Sie genau. Watch *Haltestelle 8b* with the sound off and write in German the names of the objects and people that you see. In the right column write the corresponding action being performed by that object or person(s).

Objects/People	Actions
_____	_____
_____	_____
_____	_____
_____	_____
_____	_____

J. Ihre Meinung. Watch the video segment again with the sound off and watch for information to help you complete the statements below. Circle the best choice based on what you see.

1. Das Schiff hat ...
   a. viele Passagiere°.
   b. nur acht Passagiere.
   c. keine Passagiere. | passengers

2. Die Freunde ... auf dem Schiff.
   a. tanzen
   b. singen
   c. essen und trinken

3. Auf dem Fluß sieht man ...
   a. Segelboote.
   b. andere Schiffe.
   c. kein Schiff.

K. Hören Sie zu. Read the following list of German remarks. Then view *Haltestelle 8b* with sound. Mark each question, statement, or fragment you hear.

1. _____ Die hab' ich im Bus getroffen.

2. _____ Tut mir leid.

3. _____ Wir gehen zusammen mit Tino.

4. _____ Ich freue mich.

5. _____ Ich lad' dich ein.

6. _____ ... deine Schokolade ...

L. Ich hab's verstanden. Read through the following statements. Then watch *Haltestelle 8b* again. Complete the statements by circling the letter of the correct choice.

1. Uwe hat Samia ... getroffen.
   a. im Bus   b. im Zug   c. auf dem Schiff

2. Erika ist böse auf Uwe. Er ...
   a. hat die Fahrkarten vergessen.   b. hat sich wieder verspätet.   c. sollte Erika abholen.

3. Susanne ...
   a. hat Hunger.   b. ist krank.   c. ist müde.

 **IN BACHARACH**

M. Landeskunde. The castle, **Burg Stahleck,** was built in the 12th century and is located in the hills above Bacharach. In 1925 part of the castle was converted to a youth hostel. The town of **Bacharach** has some fine examples of medieval half-timbered architecture known as **Fachwerk.** At the end of this scene the friends pose for a group photograph and say **Schneekoppe** as English speakers would say "cheese." The **Schneekoppe** is actually the highest mountain in the **Riesengebirge** on the border between the Czech Republic and Poland. **Schneekoppe** is also the name of a company that makes a cereal similar to Granola. In this scene the friends are imitating a well-known commercial for the **Schneekoppe** company.

 N. Schauen Sie genau. Watch *Haltestelle 8c* with the sound off and write in German the names of the objects which you see. In the right column write adjectives describing the objects which you have listed.

Objects	**Descriptions**
_____	_____
_____	_____
_____	_____
_____	_____

O. Ihre Meinung. Watch the video segment again with the sound off and watch for information to help you complete the statements below. Circle the best choice based on what you see.

1. In Bacharach ...
   a. wird das Wetter besser. b. bleibt das Wetter gleich. c. wird das Wetter schlechter.

2. Die Freunde besuchen ...
   a. eine alte Burg. b. eine alte Kirche. c. ein altes Museum.

3. Alex sucht etwas in ...
   a. seiner Tasche. b. seinem Rucksack. c. seinem Koffer.

4. Ein Mädchen findet ...
   a. seinen Regenschirm. b. seine Kamera. c. sein Radio.

P. Hören Sie zu. Read the following list of German remarks. Then view *Haltestelle 8c* with sound. Mark each question, statement, or fragment you hear.

1. _____ Guck mal.

2. _____ ... wir warten dann draußen ...

3. _____ ... bitte schön.

4. _____ .... herrliche Aussicht ...

5. _____ ... meine Kamera ist im Schiff.

6. _____ ... das Bild machen.

7. _____ OK, setzen Sie sich hierhin.

Q. Stimmt's? Read through the following statements. Then watch *Haltestelle 8c* again. Put a check mark before the statements which are true.

1. _____ Das Wetter in Bacharach ist sonnig und mild.

2. _____ Die Freunde übernachten in einer Jugendherberge.

3. _____ Die Mädchen schlafen im zweiten Stockwerk.

4. _____ Die Jungen schlafen im obersten Stockwerk.

5. _____ Bettwäsche° kann man für 4,— DM ausleihen. | bed linens

6. _____ Die Duschen° sind kaputt. | showers

7. _____ Das Frühstück gibt es nur im Keller.

8. _____ Alex hat seine Kamera verloren.

9. _____ Jemand hat die Kamera auf dem Schiff gefunden.

10. _____ Wenn Alex das Foto macht, sagen die Freunde „Käse".

R. Jugendherberge. Imagine that you operate a youth hostel in Salzburg, Austria which is currently under investigation by the Ministry of Tourism. The Ministry has required you to fill out the following questionnaire. Please answer honestly. Your reputation (and your license) are at stake. The video segment in the youth hostel (*Haltestelle 8c*) has the information you will need to do this. (**Note:** *Remember, the currency in Austria is the Österreichischer Schilling (öS). There are about öS 7,— in a German Mark (DM) and öS 10,— in a US dollar.*)

1. Was kostet eine Übernachtung? _____

2. Kann man Bettwäsche ausleihen? _____

3. Um wieviel Uhr schließt das Tor? _____

4. Um wieviel Uhr muß man die Jugendherberge verlassen? _____

5. Ist Rauchen verboten? _____

6. Wo ist die Dusche? _____

7. Wo ist der Frühstücksraum? _____

8. Wo schlafen die Mädchen? _____

9. Wo schlafen die Jungen? _____

NOCH EINMAL

S. Landeskunde. The **Mäuseturm** (*Mouse Tower*) is a tower on an island in the middle of the Rhine River near Bingen. It was built in the 13th century and was later turned into a signal tower to guide ships through the dangerous Binger Loch, a narrow part of the river.

T. Schilder. While watching the segment *Noch einmal*, circle the numbers of the signs below which you see.

1. Milka

2. DJH

3. Bingen

4. Wir schliessen um 21⁵⁰

5. Rauchen verboten

6. Geschlossen

Now read each description below and match it to its corresponding sign on page 245 by writing the number of the sign next to the appropriate description.

a. _____ This sign shows the name of a town on the Rhine.

b. _____ This sign tells you that smoking is not allowed.

c. _____ This sign shows the name of a chocolate company.

d. _____ This sign tells you that the establishment is closed.

e. _____ This is the sign used by German youth hostels.

f. _____ This sign tells when the gate at the youth hostel closes in the evening.

U. Dolmetscher. You are a professional interpreter in Chicago and have been hired by American Manufacturing, Inc. to interpret for Herr Kainzbauer, an Austrian manufacturer. Lisa Roth, CEO of American Manufacturing, is showing Herr Kainzbauer the sights in Chicago. Read the dialogue below and write your translation in the blanks on the right. Remember, a lot of money is riding on this.

Lisa R.:   Oh, no. It's raining again.   1. _____

Herr K.:   *Es tröpfelt nur ein bißchen.*   2. _____

Lisa R.:   That's typical for Chicago.   3. _____

Herr K.:   *Was ist das für ein Gebäude?*   4. _____

Lisa R.:   It's the Sears Tower.   5. _____ der Sears Tower.

Herr K.:   *Toll! Ich mache ein Bild davon.*   6. _____

   Oh, je. Meine Kamera ist kaputt.   7. _____

Lisa R.:   What's wrong?   8. _____

Herr K.:   *Keine Ahnung.*   9. _____

Lisa R.:   No problem. Here's my camera.   10. _____

German-English Vocabulary

The German-English vocabulary contains the basic words and expressions that appear in the video and the video workbook.

der Abend, -e evening
das Abendessen supper, dinner
abends in the evening
aber but, however
ab·holen to call for, to pick up
das Abitur final comprehensive examination at **Gymnasium**
ab·räumen to clear, to remove
der Action-Film, -e action movie
der Action-Krimi, -s crime movie
ähnlich similar
die Ahnung, -en idea, notion
die Algebra algebra
alle all, everyone
allein alone
allerdings though
allerhand quite a lot
alles all, everything
als than; as; when
also well; OK; then
alt (ä) old
älter older
altmodisch old-fashioned
das Altstadtcafé name of a café located in the old part of town
die Ananas, - pineapple
an·bauen to cultivate, to grow
ander- other
der Anfang, ⸚e beginning
an·nehmen (i; nahm an) to assume
der Anruf, -e telephone call
an·rufen (angerufen) to telephone, to call
an·sagen to announce
anscheinend apparently
die Anzeige, -n advertisement
der Apfel, ⸚ apple
die Apfelsine, -n orange
die Apotheke, -n pharmacy
die Aprikose, -n apricot
die Arbeit, -en work
arbeiten to work
die Arbeitsstelle, -n work place; job
das Armband, ⸚er bracelet
die Armbanduhr, -en wrist watch
der Armreif, -en bangle
die Artischocke, -n artichoke
auch also, too
auf·bauen to put up
die Aufgabe, -n lesson, homework
auf·passen to watch out
auf·schlagen (ä; schlug auf) to open (books)

auseinander apart
der Ausflug, ⸚e excursion, trip
der Ausflugsplan, ⸚e plan for an excursion
aus·füllen to fill out
aus·gehen (ging aus) to go out, to date
sich aus·kennen (ausgekannt) to know about something
aus·leihen (ausgeliehen) to borrow
außer besides, except for
außerdem besides, in addition
die Aussicht, -en view
ausverkauft sold out
der Ausweis, -e identity card
das Auto, -s car

backen (ä; gebacken) to bake
das Bad, ⸚er bath, bathroom
das Badezimmer, - bathroom
der Bahnhof, ⸚e train station
die Banane, -n banana
die Bandprobe, -n band rehearsal
die Bank, ⸚e bench
die Bar, -s bar
bauen to build
der Baum, ⸚e tree
sich bedanken to say thank you
beginnen (begonnen) to start, to begin
die Begrüßung, -en greeting, welcoming
beide both
das Beispiel, -e example
die Bekanntschaft, -en acquaintance
bekommen (bekommen) to get, to receive
bellen to bark
die Belohnung, -en reward
benutzen to use
bequem comfortable
der Berg, -e mountain
besser better
beste best
bestimmt certain(ly)
der Besuch, -e visit; company
das Bett, -en bed
die Bettwäsche bed sheets
bewohnt inhabited, occupied
bewölkt cloudy, overcast
das Bild, -er picture, photo
die Bildhauerin, -nen sculptress
billig cheap

bißchen a little bit
bitte please
blau blue
das Blaukraut red cabbage
bleiben (ist geblieben) to remain, to stay
der Bleistift, -e pencil
der Bleistiftspitzer, - pencil sharpener
bloß only
die Blume, -n flower
das Blumengeschäft, -e flower shop
der Blumenladen, -läden flower shop
die Bluse, -n blouse
Bord: an Bord aboard, on board
böse bad, angry, mean
brauchen to need, to require
braun brown
der Brief, -e letter
das Brot, -e bread
das Brötchen, - roll
der Bruder, ⸚ brother
das Buch, ⸚er book
bunt colorful
die Burg, -en castle
das Burgtor, -e gate of a castle
der Bus, -se bus

das Café, -s café, coffee shop
der Clown, -s clown
die Cola, -s cola drink
der Computer, - computer

dabei with (me)
das Dach, ⸚er roof
das Dachzimmer, - attic room
dadurch thereby
daher therefore
dahin (to) there
die Dame, -n lady, woman
der Dank thanks; **vielen Dank!** many thanks!
danke thanks, thank you
danken to thank
dann then
die Decke, -n blanket; ceiling
denken (gedacht) to think
denn *flavoring word;* for, because
der Dienstag, -e Tuesday
direkt direct
die Disco, -s discotheque, dance club
die Diskussion, -en discussion

DM German Marks

doch *flavoring word;* yes!

der Dom, -e dome, cathedral

der Domplatz, ¨ e square in front of a cathedral

das Dorf, ¨ er (small) town

dort there

drauf (darauf) on it/that/them, towards it/that/them, etc.

draußen outside

dringend urgent(ly)

drinnen inside

drüben on the other side

dunkel dark

dürfen (darf) may, to be permitted to

die Dusche, -n shower

(sich) duschen to take a shower

echt really, very; genuine

das Edelweiß edelweiss (*an alpine flower*)

das Ei, -er egg

eifersüchtig jealous

eigen- own

eigentlich really, actually

eilig in a hurry

der Eindruck, ¨ e impression

die Einführung, -en introduction

ein·holen to catch up with s.th./s.b.

einig agreed, in agreement

einige some, a few

ein·kaufen to shop

der Einkaufsbummel, - shopping spree

ein·laden (ä; eingeladen) to invite

einmal once, for once

einsam lonely

ein·ziehen (ist eingezogen) to move in

das Eis ice cream

eisig icy, chilly

der Eiskaffee, -s iced coffee

die Eltern (*pl.*) parents

empfehlen (ie; empfohlen) to recommend

das Ende end

endlich finally

die Entschuldigung, -en excuse; **Entschuldigung!** excuse me, sorry

entspannend relaxed

die Erdbeere, -n strawberry

erledigen to take care of

erst only; first

erwarten to expect

erzählen to tell

essen (ißt; gegessen) to eat

das Eßzimmer, - dining room

etwa about; approximately

etwas something

das Fach, ¨ er (school) subject

fahren (ä; ist gefahren) to drive, to go

das Fahrrad, ¨ er bicycle

die Fahrstunde, -n driving lesson

die Fahrtrichtung, -en direction in which one is traveling

falsch wrong

die Familie, -n family

fast almost

die Federmappe, -n pencil case

feiern to celebrate

der Feiertag, -e holiday

fein fine

das Fenster, - window

das Fernsehen television

fest firm

die Festhalle concert hall in Frankfurt/Main

der Film, -e movie

finden (gefunden) to find

flach flat

der Flur, -e hallway

der Fluß, ¨ sse river, stream

das Foto, -s photograph

das Fotoalbum, -alben photo album

die Frage, -n question

fragen to ask

die Frau, -en woman; **Frau X** Mrs. or Ms. X

frei free

der Freitag, -e Friday

die Freizeit leisure time

fressen (i; gefressen) to eat (used for animals)

die Freude, -n joy, pleasure

sich freuen to be happy, glad

der Freund, -e/die Freundin, -nen friend

freundlich friendly

frisch fresh

froh glad, happy

der Frühling spring

das Frühstück, -e breakfast

der Fuchs, ¨ e fox

füllen to fill

für for

furchtbar terrible, terribly

der Fußboden, ¨ en floor

der Fußgänger, - pedestrian

die Fußgängerzone, -n pedestrian zone

die Gabel, -n fork

ganz quite, complete(ly)

gar: gar nicht not at all

der Garten, ¨ garden

das Gebäude, - building

geben (i, gegeben) to give

der Geburtstag, -e birthday

die Geburtstagsfeier, -n birthday party

das Geburtstagskind, -er birthday girl/boy

die Geburtstagsparty, -s birthday party

gefallen (ä; gefallen) to please; **es gefällt mir** I like it

gehen (ist gegangen) to go

das Gelächter laughter

gelb yellow

das Geld money

die Geldtasche, -n billfold

gemeinsam together, communally

gemischt mixed

das Gemurmel mumbling

das Gemüse, - vegetable

der Gemüsehändler, - vegetable grocer

genau exactly, just

gerade exact(ly), just

das Geräusch, -e noise

gern gladly, with pleasure; **gern haben** to like, to be fond of

der Gesang singing

das Geschäft, -e store

das Geschenk, -e present, gift

das Geschirr dishes

die Geschwister (*pl.*) brothers and sisters, siblings

gestern yesterday

gestreift striped

gesund healthy

das Getränk, -e beverage

gießen (gegossen) to pour

glauben to believe

gleich like, similar, alike

glücklich happy

der Goldschmied, -e goldsmith

grau grey

groß (ö) big, tall, large

die Größe, -n size; **welche Größe trägst du?** what size do you wear?

die Großeltern (*pl.*) grandparents

der Großvater, ¨ grandfather

grün green

Grüß dich hello, hi (*informal*)

grüßen to greet

gucken to look

günstig reasonable

gut good

das Haar, -e hair

haben to have; **gern haben** to like

halb half

hallo hello

die Halskette, -n necklace

halten (ä; gehalten) to hold; to stop

die Haltestelle, -n (bus or streetcar) stop

die Hand, ⸚e hand
häßlich ugly
der Hauptbahnhof, -höfe main train station
das Hauptgericht, -e main dish
das Haus, ⸚er house; nach Hause home (*direction*); zu Hause (at) home
die Hausarbeit, -en housework
die Hausaufgabe, -n homework
die Hauspflicht, -en house duty
das Heft, -e notebook
heim home
heiß hot
heißen (geheißen) to be named, called
die Heizanlage, -n heating system
helfen (i; geholfen) to help
hell light; hellorange light-orange
das Hemd, -en shirt
herauf·stellen to put on top, to put up
heraus out
der Herbst autumn, fall
der Herr, -n, -en gentleman, man; Mr.
der Herrenhut, ⸚e man's hat
herrlich marvellous, gorgeous
heute today
hier here
hierher·kommen (ist hierhergekommen) to come over here
hierhin (over) here
die Himbeere, -n raspberry
der Himmel sky, heaven
hin·fahren (ä; ist hingefahren) to drive there
hin·gehen (ist hingegangen) to go there
sich hin·setzen to sit down
hinten in the back, behind
der Hintergrund back-ground
hinterher afterwards
hoch (höher) high
das Hochgebirge high mountains
hoch·gehen (ist hochgegangen) to go up
hoffen to hope
hoffentlich I hope, let's hope
holen to pick up
hören to hear; to listen
die Hose, -n pants, slacks
das Huhn, ⸚er chicken
der Hund, -e dog
hundemüde dog-tired
der Hut, ⸚e hat

ideal ideal
die Idee, -n idea
immer always

informieren to inform
die Innenstadt center of town
interessant interesting
interessiert interested
irgendwelch- some, any
der Italiener, -/die Italienerin, -nen Italian (person)
italienisch Italian

ja yes; *flavoring particle*
die Jacke, -n suit coat, jacket
das Jahr, -e year
die Jeans jeans
die Jeans-Jacke, -n jeans-jacket
jeder each, everyone
jemand someone
jetzt now
die Jugendherberge, -n youth hostel
jung (ü) young
der Junge, -n, -n boy
der Juwelier, -e jeweler

der Kaffee coffee
kalt (ä) cold
die Kamera, -s camera
das Kapitel, - chapter
kaputt broken
die Karotte; -n carrot
die Karte, -n ticket; postcard; menu; cards
die Kartoffel, -n potato
der Käse cheese
die Kasse, -n box office, cashier
die Katze, -n cat
kaufen to buy
kein not a, not any
der Keller, - cellar, basement
kennen (gekannt) to know, to be acquainted with
kennen·lernen to get to know
das Kilo, -s kilogram (= 2.2 American pounds)
das Kind, -er child
der Kindergesang children's singing
der Kinderwagen, - baby carriage
die Kindheit childhood
das Kino, -s movie theater
der Kinoteil movie listings in a newspaper or magazine
die Kirche, -n church
die Kirmes fair (country fair, carnival)
die Kirsche, -n cherry (fruit)
klappen to work
klar clear
klasse! terrific!
die Klasse, -n grade, class
die Klassenfahrt, -en class trip

der Klassenlehrer, -/die Klassenlehrerin, -nen homeroom teacher
das Klassenzimmer, - classroom
der Klavierunterricht, -e piano lessons
das Kleid, -er dress; *pl.* clothes
klein small, little, short
die Klingel, -n bell
kochen to cook
kommen (ist gekommen) to come
die Kommode, -n dresser
die Konditorei, -en shop serving pastries and coffee
können (kann) can, to be able to
das Konzert, -e concert
der Kopf, ⸚e head
der Kopfsalat, -e green lettuce
der Korb, ⸚e basket
das Kosmetikgeschäft, -e cosmetic store
kosten to cost
krank sick, ill
die Kreide, -n chalk
kriegen to get
die Küche, -n kitchen
der Kuchen, - cake, pie
der Kugelschreiber, - ball-point pen
kühl cool
die Kunst, ⸚e art
der Kunstlehrer, -/die Kunstlehrerin, -nen art teacher
kurz (ü) short
die Kusine, -n (female) cousin
der Kuß, ⸚sse kiss

lachen to laugh
der Laden, ⸚ store
das Land, ⸚er country, land; state
die Landkarte, -n map
lang (ä) long
langweilig boring
lassen (gelassen) to let
die Laterne, -n lantern
die Latzhose, -n overalls
laufen (äu; ist gelaufen) to run; to walk
leben to live
der Lehrer, -/die Lehrerin, -nen teacher
leicht easy
leichtgläubig gullible
leid: das tut mir leid I'm sorry
leider unfortunately
das Licht, -er light
lieber (*comp. of* gern) rather; lieber haben to like better, to prefer
der Liebesfilm, -e love film
das Lieblingsfach, ⸚er favorite subject

die Lieblingssachen (*pl.*) favorite things, clothes
das Lied, -er song
liegen (gelegen) to lie
das Lineal, -e ruler
links (to the) left
die Litfaßsäule, -n column structure for announcements
der Löffel, - spoon
los: was ist los? what's up?
los·gehen (ist losgegangen) to begin
die Lust pleasure, enjoyment; Lust haben to feel like doing something
lustig funny

machen to make, to do
das Mädchen, - girl
mähen to mow
mal times; *flavoring word*
man one, you, they, people
der Mann, ¨er man; husband
die Mappe, -n briefcase, book bag
Mark mark, (DM) German mark
der Markt, ¨e market
die Marktfrau, -en market vendor (*f.*)
der Marktplatz, ¨e market square
die Marmelade, -n jam
die Mathe math
das Mathebuch, ¨er math book
der Mathelehrer, -/die Mathelehrerin,-nen math teacher
die Mathematik mathematics
mehr more
die Meinung, -en opinion
der Mensch, -en, -en man, human being; Mensch! wow! brother! oh boy!
merken to notice
der Meter, - meter (= 39.37 inches)
die Metzgerei, -en butcher shop
der Mime, -n mime
mischen to mix
mit with
miteinander together
mit·fahren (ä; ist mitgefahren) to go, to drive with someone
mit·kommen (ist mitgekommen) to come along
mit·machen to join in
mit·schicken to send with
das Mittelgebirge low mountain range
der Mittwoch Wednesday
möchte (*form of* mögen) would like to
die Mode, -n fashion
modern modern
modisch fashionable, stylish
mögen (mag; gemocht) to like

möglich possible(ly)
die Möglichkeit, -en possibility
der Moment, -e moment
der Monat, -e month
der Montag Monday
der Morgen, - morning; guten Morgen good morning
morgen tomorrow
müde tired
die Musik music
müssen (muß) to have to, must
die Mutter, ¨ mother
Mutti mom

nach after; to
nachdem afterwards; je nachdem it depends
nach·feiern to celebrate at a later date
nachher afterwards
nach·lassen (nachgelassen) to reduce, to give in
nach·messen (nachgemessen) to measure
der Nachmittag, -e afternoon
nachmittags in the afternoon
nächst- next
die Nacht, ¨e night
nachts in the night, at night
die Nähe proximity; in der Nähe nearby
der Name, -n, -n name
nämlich namely, you know
naß wet
natürlich naturally, of course
neben next to, beside
nebeneinander next to each other
neblig foggy
nee nope (*coll.*)
nehmen (nimmt, genommen) to take
die Nektarine, -n nectarine
nervös nervous
nett nice
neu new
nicht not; nicht? = nicht wahr? isn't that so?
nichts nothing
nie never
noch still, yet
nochmal again
notwendig necessary
die Nummer, -n number
nur only, just

oben on top
oberst- highest
das Obst fruit

der Obsthändler, -/die Obsthändlerin, -nen salesperson in a fruit store
der Obstsalat, -e fruit salad
oder or
offen open
öffentlich public, openly
oft (ö) often
die Oma, -s grandma
der Onkel, - uncle
der Opa, -s grandpa
orange orange

das Papier, -e paper
der Paprika, -s pepper, paprika
die Paprikaschote, -n green, red, yellow pepper
die Party, -s party
der Passagier, -e passenger
passen to fit; to match
passieren (ist passiert) to happen; to pass
das Pech bad luck
die Person, -en person
der Pfirsich, -e peach
pink pink
die Pizza, -s pizza
der Plan, ¨e plan; schedule
der Platz, ¨e seat; square
plötzlich suddenly
politisch political
positiv positive
der Preis, -e price
prima excellent, fine, great
pro per
probieren to try (on)
das Problem, -e problem
das Programm, -e program
der Pulli, -s sweater
die Puppe, -n doll
pur pure, clean
putzen to clean
die Putzfrau, -en cleaning lady

Quatsch! nonsense! rubbish!

der Radiergummi, -s eraser
das Radio, -s radio
der Rasen, - lawn
raus out
raus·gehen (ist rausgegangen) to go out
rechts (to the) right
reden to talk, to speak
der Regenschirm, -e umbrella
regnen: es regnet it's raining
regnerisch rainy
reichen to pass somebody something

rein·gehen (ist reingegangen) to go in

reinigen to clean

reservieren to reserve

das Restaurant, -s restaurant

der Rhein Rhine river

die Rheinfahrt, -en boat trip on the Rhine

richtig right; **gerade richtig** just right

der Rock, ¨ e skirt

das Rockkonzert, -e rock concert

rot red

rufen (gerufen) to call

die Ruhe quietness; **laß mich in Ruhe** leave me alone

rund round

runter·kommen (ist runterge-kommen) to come down

die Sache, -n thing; *pl.* clothes

das Säckelchen, - little bag

sagen to say, to tell

die Salami, - salami

der Salat, -e salad; lettuce

der Samstag Saturday

die Sardelle, -n anchovy

sauer cross, annoyed; sour

der Sauerbraten, - sauerbraten

schade too bad

schauen to look

der Schauspieler, -/die Schauspie-lerin, -nen actor

scheinen (geschienen) to shine; to seem

schieben (geschoben) to push

das Schiff, -e ship

das Schild, -er sign

schlafen (ä; geschlafen) to sleep

schlecht bad

schließen (geschlossen) to close

das Schloß, ¨ sser castle, palace

der Schlüssel, - key

schmecken to taste (good)

schneiden (geschnitten) to cut, slice

schnell fast

das Schnitzel, - cutlet

die Schokolade, -n chocolate

schon already

schön beautiful; nice

der Schrank, ¨ e closet, cupboard

schreiben (geschrieben) to write

der Schreibschrank, ¨ e writing desk

schüchtern shy

der Schuh, -e shoe

die Schularbeit, -en school work

die Schule, -n school

das Schuljahr, -e school year

die Schultasche, -n schoolbag, bookbag

schütteln to shake

schwarz (ä) black

die Schwester, -n sister

das Segelboot, -e sailboat

sehen (ie; gesehen) to see, to watch, to look

sehr very

sein (ist; ist gewesen) to be

seit since, for

die Seite, -n side; page

selbst oneself, myself, *etc.*

das Semester, - semester

der Sender, - (TV or radio) station

sich setzen to sit

sicher sure, certain(ly)

sitzen (gesessen) to sit

sitzen·bleiben (ist sitzengeblieben) to repeat one year of school

so so

sogar even

der Sohn, ¨ e son

sollen (soll) should, to be supposed to

der Sommer summer

die Sonne, -n sun

sich sonnen to sunbathe

sonnig sunny

sonst in addition

spät late

später later

der Speck bacon

die Speise, -n food

die Speisekarte, -n menu

der Spiegel, - mirror

spielen to play

der Spielverderber, - spoilsport

der Spinat spinach

spinnen (gesponnen) to spin; **du spinnst** you're crazy

sprechen (i; gesprochen) to speak

spülen to rinse, to wash

die Stadt, ¨ e city, town

staubsaugen (staubsaugte, staubgesaugt) to vacuum

Staub wischen to dust

stehen (gestanden) to stand

stehen·bleiben (ist stehen-geblieben) to stop

die Stimme, -n voice

stimmen to be true, correct; **das stimmt** that's right

das Stockwerk, -e floor, story

stoßen (ö; gestoßen) to push

die Straße, -n street

die Straßenbahn, -en streetcar

der Streit, -e dispute, argument

streiten (gestritten) to argue

streng strict

der Strom, ¨ e river; **es gießt in Strömen** it's pouring

das Stück, -e piece

das Studentenheim, -e student dormitory

studieren to study

die Stunde, -n hour; class

der Stundenplan, ¨ e class schedule

suchen to look for

super great

die Suppe, -n soup

süß sweet

die Süßigkeit, -en sweet, candy

der Tag, -e day; **guten Tag** hello

der Tagesraum, ¨ e common room

die Tante, -n aunt

tanzen to dance

der Tanzkurs, -e dance lesson

die Tasche, -n pocket

die Tasse, -n cup

tauschen to exchange

die Telefonzelle, -n telephone booth

teuer expensive

das Theater, - theater

die Theatergruppe, -n theater group

der Tisch, -e table

die Tochter, ¨ daughter

die Toilette, -n restroom

toll great, fantastic

die Tomate, -n tomato

die Torte, -n (fancy layer) cake

total total, complete(ly)

tragen (ä; getragen) to wear; to carry

die Traube, -n grape

traurig sad

treffen (i; getroffen) to meet

der Treffpunkt, -e meeting place, hangout

die Treppe, -n stairs

trinken (getrunken) to drink

tröpfeln to drip; to drizzle

trotzdem nevertheless

tschüs so long, bye (*informal*)

tun (getan) to do

die Tür, -en door

die Türklinke, -n door handle

typisch typical

über about, above, over

überall everywhere

überhaupt in general, anyway

sich überlegen to think about

übermorgen the day after tomorrow

die Übernachtung, -en overnight stay

das Ufer, - shore

die Uhr, -en clock, watch

umweltfreundlich ecologically harmless

um·ziehen (ist umgezogen) to move

ungeduldig impatient

unglücklich unhappy
unheimlich eerie; tremendous(ly) (*coll.*)
uninteressant uninteresting
die Universität, -en university
der Unsinn nonsense
unten underneath, below
sich unterhalten (ä; unterhalten) to talk with someone
der Unterricht, -e lesson, instruction
unterrichten (unterrichtet) to teach
unterschreiben (unterschrieben) to sign
unverläßlich unreliable

der Vater, ⸗ father
Vati dad
verboten prohibited
vergessen (i; vergessen) to forget
der Verkäufer, -/die Verkäuferin, -nen salesperson
das Verkehrsmittel, - transportation
verlangen to demand, to request
verlieben to fall in love
verlieren (verloren) to lose
sich verspäten to be late
versprechen (i; versprochen) to promise
verstehen (verstanden) to understand
viel much, many, a lot; **vielen Dank** thanks a lot
vielleicht maybe, perhaps
das Viertel, - quarter
vorbei over
die Vorhersage, -n forecast
vorhin before
vor·stellen to introduce

die Vorstellung, -en performance

die Waage, -n scale
wahrscheinlich probably
die Wand, ⸗e wall
wandern (ist gewandert) to hike, to go hiking
das Wanderwetter hiking weather
warm (ä) warm
warten to wait
wechseln to change
weg away
weg·fahren (ä; ist weggefahren) to drive away
die Weintraube, -n grape
weiß white
weit far
weiter further
welch- which
wenig less, little
wenn if; when
werden (wird; ist geworden) to become
werfen (i; geworfen) to throw
wetten to bet
das Wetter weather
die Wettervorhersage, -n weather forecast
wichtig important
wieder again
Wiederhören: auf Wiederhören good-bye (on the phone)
Wiedersehen: auf Wiedersehen good-bye
wieviel how much
windig windy
der Winter winter
wirklich really

der Wirt, -e/die Wirtin, -nen landlord; pub owner
wischen to wipe
wissen (weiß; gewußt) to know
die Woche, -n week
das Wochenende, -n weekend
wohl indeed, probably
wohnen to live
die Wohnung, -en apartment
die Wohnungsanzeige, -n real estate ad
die Wohnungssuche search for an apartment
das Wohnzimmer, - living room
der Wolf, ⸗e wolf
wollen (will) to want, to intend to, to wish
die Wurst, ⸗e sausage

zahlen to pay
der Zauberer, - magician
das Zeichen, - symbol
zeigen to show
die Zeit, -en time
die Zeitschrift, -en magazine
die Zeitung, -en newspaper
ziehen (nach) to move (to)
ziemlich quite
das Zimmer, - room
die Zitrone, -n lemon
der Zufall, ⸗e chance, coincidence
zunächst first of all
zurück back
zusammen together
zwar in fact, actually
die Zwiebel, -n onion

Proficiency Cards

1. Warm-up

Walk around the room getting to know your fellow classmates. Give your name and ask for their names.

---

2. Spelling names

Go back to people you have met and try to remember their names. Spell their last names:

Man schreibt das S-C-H-M-I-D-T, ja?

---

3. Getting acquainted

Walk around the classroom.

1. Talk to people whose names you remember. Ask their telephone numbers and addresses.
2. Introduce yourself to people you don't know.

---

4. Asking for personal information

Make a list with the names of five people in the class.

1. Ask their telephone numbers and addresses.
2. Ask about their ages.

5. Warm-up

You are at a party with your fellow classmates. Greet people and ask how they are.

✂

6. Getting acquainted

You meet a fellow student for the first time. Get to know her/him. Find out what sports and activities she/he likes to do.

✂

7. Meeting and greeting people

You meet a fellow classmate on campus. Work out the following dialogue with a partner.

1. Greet her/him.
2. Ask how she/he is.
3. Ask what she/he is doing this afternoon.
4. Tell what you are doing.
5. Ask if she/he likes to play tennis.
6. Arrange a time to play together tomorrow.

✂

8. *Kaffeestunde*

1. Talk about the different people in your class. Make comments.
2. Ask your partner what activities she/he will engage in today and at what time.

9. Warm-up

Your partner names a month or a geographical location. You must make an appropriate comment about the weather.

---

10. Discussing the weather

With a partner, role-play the following situations. Each of you takes a role. Then reverse the roles.

1. You are visiting a friend far away from where you live. You are on the phone with someone from home. Tell her/him what the weather is like.
2. You meet a friend walking on campus during a blizzard/heat wave. Talk about the weather.
3. You see an interesting-looking person you want to meet on the beach. Start a conversation.
4. You are talking to a travel agent. You can't decide where you want to spend your next vacation. Ask about the weather in various places.

---

11. Describing people and objects

You are talking with a German friend. She/he wants to know about your first weeks at school. Tell her/him about:

1. a friend/a classmate.
2. the weather.
3. your room and its contents (size, color).

---

12. *Kaffeestunde*

1. Talk about the activities you engage in regularly.
2. Talk about the weather.
3. With your partner, look around the room. Comment on a few of the objects you see.
4. Comment on people's moods yesterday.

Pretend you are on a busy street. You are looking for a store. Walk around the room. When your instructor signals, stop. A person close to you will ask you what you are looking for. Tell her/him. Walk around until your instructor signals again. Use the name of a different store each time.

You invite a classmate back to your room or apartment for dinner.

1. She/he makes comments on your room/apartment.
2. Ask her/him what she/he likes to eat.
3. Either you don't have what she/he has mentioned or what you have is not fresh.
4. She/he asks if there is a grocery store nearby.
5. Make a list of what you will buy together for dinner.

You and your friend are in a large department store. You need to buy three items for your room. You look at different items and express your opinion about them. Your friend disagrees with you about everything.

---

1. Ask your partner about what she/he likes to eat and what she/he normally buys every week at the grocery store.
2. Ask your partner about what she/he needs to buy.

17. Warm-up

Sit in a circle of five. Each person:

1. names a subject she/he is studying.
2. says whether or not it is her/his major or minor.
3. tells what work she/he must prepare now—either a test or a report.

✂

18. Getting acquainted

You meet a fellow student in the library.

1. Ask what she/he is doing here.
2. Ask which classes she/he is taking.
3. Ask what her/his major is.
4. Ask if she/he would like to go out for coffee.
5. She/he has a test tomorrow and must study.

✂

19. Talking with fellow students

With a partner, role-play the following situations. When you are finished, switch roles.

1. You are interested in a class that your friend is taking. Ask about what work is required for the class. Ask if you can borrow her/his notes.
2. You are trying to find someone who will lend you her/his notes for last week's German class. Everyone you meet has a different reason for not lending them to you.
3. You and your roommate are discussing what you can, should, want to, and are supposed to do tonight. You decide however to go drink some coffee and listen to music.

✂

20. *Kaffeestunde*

1. Ask your partner about her/his studies.
2. Ask your partner about her/his family.
3. Use the following phrases to start conversations with your partner:

> **Ich kann ...**
> **Ich soll ...**
> **Magst du ... ?**
> **Ich muß heute ...**
> **Darfst du ... ?**

21. Warm-up

Sit in a circle of four. Two people stand in the center. One person asks questions and the other person answers. The person who runs out of things to say first (either questions or answers) sits down and is replaced by another person. In the new round, question and answer roles are reversed.

22. Discussing vacation plans

You are going home during the next vacation for someone's birthday. A friend/your roommate is interested in going with you.

1. She/he wants to know how you are getting home and where she/he can stay.
2. Tell her/him about the weather.
3. Tell her/him how she/he can get around town.
4. She/he asks what there is to do in your town.
5. She/he asks what you are giving the person with the birthday. She/he wants to give a gift as well.

She/he may ask you for further information.

23. Convincing a friend to participate in activities

You are trying to convince a friend of yours to go with you as an exchange student to Austria. Tell her/him what you know about Austria and what she/he can do there.

24. *Kaffeestunde*

1. Ask about your partner's daily routine.
2. Ask where your partner is going on her/his next vacation and with whom.
3. Discuss public transportation here. (Compare to Europe)

25. Warm-up

Sit in a group of five. One person names a room. Each of the others must name an activity or household chore that is done in that room.

---

26. Ordering in a restaurant

Role-play the following situations in groups of three. Each person takes a role. When you are finished, switch roles.

1. You are at a restaurant with a friend of yours. You are a vegetarian and she/he can't eat salt (**das Salz**) or sugar (**der Zucker**). Order accordingly.
2. You and your partner are in your favorite restaurant. Order what you like to eat most. Unfortunately the waiter doesn't have what you want.

---

27. Reporting about recent events

Your friend/roommate has just returned from a wonderful evening out with a special person. Ask her/him about it.

---

28. *Kaffeestunde*

1. Ask your partner about the last meal she/he had in a restaurant.
2. Ask your partner what she/he likes and doesn't like about the town or city your college/university is in.
3. Talk about the clothes your classmates are wearing today.

29. Warm-up

1. Walk around the room. When your teacher signals, stop. Tell the person closest to you what you are doing this afternoon and invite her/him to join you.
2. With a partner, list five things you consider characteristic of life in German-speaking countries and five you consider characteristic of life where you live. Share your ideas with another group.

✂

30. Describing spatial location

a. Draw your room

b. Draw your partner's room

When you have finished drawing your own room, describe it to your partner without showing her/him your drawing. She/he must draw according to how you describe the location of various objects. When she/he is finished, compare drawings.

Fold here

Fold here

31. Discussing vacation activities

You meet a young German traveler in a café. With a partner, prepare the conversation.

1. Ask her/him where she/he is from.
2. She/he is from Munich.
3. You were in Europe last year. Your family goes there once a year.
4. She/he asks why you go so often.
5. Your sister lives near Munich.
6. She/he asks you what you do when you are at your sister's.
7. You go into Munich everyday. On Sundays you go to the mountains. Your family likes to go hiking in the Alps.
8. Ask her/him where she/he is going in the States.
9. She/he was in New York a week ago. On Monday she/he is going to the Rockies. She/he likes to hike and will be hiking four weeks in the mountains.
10. You think that's great.
11. She/he invites you to come along.
12. Unfortunately, you have to study for tests.
13. Ask her/his name, address, and phone number for the next time you are in Europe.

---

32. *Kaffeestunde*

1. Think of how you would complete each of the following phrases. Use one of the completed sentences to start a conversation with your partner.

    Ich denke oft an ...
    Ich rede gern über ...
    Ich habe Angst vor ...
    Meine Großmutter erzählt immer von ...
    Ich höre mit ... auf./Ich höre auf mit ...
    Ich helfe meinen Freunden gern bei ...

2. Ask your partner what she/he will be doing
    a. next Monday.
    b. Saturday evening.
    c. in a year.

3. Ask what she/he was doing a year ago.

33. Warm-up

Sit in a group of five. Each person names a profession she/he would like to follow and states why.

- ✂ -

34. Interviewing for a job

You are interviewing a prospective candidate for a sales position in your computer store. Your partner is the prospective applicant. She/he has had summer sales experience during college and has a degree in computer programming. You think she/he is the right person for the job but she/he is reluctant to work Saturdays. Ask her/him about:
1. her/his educational background.
2. her/his previous work experience.
3. why she/he wants to go into sales.
4. working on Saturdays.

Offer her/him some interesting incentives to ensure that she/he accepts the position.

- ✂ -

35. Discussing housing

You are a real-estate agent with a beautiful house to sell. Describe it for your partner who is a reluctant customer. Your glowing description finally convinces her/him to buy.

- ✂ -

36. *Kaffeestunde*

1. With a partner, make comments about objects in the classroom and what people are wearing.
2. Think of how you would complete the following phrases. Use one of your completed sentences to start a conversation with your partner.

Eines Tages ...	**Wegen ...**	**Statt ...**
Trotz ...	**Während ...**	

3. Point out various objects in the room to a partner. **Wessen ... ist das? Wem gehört das?** She/he will answer.

37. Warm-up

Six people participate in a quiz game on Switzerland. Form teams of three and prepare five questions on Switzerland. The teams take turns asking their questions.

✄

38. Discussing one's health

With a partner, role-play the following conversations.

1. Your partner doesn't feel well. She/he has been up all night cramming for an exam. Ask her/him what's wrong.
2. You went skiing last weekend. It was very sunny and you fell quite a bit. Your partner asks you on Monday how you are feeling.
3. Your roommate has all the symptoms of pneumonia. Ask her/him how she/he feels and suggests she/he see a doctor.
4. You are a doctor. A patient comes to you not feeling well. She/he complains of many different symptoms. You suspect stress and suggest changes in her/his daily routine.

✄

39. Comparing academic and personal achievement

You and your partner are members of a university admissions committee. You have to decide which of the following three students you will award an athletic scholarship to.

	Noten	Tennis	Anderes
Brita Feyler	3, 7	**	Preis für Computer-Programm
Günther Weyl	3, 5	***	spielt Schach/hilft Kindern beim Lesen
Peter Weiß	3, 2	****	Präsident der Klasse

✄

40. *Kaffeestunde*

1. Talk about your daily routine.
2. **Es ist schwer / leicht / schön ...**
3. Think about a friend you know well. Your partner will ask you questions comparing the two of you, e.g., **Ist er/sie älter?**

Sit in a circle of five. One person starts a story by completing the sentence: **Als Frau Schmidt mit dem Bus zur Arbeit fahren wollte, ...** The other students must each contribute a sentence to the story's continuation.

You travel to Germany for the first time. Your partner is a young student you meet in a café.

1. Introduce yourself.
2. Ask about where and what she/he studies.
3. Ask about her/his family.
4. Ask about life in Germany.
5. She/he wants to know what you think of the country.
6. She/he invites you to meet her/his friends.

You are a television talk show host. Your guest is a well-known film star. Ask her/him about her/his life. Be sure to ask specifically about:

1. her/his life before she/he became a film star.
2. her/his career before she/he became famous.
3. the highlights of her/his career.
4. any interesting stories she/he would like to share.

---

1. Tell your partner about a funny incident that happened when you were young.
2. Think of how you would complete each of the following sentences. Then use one of the sentences to start a conversation with your partner.

> **Als ich jung war, dachte ich ...**
> **hatte ich ...**
> **wollte ich ...**
> **mußte ich ...**

Try to sell something you no longer need. Your partner is reluctant to buy it so you must convince her/him of the good qualities it has and of the advantage of owning it.

- ✂ -

You and your friend/roommate are talking about how you would live differently if you were rich (**reich**) and famous. Discuss the advantages and disadvantages.

- ✂ -

Role-play the following situations with your partner. When you are finished reverse roles.
1. Go and talk to your instructor. You have a difficult paper to write and you don't know how to approach it.
2. You are sick. Ask your friend/roommate for a glass of water. You also want something to eat.
3. You need to borrow five dollars from your aunt/uncle. Your aunt/uncle is hard of hearing and doesn't always hear what you say.
4. You want to ask a new group of friends if you can go to the movies with them.
5. Your grandmother/grandfather has to go to the bank. Suggest that she/he should be going. She/he is also hard of hearing and doesn't always take kindly to suggestions.
6. You have been paying your own tuition but you couldn't work last summer and you need money. Ask a relative if you could borrow money from her/him for next semester's tuition.

- ✂ -

Think of how you would complete the following phrases. Then use one of the sentences to start a conversation with your partner.

1. **Könnten Sie ... ?**
    Dürfte ich ... ?
    Ich wollte ...
    Sie sollten ...
    Müßte ich ... ?
2. **Wenn jetzt Ferien wären, ...**
    Wenn jetzt Samstag abend wäre, ...

49.   Warm-up

In a group of five, each person tells how she/he envisions her/his life in ten years.

---

50.   Discussing cultural events

You meet someone who loves cultural events as much as you do.

1.   Ask her/his preferences.
2.   Ask about the last event she/he attended.
3.   Invite her/him for [the opera] next week.
4.   She/he is reluctant and asks you what is playing.
5.   You tell her/him that it is [Mozart's *Magic Flute*].
6.   It's her/his favorite opera. She/he'd love to go.
7.   Arrange a time and place to meet beforehand.

---

51.   Assessing cultural acclimatization

You are a journalist for a major German news weekly. You are interviewing a foreign worker about her/his impressions of life in Germany. Be sure to ask her/him:

1.   about working conditions.
2.   about cultural differences.
3.   about family life.

---

52.   *Kaffeestunde*

1.   Make comments about different people and objects in the classroom. **Das ist die Frau, die ...**
2.   Ask your partner to tell you about:
     a.   a film she/he would like to see.
     b.   a book she/he would like to read.
     c.   a trip she/he would like to take.
     d.   a concert she/he would like to attend.

Sit in a circle of five. Each person states something that can be done to save or improve the environment.

In a group of four, each person states what aspects of the environment she/he thinks the group should concentrate on improving or saving. The members then negotiate with each other to determine the group's focus and actions.

With a partner, role-play the following dialogue. Your roommate doesn't share enough of the responsibility. Tell her/him what must be done:

1. the room must be cleaned.
2. food must be bought.
3. laundry must be washed.
4. the bathroom must be cleaned.
5. [...]

Your roommate will say why she/he can't do the chores.

---

1. Talk about a celebration or activity you or your friends are arranging. Tell who will do the different tasks.
2. Talk about what you have learned about Germany.
3. Ask your partner if she/he would like to study in a German-speaking country for a year. Why?
4. Talk about what you have learned about the German-speaking countries this year.
5. Talk about ways in which you can continue to learn more about the German language and culture.